KT-527-502

No Nonsense XML Web Development With PHP

by Thomas Myer

NORTH NOTTS. COLLEGE

S81 S21 S23.

WITHDRAWN FROM

LIBRARY STOCK

-6. JUL

25. JUL

-3. JU

No Nonsense XML Web Development With PHP

by Thomas Myer

Copyright © 2005 SitePoint Pty. Ltd.

Managing Editor: Simon Mackie　　**Index Editor**: Bill Johncocks
Technical Director: Kevin Yank　　**Cover Designer**: Julian Carroll
Technical Editor: Joe Marini　　　**Cover Illustrator**: Lucas Licata
Editor: Georgina Laidlaw
Printing History:　　　　　　　　**Latest Update**: April 2006
　First Edition: July 2005

Notice of Rights

All rights reserved. No part of this book may be reproduced, stored in a retrieval system or transmitted in any form or by any means, without the prior written permission of the publisher, except in the case of brief quotations embodied in critical articles or reviews.

Notice of Liability

The author and publisher have made every effort to ensure the accuracy of the information herein. However, the information contained in this book is sold without warranty, either express or implied. Neither the authors and SitePoint Pty. Ltd., nor its dealers or distributors will be held liable for any damages to be caused either directly or indirectly by the instructions contained in this book, or by the software or hardware products described herein.

Trademark Notice

Rather than indicating every occurrence of a trademarked name as such, this book uses the names only in an editorial fashion and to the benefit of the trademark owner with no intention of infringement of the trademark.

Published by SitePoint Pty. Ltd.

424 Smith Street Collingwood
VIC Australia 3066.
Web: www.sitepoint.com
Email: business@sitepoint.com

ISBN 0-9752402-0-X
Printed and bound in the United States of America

About The Author

Thomas Myer is the founding principal of Triple Dog Dare Media, an Austin, TX-based Web consultancy that specializes in building database- and XML-driven dynamic sites. He first entered the field of Web development in 1996 when he learned Perl. He was introduced to XML shortly thereafter and has worked with it extensively to build document repositories, search engine indexes, content portal taxonomies, online product catalogs, and business logic frameworks.

About The Technical Editor

Joe Marini has been active in the Web and graphics software industries for more than 15 years. He was an original member of the Dreamweaver engineering team at Macromedia, and has also held prominent roles in creating products such as QuarkXPress, mFactory's mTropolis, and Extensis QX-Tools. Today Joe is a Senior Program Manager at Microsoft.

About The Technical Director

As Technical Director for SitePoint, Kevin Yank oversees all of its technical publications—books, articles, newsletters and blogs. He has written over 50 articles for SitePoint on technologies including PHP, XML, ASP.NET, Java, JavaScript and CSS, but is perhaps best known for his book, *Build Your Own Database Driven Website Using PHP & MySQL*, also from SitePoint. Kevin now lives in Melbourne, Australia. In his spare time he enjoys flying light aircraft and learning the fine art of improvised acting. Go you big red fire engine!

About SitePoint

SitePoint specializes in publishing fun, practical and easy-to-understand content for Web professionals.

Visit http://www.sitepoint.com/ to access our books, newsletters, articles and community forums.

NORTH NOTTS. COLLEGE

006.76

27-99

LIBRARY / LRC

To my wife Hope, for loving me anyway.

To my three pups: big quiet Kafka, little rascal Marlowe, and for regal Vladimir, who passed away the day after I finished Chapter 5.

Table of Contents

Preface

Off and on, I run a workshop called *XML for Mere Mortals*. The title attracts an audience that's much wider than your typical Web developer needing to bone up on the subject. I train technical writers, project managers, database geeks—even the occasional business owner who's trying to get a handle on the exciting possibilities of XML.

If I had to give this book a subtitle, it would be, "XML for Mere Mortals," because every time I sat down to write a chapter, I tried to picture the kind of folks who show up at my workshops—intelligent and curious, with a wide range of technical proficiency, but all of them feeling a little overwhelmed by the terminology, processes, and technologies surrounding XML. With any luck, this approach will serve you well.

This book has two goals: to introduce readers to a large part of the XML world, and to walk them, step by step, through the creation of an XML-powered Website. Let's talk about each of those goals in more detail.

If we were to take the time to introduce you to the entire spectrum of XML technologies, it would take a book twice (or thrice) as big as the one you're currently holding. There's a lot to talk about when you start looking at XML, so I had to pick my battles. For instance, you'll notice that we discuss DTDs, but not XML Schemas. We talk a lot about XPath, but we don't cover XQuery or XLink. The idea of this title is to get your feet (and perhaps your ankles, shins, and knees) wet in the topic of XML, and to make you feel comfortable to go out and learn even more.

The second goal involves building your own XML-powered Website. I build both XML- and database-powered dynamic Websites for a living, and I tried to pour as much as I know about the process into the limited space available. As we work to build the project that's developed through the course of this book, I'll take you through the requirements gathering and analysis phases, then show you how to convert that information into real XML documents and working code. Yes, we are building a content management system, but a simplified one without the heavy workflow or other capabilities you see in other systems. Nevertheless, what you'll end up with is a simple, powerful system that can get a Website up and running quickly.

Every time I teach a class or workshop, I feel that I learn as much from my students as they learn from me—that, in fact, I learn more as I continue to teach.

Writing this book was very much like that, because it forced me to organize my thoughts and approaches into a more coherent fashion.

I hope you find the book a useful introduction to the incredibly fascinating topic of XML. I know that many experts won't agree with the approaches I took here, and I'd like to say that I can understand all your disagreements, but writing a book for the novice requires that the concepts be presented from a slightly different perspective. If you wish to provide me with feedback, or you have any questions, feel free to drop me a line: `tom@tripledogdaremedia.com`.

Who Should Read this Book?

This book is intended for the XML beginner. You should have some working knowledge of the Web, including HTML and some JavaScript skills, and experience with a server-side programming language.

In this book, we use PHP 5 on the server side, and I'll assume that you have had some exposure to PHP. However, I always try to explain what's going on, particularly as I work with XML concepts with which you may have little or no past experience.

If you've ever fiddled with JavaScript, worked with a database, set up an ecommerce system, or programmed in PHP, ASP, or Perl, you'll likely have no problem following what we do within these pages.

What's in this Book?

Here's what we'll cover:

Chapter 1: *Introduction to XML*
This chapter introduces XML. We talk about elements, tags, attributes, entities, and we get into semantics. We explore the difference between well-formedness and validity, then get our hands dirty with some examples. We also start gathering requirements for our project.

Chapter 2: *XML in Practice*
It's time to meet the XML family, namely XHTML, XML Namespaces, and Extensible Stylesheet Language Transformations (XSLT). In addition to playing with these technologies, we gather the final requirements for our project.

Chapter 3: *DTDs for Consistency*

This chapter is all about consistency. In particular, we look at Document Type Definitions (DTDs), a language that describes the requirements that are necessary for an XML document to be valid; that is, suitable for use in a particular system. We finish the chapter by refining some of the requirements we've gathered for our project.

Chapter 4: *Displaying XML in a Browser*

In this chapter, we talk about XSLT and how to use it to transform XML for display in a browser. We explore some of the basics of XSLT and introduce XPath. At the end of the chapter, we build many of the public display templates we'll need for our project.

Chapter 5: *XSLT in Detail*

This chapter picks up where the last one left off. We delve much deeper into the programmatic aspects of XSLT, such as `foreach` loops, conditionals, sorting, counting, and using XPath. In our project, we use this knowledge to leverage XPath on the server side, and to create an XSLT-driven site map.

Chapter 6: *Manipulating XML with JavaScript/DHTML*

Here, we learn how to manipulate XML with client-side tools. We learn about the Document Object Model (DOM) and the differences between the handling of XML in Internet Explorer as compared to Firefox and other Mozilla-based browsers. On the project side of things, we add categories to our content structure, and use client-side XML processing to allow users to browse the site's content by category.

Chapter 7: *Manipulating XML with PHP*

In the previous chapter, our work was mostly on the client side. Now we tackle the server side, specifically addressing the question of PHP 5 as we explore the differences between SAX, DOM, and SimpleXML function libraries for working with XML. We further our project work as we start to build our administrative tool files, including login/verification templates and article create/update/delete templates.

Chapter 8: *RSS and RDF*

RSS is a hot topic right now. It provides a means for Website users to monitor sites they don't have time to visit regularly, and for Web applications to make use of content that's syndicated from third-party Websites and other information sources. In this chapter, we delve into the specifics of the different varieties of RSS that are available (including RDF, which forms the basis of RSS 1.0), and discuss news aggregators, the parsing of feeds with PHP, and

more. We finish the chapter with the addition of an RSS feed to our Web
project.

Chapter 9: *XML and Web Services*

It's time to look at Web Services. The emphasis of this chapter is XML-RPC,
an older standard for Web Services that's easy to work with, but we do
mention SOAP, a newer standard in this area. On the project side, we create
an XML-RPC server (and clients) that search for articles on our site.

Chapter 10: *XML and Databases*

This final chapter considers XML and databases. We talk about the need to
use databases and XML together, explore the differences between relational
and native XML databases, and investigate the task of storing XML information in a database. We hand-roll an SQL-to-XML converter, then do the
same thing using a ready-made solution, phpMyAdmin. Lastly, we create a
MySQL backup system for our XML project files.

Appendix A: *PHP XML Functions*

This appendix contains a complete reference to the SAX, DOM, and SimpleXML functions that PHP 5 supports for working with XML.

Appendix B: *CMS Administration Tool*

This appendix completes our work on the project's administrative tools. We'll
build forms and scripts to handle news items, Web copy, authors, administrators, and categories.

The Book's Website

Located at http://www.sitepoint.com/books/xml1/, the Website supporting this
book will give you access to the following facilities:

The Code Archive

As you progress through the text, you'll note that most of the code listings are
labelled with filenames, and a number of references are made to the code archive.
This is a downloadable ZIP archive that contains complete code for all the examples presented in this book.

Updates and Errata

The Errata page on the book's Website will always have the latest information about known typographical and code errors, and necessary updates for changes to technologies.

The SitePoint Forums

While I've made every attempt to anticipate any questions you may have, and answer them in this book, there is no way that *any* book could cover everything there is to know about XML. If you have a question about anything in this book, the best place to go for a quick answer is http://www.sitepoint.com/forums/—SitePoint's vibrant and knowledgeable community.

The SitePoint Newsletters

In addition to books like this one, SitePoint offers free email newsletters.

The SitePoint Tech Times covers the latest news, product releases, trends, tips, and techniques for all technical aspects of Web development. Anything newsworthy in the worlds of XML or PHP will find its way into the pages of this newsletter.

The long-running *SitePoint Tribune* is a biweekly digest of the business and moneymaking aspects of the Web. Whether you're a freelance developer looking for tips to score that dream contract, or a marketing major striving to keep abreast of changes to the major search engines, this is the newsletter for you.

The SitePoint Design View is a monthly compilation of the best in Web design. From new CSS layout methods to subtle PhotoShop techniques, SitePoint's chief designer shares his years of experience in its pages.

Browse the archives or sign up to any of SitePoint's free newsletters at http://www.sitepoint.com/newsletter/.

Your Feedback

If you can't find an answer through the forums, or you wish to contact us for any other reason, the best place to write is `books@sitepoint.com`. We have a well-manned email support system set up to track your inquiries, and if our support staff are unable to answer your question, they send it straight to me. Suggestions for improvement as well as notices of any mistakes you may find are especially welcome.

Acknowledgements

Picture this scene: Simon Mackie (my very talented editor) calls me from Australia, basically to tell me to buck up, stop whining, and please just finish the darn book. Without Simon's perseverance none of this would have been possible, especially when I hit the wall around Chapter 8.

A colleague once told me that without deadlines, nothing would get done; that's still true, but I'd like to add that without great editing, no book would ever get done.

Simon had a team of very smart reviewers who pored over every sentence and illustration in this book. Without their sharp eyes, this book would have been a shambling mess; their sound advice and good humor allowed me to stay on track and keep the book to the highest standards of technical accuracy. Of course, I'm pretty feisty and put up a good fight, but 90% of the time their logical good sense prevailed over my natural instinct to bargain my way out of any compromise. To make a long story short, any errors in this book are my fault, not theirs.

Of course, Simon had help, namely my wife Hope, who is herself one heck of an editor. She cheerfully put up with my long absences as I plugged away on the book. She celebrated when I met deadlines and hassled me if she caught me slacking. She read over drafts and made suggestions, asked questions, and basically pushed me when I most needed it. She is everything to me.

1

Introduction to XML

In this chapter, we'll cover the basics of XML—essentially, most of the information you'll need to know to get a handle on this exciting technology. After we're done exploring some terminology and examples, we'll jump right in and start working with XML documents. Then, we'll spend some time starting the project we'll develop through the course of this book: building an XML-powered content management system.

An Introduction to XML

Who here has heard of XML? Okay, just about everybody. If ever there were a candidate for "Most Hyped Technology" during the late 90s and the current decade, it's XML (though Java would be a close contender for the title).

Whenever I talk about XML with developers, designers, technical writers, or other Web professionals, the most common question I'm asked is, "What's the big deal?" In this book, I'll explain exactly what the big deal is—how XML can be used to make your Web applications smarter, more versatile, and more powerful. I'll try to stay away from the grandstanding hoopla that has character-ized much of the discussion of XML; instead, I'll give you the background and know-how you'll need to make XML a part of your professional skillset.

What is XML?

So, what is XML? Whenever a group of people asks this question, I always look at the individuals' body language. A significant portion of the group leans forward eagerly, wanting to learn more. The others either roll their eyes in anticipation of hype and half-formed theories, or cringe in fear of a long, dry history of markup languages. As a result, I've learned to keep my explanation brief.

The essence of XML is in its name: Extensible Markup Language.

Extensible   XML is extensible. It lets you define your own tags, the order in which they occur, and how they should be processed or displayed. Another way to think about extensibility is to consider that XML allows all of us to extend our notion of what a document is: it can be a file that lives on a file server, or it can be a transient piece of data that flows between two computer systems (as in the case of Web Services).

Markup   The most recognizable feature of XML is its tags, or elements (to be more accurate). In fact, the elements you'll create in XML will be very similar to the elements you've already been creating in your HTML documents. However, XML allows you to define your own set of tags.

Language   XML is a language that's very similar to HTML. It's much more flexible than HTML because it allows you to create your own custom tags. However, it's important to realize that XML is not just a language. XML is a meta-language: a language that allows us to create or define other languages. For example, with XML we can create other languages, such as RSS, MathML (a mathematical markup language), and even tools like XSLT. More on this later.

Why Do We Need XML?

Okay, we know what it is, but why do we need XML? We need it because HTML is specifically designed to describe documents for display in a Web browser, and not much else. It becomes cumbersome if you want to display documents in a mobile device or do anything that's even slightly complicated, such as translating the content from German to English. HTML's sole purpose is to allow anyone to quickly create Web documents that can be shared with other people. XML, on the other hand, isn't just suited to the Web—it can be used in a variety of different contexts, some of which may not have anything to do with humans interacting with content (for example, Web Services use XML to send requests and responses back and forth).

HTML rarely (if ever) provides information about how the document is structured or what it means. In layman's terms, HTML is a presentation language, whereas XML is a data-description language.

For example, if you were to go to any ecommerce Website and download a product listing, you'd probably get something like this:

```
<!DOCTYPE html PUBLIC "-//W3C//DTD XHTML 1.0 Transitional//EN"
    "http://www.w3.org/TR/xhtml1/DTD/xhtml1-transitional.dtd">
<html xmlns="http://www.w3.org/1999/xhtml">
<head>
<title>ABC Products</title>
<meta http-equiv="Content-Type"
    content="text/html; charset=iso-8859-1" />
</head>
<body>
<h1>ABC Products</h1>
<h2>Product One</h2>
<p>Product One is an exciting new widget that will simplify your
  life.</p>
<p><b>Cost: $19.95</b></p>
<p><b>Shipping: $2.95</b></p>
<h2>Product Two</h2>
...
<h3>Product Three</h3>
<p><i>Cost: $24.95</i></p>
<p>This is such a terrific widget that you will most certainly
  want to buy one for your home and another one for your
  office!</p>
...
</body>
</html>
```

Take a good look at this—admittedly simple—code sample from a computer's perspective. A human can certainly read this document and make the necessary semantic leaps to understand it, but a computer couldn't.

> **Semantics and Other Jargon**
>
> You're going to be hearing a lot of talk about "semantics" and other linguistics terms in this chapter. It's unavoidable, so bear with me. Semantics is the study of meaning in language.
>
> Humans are much better at semantics than computers, because humans are really good at deriving meaning. For example, if I asked you to list as many names for "female animals" as you could, you'd probably start with "lioness", "tigress", "ewe", "doe" and so on. If you were presented with a list of these names and asked to provide a category that contained them all, it's likely you'd say something like "female animals." Furthermore, if I asked you what a lioness was, you'd say, "female lion."
>
> If I further asked you to list associated words, you might say "pride," "hunt," "savannah," "Africa," and the like. From there, you could make the leap to other wild cats, then to house cats and maybe even dogs (cats and dogs are both pets, after all). With very little effort, you'd be able to build a stunning semantic landscape, as it were.
>
> Needless to say, computers are really bad at this game, which is a shame, as many computing tasks require semantic skill. That's why we need to give computers as much help as we can.

For example, a human can probably deduce that the <h2> tag in the above document has been used to tag a product name within a product listing. Furthermore, a human might be able to guess that the first paragraph after an <h2> holds the description, and that the next two paragraphs contain price and shipping information, in bold.

However, even a cursory glance at the rest of the document reveals some very human errors. For example, the last product name is encapsulated in <h3> tags, not <h2> tags. This last product listing also displays a price before the description, and the price is italicized instead of appearing in bold.

A computer program (and even some humans) that tried to decipher this document wouldn't be able to make the kinds of semantic leaps required to make sense of it. The computer would be able only to render the document to a browser with the styles associated with each tag. HTML is chiefly a set of instructions for rendering documents inside a Web browser; it's not a method of structuring documents to bring out their meaning.

If the above document were created in XML, it might look a little like this:

```
<?xml version="1.0"?>
<productListing title="ABC Products">
  <product>
    <name>Product One</name>
    <description>Product One is an exciting new widget that will
      simplify your life.</description>
    <cost>$19.95</cost>
    <shipping>$2.95</shipping>
  </product>
  <product>
    <name>Product Two</name>
    ...
  </product>
  <product>
    <name>Product Three</name>
    <description>This is such a terrific widget that you will
      most certainly want to buy one for your home and another one
      for your office!</p>
    <cost>$24.95</cost>
    <shipping>$0.00</shipping>
  </product>
  ...
</productListing>
```

Notice that this new document contains absolutely no information about display. What does a `<product>` tag look like in a browser? Beats me—we haven't defined that yet. Later on, we'll see how you can use technologies like CSS and XSLT to transform your XML into any format you like. Essentially, XML allows you to *separate information from presentation*—just one of its many powerful abilities.

When we concentrate on a document's structure, as we've done here, we are better able to ensure that our information is correct. In theory, we should be able to look at any XML document and understand instantly what's going on. In the example above, we know that a product listing contains products, and that each product has a name, a description, a price, and a shipping cost. You could say, rightly, that each XML document is *self-describing*, and is readable by both humans and software.

Now, everyone makes mistakes, and XML programmers are no exception. Imagine that you start to share your XML documents with another developer or company, and, somewhere along the line, someone places a product's description after its price. Normally, this wouldn't be a big deal, but perhaps your Web application requires that the description appears after the product name *every* time.

To ensure that everyone plays by the rules, you need a **DTD** (a document type definition), or schema. Basically, a DTD provides instructions about the structure of your particular XML document. It's a lot like a rule book that states which tags are legal, and where. Once you have a DTD in place, anyone who creates product listings for your application will have to follow the rules. We'll get into DTDs a little later. For now, though, let's continue with the basics.

A Closer Look at the XML Example

From the casual observer's viewpoint, a given XML document, such as the one we saw in the previous section, appears to be no more than a bunch of tags and letters. But there's more to it than that!

A Structural Viewpoint

Let's consider our XML example from a structural standpoint. No, not the kind of structure we bring to a document by marking it up with XML tags; let's look at this example on a more granular level. I want to examine the contents of a typical XML file, character by character.

The simplest XML elements contain an opening tag, a closing tag, and some content. The opening tag begins with a left angle bracket (<), followed by an element name that contains letters and numbers (but no spaces), and finishes with a right angle bracket (>). In XML, content is usually parsed character data. It could consist of plain text, other XML elements, and more exotic things like XML entities, comments, and processing instructions (all of which we'll see later). Following the content is the closing tag, which exhibits the same spelling and capitalization as your opening tag, but with one tiny change: a / appears right before the element name.

Here are a few examples of valid XML elements:

```
<myElement>some content here</myElement>
<elements>
  <myelement>one</myelement>
  <myelement>two</myelement>
</elements>
```

> **Elements, Tags, or Nodes?**
>
> I'll refer to XML elements, XML tags, and XML nodes at different points in this book. What's the deal? Well, for the layman, these terms are interchangeable, but if you want to get technical (and who'd want to do that in a technical book?) each has a very precise meaning:
>
> ❏ An element consists of an opening tag, its attributes, any content, and a closing tag.
>
> ❏ A tag—either opening or closing—is used to mark the start or end of an element.
>
> ❏ A node is a part of the hierarchical structure that makes up an XML document. "Node" is a generic term that applies to any type of XML document object, including elements, attributes, comments, processing instructions, and plain text.

If you're used to working with HTML, you've probably created many documents that are missing end tags, use different capitalization in opening and closing tags, and contain improperly nested tags.

You won't be able to get away with any of that in XML! In this language, the `<myElement>` tag is different from the `<MYELEMENT>` tag, and both are different from the `<myELEMENT>` tag. If your opening tag is `<myELEMENT>` and your closing tag is `</Myelement>`, your document won't be valid.

If you use attributes on any elements, then attribute values must be single- or double-quoted. No longer can you get by with bare attribute values like you did in HTML! Let's see an example. The following is okay in HTML:

```
<h1 class=topHeader>
```

In XML, you'd have to put quotes (either single or double) around the attribute value, like this:

```
<h1 class="topHeader">
```

Also, if you nest your elements improperly (i.e. close an element before closing another element that is inside it), your document won't be valid. (I know I keep mentioning validity—we'll talk about it in detail soon!) For example, Web browsers don't generally complain about the following:

```
<b>Some text that is bolded, some that is <i>italicized</b></i>.
```

In XML, this improper nesting of elements would cause the program reading the document to raise an error.

As XML allows you to create any language you want, the inventors of XML had to institute a special rule, which happens to be closely related to the proper nesting rule. The rule states that each XML document must contain a single root element in which all the document's other elements are contained. As we'll see later, almost every single piece of XML development you'll do is facilitated by this one simple rule.

Attributes

Did you notice the `<productListing>` opening tag in our example? Inside the tag, following the element name, was the data `title="ABC Products"`. This is called an attribute.

You can think of attributes as adjectives—they provide additional information about the element that may not make any sense as content. If you've worked with HTML, you're familiar with such attributes as the `src` (file source) on the `<img>` tag.

What information should be contained in an attribute? What should appear between the tags of an element? This is a subject of much debate, but don't worry, there really are no wrong answers here. Remember: you're the one defining your own language. Some developers (including me!) apply this rule of thumb: use attributes to store data that doesn't necessarily need to be displayed to a user of the information. Another common rule of thumb is to consider the length of the data. Potentially large data should be placed inside a tag; shorter data can be placed in an attribute. Typically, attributes are used to "embellish" the data contained within the tag.

Let's examine this issue a little more closely. Let's say that you wanted to create an XML document to keep track of your DVD collection. Here's a short snippet of the code you might use:

```
<dvdCollection>
  <dvd>
    <id>1</id>
    <title>Raiders of the Lost Ark</title>
    <release-year>1981</release-year>
    <director>Steven Spielberg</director>
    <actors>
      <actor>Harrison Ford</actor>
```

```
      <actor>Karen Allen</actor>
      <actor>John Rhys-Davies</actor>
   </actors>
  </dvd>
  ….
</dvdCollection>
```

It's unlikely that anyone who reads this document would need to know the ID of any of the DVDs in your collection. So, we could safely store the ID as an attribute of the <dvd> element instead, like this:

```
<dvd id="1">
```

In other parts of our DVD listing, the information seems a little bare. For instance, we're only displaying an actor's name between the <actor> tags—we could include much more information here. One way to do so is with the addition of attributes:

```
<actor type="superstar" gender="male" age="50">Harrison Ford
</actor>
```

In this case, though, I'd probably revert to our rule of thumb—most users would probably want to know at least some of this information. So, let's convert some of these attributes to elements:

```
<actor type="superstar">
  <name>Harrison Ford</name>
  <gender>male</gender>
  <age>50</age>
</actor>
```

Beware of Redundant Data

From a completely different perspective, one could argue that you shouldn't have all this repetitive information in your XML file. For example, your collection's bound to include at least one other movie that stars Harrison Ford. It would be smarter, from an architectural point of view, to have a separate listing of actors with unique IDs to which you could link. We'll discuss these questions at length throughout this book.

Empty-Element Tags

Some XML elements are said to be empty—they contain no content whatsoever. Familiar examples are the img and br elements in HTML. In the case of img, for example, all the element's information is contained in its tag's attributes. The

`<br>` tag, on the other hand, does not normally contain any attributes—it just signifies a line break.

Remember that in XML all opening tags must be matched by a closing tag. For empty elements, you can use a single empty-element tag to replace this:

```
<myEmptyElement></myEmptyElement>
```

with this:

```
<myEmptyElement/>
```

The / at the end of this tag basically tells the parser that the element starts and ends right here. It's an efficient shorthand method that you can use to mark up empty elements quickly.

The XML Declaration

The line right at the top of our example is called the XML declaration:

```
<?xml version="1.0"?>
```

It's not strictly necessary to include this line, but it's the best way to make sure that any device that reads the document will know that it's an XML document, and to which version of XML it conforms.

Entities

I mentioned entities earlier. An entity is a handy construct that, at its simplest, allows you to define special characters for insertion into your documents. If you've worked with HTML, you know that the `&lt;` entity inserts a literal < character into a document. You can't use the actual character because it would be treated as the start of a tag, so you replace it with the appropriate entity instead.

XML, true to its extensible nature, allows you to create your own entities. Let's say that your company's copyright notice has to go on every single document. Instead of typing this notice over and over again, you could create an entity reference called `copyright_notice` with the proper text, then use it in your XML documents as `&copyright_notice;`. What a time-saver!

We'll cover entities in more detail later on.

More than Structure...

XML documents are more then just a sequence of elements. If you take another, closer look at our product or DVD listing examples, you'll notice two things:

❑ The documents are self-describing, as we've already discussed.

❑ The documents are really a hierarchy of nested objects.

Let's elaborate on the first point very quickly. We've already said that most (if not all) XML documents are self-describing. This feature, combined with all that content encapsulated in opening and closing tags, takes all XML documents far past the realm of mere data and into the revered halls of *information*.

Data can comprise a string of characters or numbers, such as **5551238888**. This string can represent anything from a laptop's serial number, to a pharmacy's prescription ID, to a phone number in the United States. But the only way to turn this data into information (and therefore make it useful) is to add context to it—once you have context, you can be sure about what the data represents. In short, `<phone country="us">5551238888</phone>` leaves no doubt that this seemingly arbitrary string of numbers is in fact a U.S. phone number.

When you take into account the second point—that an XML document is really a hierarchy of objects—all sorts of possibilities open up. Remember what we discussed before—that, in an XML document, one element contains all the others? Well, that root element becomes the root of our hierarchical tree. You can think of that tree as a family tree, with the root element having various children (in this case, product elements), and each of those having various children (name, description, and so on). In turn, each product element has various siblings (other product elements) and a parent (the root), as shown in Figure 1.1.

Figure 1.1. The logical structure of an XML document.

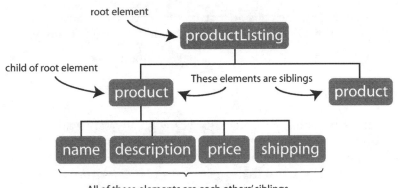

Because what we have is a tree, we should be able to travel up and down it, and from side to side, with relative ease. From a programmatic stance, most of your work with XML will focus on properly creating and navigating XML structures.

There's one final point about hierarchical trees that you should note. Before, we talked about transforming data into information by adding context. Well, when we start building hierarchies of information that indicate natural relationships (known as **taxonomies**), we've just taken the first giant leap toward turning information into knowledge. That statement itself could spawn a whole other book, so we'll just have to leave it at that and move on!

Formatting Issues

Earlier in this chapter, I made a point about XML allowing you to separate information from presentation. I also mentioned that you could use other technologies, like CSS (Cascading Style Sheets) and XSLT (Extensible Stylesheet Language Transformations), to make the information display in different contexts.

 Notice that in XSLT, it's "stylesheet," but in CSS it's "style sheet"! For the sake of consistency, we'll call them all "style sheets" in this book.

In later chapters, I'll go into plenty of detail on both CSS and XSLT, but I wanted to make a brief point here. Because we've taken the time to create XML documents, our information is no longer locked up inside proprietary formats such as word processors or spreadsheets. Furthermore, it no longer has to be "re-created" every time you want to create alternate displays of that information: all you have to do is create a style sheet or transformation to make your XML presentable in a given medium.

For example, if you stored your information in a word processing program, it would contain all kinds of information about the way it should appear on the printed page—lots of bolding, font sizes, and tables. Unfortunately, if that document also had to be posted to the Web as an HTML document, someone would have to convert it (either manually or via software), clean it up, and test it. Then, if someone else made changes to the original document, those changes wouldn't cascade to the HTML version. If yet another person wanted to take the same information and use it in a slide presentation, they might run the risk of using outdated information from the HTML version. Even if they did get the right information into their presentation, you'd still need to track three locations in which your information lived. As you can see, it can get pretty messy!

Now, if the same information were stored in XML, you could create three different XSLT files to transform the XML into HTML, a slide presentation, and a printer-friendly file format such as PostScript. If you made changes to the XML file, the other files would also change automatically once you passed the XML file through the process. (This notion, by the way, is an essential component of single-sourcing—i.e. having a "single source" for any given information that's reused in another application.)

As you can see, separating information from presentation makes your XML documents reusable, and can save hassles and headaches in environments in which a lot of information needs to be stored, processed, handled, and exchanged.

Here's another example. This book will actually be stored as XML (in the DocBook schema). That means the publisher can generate sample PDFs for its Website, make print-ready files for the printer, and potentially create ebooks in the future. All formats will be generated from the same source, and all will be created using different style sheets to process the base XML files.

Well-Formedness and Validity

We've talked a little bit about XML, what it's used for, how it looks, how to conceptualize it, and how to transform it. One of the most powerful advantages of XML, of course, is that it allows you to define your own language.

However, this most powerful feature also exposes a great weakness of XML. If all of us start defining our own languages, we run the risk of being unable to understand anything anyone else says. Thus, the creators of XML had to set down some rules that would describe a "legal" XML document.

There are two levels of "legality" in XML:

❑ Well-formedness

❑ Validity

A **well-formed** XML document follows these rules (most of which we've already discussed):

❑ An XML document must contain a single root element that contains all other elements.

❑ All elements must be properly nested.

❑ All elements must be closed either with a closing tag or with a "self-closing" empty-element tag (i.e. *<tag/>*).

❑ All attribute values must be quoted.

A **valid** XML document is both well-formed and follows all the rules set down in that document's DTD (document type definition). A valid document, then, is nothing more then a well-formed document that adheres to its DTD.

The question then becomes, why have two levels of legality? A good question, indeed!

For the most part, you will only care that your documents are well formed. In fact, most XML parsers (software that reads your XML documents) are non-validating (i.e. they don't care if your documents are valid)—and that includes those found in Web browsers like Firefox and Internet Explorer. Well-formedness alone allows you to create ad hoc XML documents that can be generated, added to an application, and tested quickly.

For other applications that are more mission-critical, you'll want to use a DTD within your XML documents, then run those documents through a validating parser.

The bottom line? Well-formedness is mandatory, but validity is an extra, optional step.

In the next section, we'll practice using both validating and non-validating parsers to get the hang of these tools.

Getting Your Hands Dirty

Okay, we've spent some time talking about XML and its potential, and examining some of the neater aspects of it. Now, it's time to do what I like best, and get our hands dirty as we actually work on some documents.

The first thing we want to do is to create an XML document. For our purposes, any XML document will do, but for the sake of continuity, let's use the product listing document we saw earlier in the chapter.

Here it is again, with a few more nodes added to it:

File: **myFirstXML.xml**

```
<productListing title="ABC Products">
  <product>
    <name>Product One</name>
    <description>Product One is an exciting new widget that will
      simplify your life.</description>
    <cost>$19.95</cost>
    <shipping>$2.95</shipping>
  </product>
  <product>
    <name>Product Two</name>
    <description>Product Two is an exciting new widget that will
      make you jump up and down.</description>
    <cost>$29.95</cost>
    <shipping>$5.95</shipping>
  </product>
  <product>
    <name>Product Three</name>
    <description>Product Three is better than Product One and
      Product Two combined! It really is as good as we say it
is--or your money back. </description>
    <cost>$39.95</cost>
    <shipping>$5.95</shipping>
  </product>
</productListing>
```

Save this XML markup into a file and name it myFirstXML.xml. In the next few sections, we'll be viewing the file in different browsers and experimenting with parsers.

Viewing Raw XML in Internet Explorer

If you have Internet Explorer 5 or higher installed on your machine, you can view your newly-created XML file. As Figure 1.2 illustrates, Internet Explorer simply displays XML files as a series of indented nodes.

Figure 1.2. Viewing an XML file in Internet Explorer.

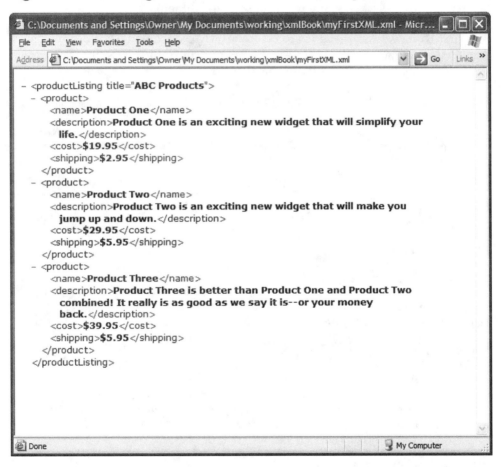

Notice the little minus signs next to some of the XML nodes? A minus sign in front of a node indicates that the node contains other nodes. If you click the minus sign, Internet Explorer will collapse all the child nodes belonging to that node, as shown in Figure 1.3.

Figure 1.3. Collapsing nodes displaying in Internet Explorer.

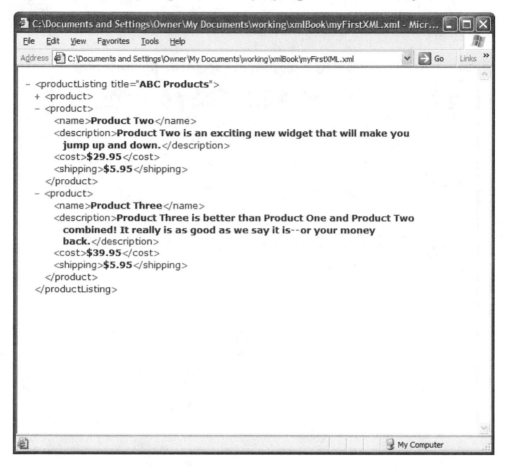

The little plus sign next to the first product node indicates that the node has children. Clicking on the plus sign will expand any nodes under that particular node. In this way, you can easily display the parts of the document on which you want to focus.

Now, open your XML document in any text editing tool and scroll down to the cost node of the second product. The line we're interested in should read:

File: **myFirstXML.xml** (excerpt)

```
<cost>$29.95</cost>
```

Capitalize the "c" on the opening tag, so that the line reads like this:

```
<Cost>$29.95</cost>
```

Save your work and reload Internet Explorer. You should see an error message that looks like the one pictured in Figure 1.4.

Figure 1.4. Error message displaying in Internet Explorer.

As you can see, Internet Explorer provides a rather verbose explanation of the error it ran into: the end tag, `</cost>`, does not match the start tag, `<Cost>`.

Furthermore, it provides a nice visual of the offending line, a little arrow pointing to the spot at which the parser thinks the problem arose.

```
<Cost>$29.95</cost>
--------------^
```

Even though the problem is really with the start tag, the arrow points to the end tag. Because Internet Explorer uses a non-validating parser by default (remember, this means it only cares about well-formedness rules), it runs into problems at the end tag. You now have to backtrack to find out why that particular end tag caused such a problem. Once you get the hang of this debugging method, you'll find it a great help in tracking down problems.

Let's introduce a slightly more complex problem. Open your XML document in an editor once more, and fix the problem we introduced above. Then, go to the second-last line of the document (it should read `</product>`) and add a `<product>` tag in front of it. Save your work and reload your browser.

You should see an error message similar to the one shown in Figure 1.5.

Figure 1.5. Debugging a more complex error.

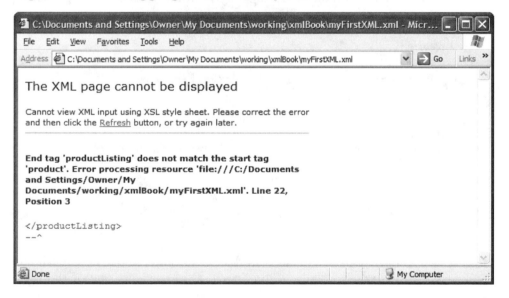

At first glance, this error message seems a bit more obscure than the previous one. For starters, this message seems to indicate a problem with the `</product-Listing>` end tag. However, look closely and what do you see? It says that the `</productListing>` end tag does not match the `<product>` start tag. That's exactly what's wrong! Someone introduced a `<product>` start tag and didn't close it properly.

I'm including this example because bad nesting is one of the most common errors introduced to XML documents. This kind of error can be subtle and hard to find, especially if you're doing a lot of editing, or if your document is complex or long.

Viewing Raw XML in Firefox

You can also use Firefox (and other Mozilla browsers like Netscape 8) to view your XML files. Firefox is a popular open-source browser, and at the time this book went to print the latest version was 1.0.4. You can download a free copy from the Mozilla website[1].

Viewing raw XML in Firefox is basically the same as viewing it in Internet Explorer, as you can see from Figure 1.6.

Firefox's built-in parser is non-validating, so you won't be able to use it to check for document validity. However, it's comforting to know that the good folks at the Mozilla Foundation are planning to add a validating parser in a future release of the browser.

Options for Using a Validating Parser

Okay, so both Internet Explorer and Firefox will check your XML for well-formedness, but you need to know for future reference how to check that an XML file is valid (i.e. conforms to a DTD).[2] How do you do that?

Well, there are a couple of options, listed below.

Using an Online Validating Parser

There are various well-known online validating XML parsers. All you have to do is visit the appropriate page, upload your document, and the parser will validate it. Brown University's Scholarly Technology Group sponsors one of the most famous parsers:

http://www.stg.brown.edu/service/xmlvalid/

---

[1] http://www.mozilla.org/
[2] Our current product listing example does not have an associated DTD, and thus cannot be validated. We'll look at DTDs in Chapter 3, at which point you'll be able to try validating your XML.

Figure 1.6. Viewing raw XML in Firefox.

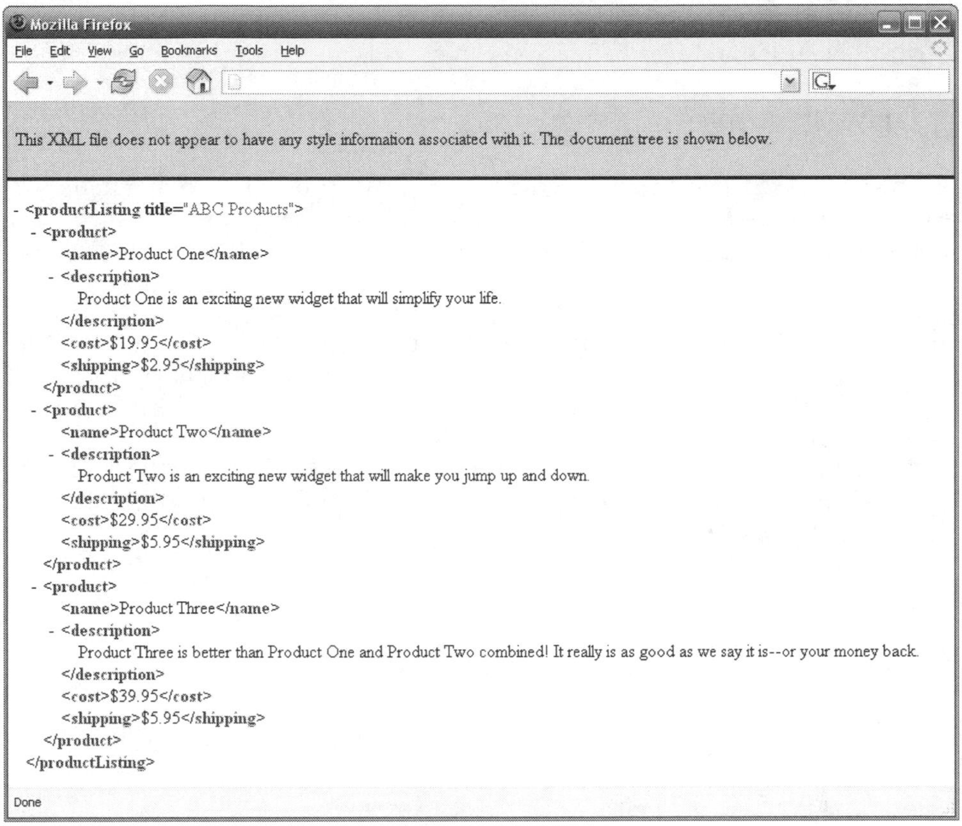

```
Mozilla Firefox
File  Edit  View  Go  Bookmarks  Tools  Help

This XML file does not appear to have any style information associated with it. The document tree is shown below.

- <productListing title="ABC Products">
   - <product>
        <name>Product One</name>
      - <description>
           Product One is an exciting new widget that will simplify your life.
        </description>
        <cost>$19.95</cost>
        <shipping>$2.95</shipping>
     </product>
   - <product>
        <name>Product Two</name>
      - <description>
           Product Two is an exciting new widget that will make you jump up and down.
        </description>
        <cost>$29.95</cost>
        <shipping>$5.95</shipping>
     </product>
   - <product>
        <name>Product Three</name>
      - <description>
           Product Three is better than Product One and Product Two combined! It really is as good as we say it is--or your money back.
        </description>
        <cost>$39.95</cost>
        <shipping>$5.95</shipping>
     </product>
  </productListing>

Done
```

Using a Local Validating Parser

Sometimes, it may be impractical to use a Website to validate your XML because of issues relating to connectivity, privacy, or security. In any of these cases, it's a good idea to download one of the freely available solutions.

❑ If you're familiar with Perl, you can use any of the outstanding parser modules written for that language, all of which are available at CPAN.org[3].

❑ If you're comfortable with C++ or Visual Basic, then give MSXML by Microsoft[4] a try.

---

[3] http://www.cpan.org
[4] http://www.microsoft.com/

❑ IBM offers a very good standalone validating parser called XML4J[5]. Just download the package and install it by following the instructions provided. Be warned, however, that you will have to know something about working with Java tools and files before you can get this one installed successfully.

Using Dreamweaver

Dreamweaver isn't just a tool for creating Web pages; it's also an integrated development environment (IDE) that offers a suite of development tools to the interested Web developer.

One of Dreamweaver's more interesting capabilities is its built-in XML validator. This checks for well-formedness if the document has no DTD, and for well-formedness and validity if a DTD is specified. If you don't have a copy of Dreamweaver, you can get a trial version[6] to play with.

To validate an XML document, choose File > Check Page in Dreamweaver, then select Validate as XML. Results of the validation will appear under the Results area, as illustrated in Figure 1.7.

Figure 1.7. Dreamweaver MX's validating XML parser.

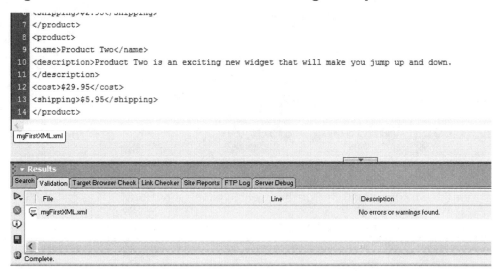

---

[5] http://www.alphaworks.ibm.com/tech/xml4j
[6] http://www.macromedia.com/go/trydreamweaver

What if I Can't Get a Validating Parser?

If you can't get your hands on a validating parser, don't panic. For most purposes, an online resource will do the job nicely. If you work in a company that has an established software development group, chances are that one of the XML-savvy developers has already set up a good validating parser.

What about the content management system we'll work on through the course of this book? Well, we won't need to validate our XML documents until we get close to the project's end, when we start to deal with Web Services, and need to figure out how to accept XML content from (and send content to) organizations in the world at large.

Starting Our CMS Project

Now that we've introduced XML and played around with some documents and parsers, it's time to start our project. Throughout this book, we'll spend time building an XML-powered Website. Specifically, we're going to build an XML-powered content management system. This project will help ground your skills as you obtain firsthand experience with practical XML development techniques, issues, and processes.

So... What's a Content Management System?

A content management system (henceforth referred to as a CMS) is a piece of server-side software that's used to create, publish, and maintain content easily and efficiently on a Website. It usually consists of the following components:

❑ A data back-end (comprising XML or database tables) that contains all your articles, news stories, images, and other content.

❑ A data display component—usually templates or other pages—onto which your articles, images, etc., are "painted" by the CMS for display to site visitors.

❑ A data administration component. This usually comprises easy-to-use HTML forms that allow site administrators to create, edit, publish, and delete articles in some kind of secure workflow. The data administration portion of a CMS is usually the most complicated, and this is the section on which you'll likely spend most of your development time.

Over the past decade, CMSs have been created using a range of different scripting languages including Perl/CGI, ASP, TCL, JSP, Python, and PHP. Each of these languages has its own pros and cons, but we'll use PHP with XML to build our CMS.

Requirements Gathering

Before you build any kind of CMS, first you must gather information that defines the basic requirements for the project.

The goal of the CMS is to make things easier for those who need to develop and run the site. And making things easier means having to do more homework beforehand! Although you may groan at the thought of this kind of exercise, a set of well-defined requirements can make the project run a lot more smoothly.

What kind of requirements do we need to gather? Essentially, requirements fall into three major categories:

❑ What kind of content will the CMS handle? How is each type of content broken down? (The more complete your understanding of this issue, the easier it'll be to create and manage your XML files.)

❑ Who will be visiting the site, and what behaviors do these users expect to find? (For example, will they want to browse a hierarchical list of articles, search for articles by keyword, see links to related articles, or all three?)

❑ What do the site administrators need to do? (For example, they may need to log in securely, create content, edit content, publish content, and delete content. If your CMS will provide different roles for administrative users—such as site administrators, editors, and writers—your system will become more complex.)

As you can see, we've barely scratched the surface, and already we've uncovered a number of issues that need addressing. Let's tackle them one at a time.

CMS Content and Metadata

If you're going to build a content management system, it's logical to expect that you're going to want to put content into it. However, it's not always that easy!

The most common failing I've seen on dozens of CMS engagements on which I've worked is that most of the companies that actually take the time to think about content only think about one thing: "articles!" I'm not exactly sure why that is, but I'd venture to guess that articles are what most folks are exposed to when they read newspapers, magazines, or Websites, so it's the first—and only—content type that comes to mind.

But if you're going to build a workable CMS, you'll have to think beyond "articles" and define your content types more clearly. There's a whole range of content types that need management: PDFs, images, news stories, multimedia presentations, user reviews of whitepapers/PDFs, and much, much more. In the world of XML, each of these different types of content is, naturally enough, called a **document type**.

The second most common failing I see is an inability to successfully convince site owners that content means more than just "articles." What's even harder is to convince them that you have to know as much as you possibly can about each content type if you're going to successfully build their CMS.

It's not good enough to know that you'll be serving PDF files, news stories, images, and so on. You also have to know how each of these content types will break out into its separate components, or **metadata**. Metadata means "data about data" and it is immensely useful to the CMS developer. Each article, for instance, will have various pieces of metadata, such as a headline, author name, and keywords, each of which the CMS needs to track.

The only way to understand a content type's metadata is to research it—in other words, ask yourself and others a whole lot of questions about that piece of content.

The final challenge—to define various types of metadata—can be a blessing in disguise. In my experience, once people grasp the importance of metadata, they race off in every direction and collect every single piece of metadata they can find about a given content type. Usually, we developers end up with random bits of information that aren't very useful and will never be used. For example, the client might start to track the date on which an article is first drafted. In most cases, this is unimportant information—the reader certainly doesn't care!

Obviously, it's important to look for the right kinds of metadata, like these:

Provenance Metadata
> Who created the content? When? When was it first published? When should it automatically be removed from the site, or archived? How is this document uniquely identified in the system? Who holds the copyright to it?

Organizational/Administrative Metadata

If you're using category listings for your content, where will any individual piece of content live within that category system? What other content is it related to? Which keywords describe the content for indexing or search purposes (in other words, how do we find the content)? Who should have access to the content (the entire public, only site subscribers, or company staff)?

Physical/Structural Metadata

Is the content ASCII text, an XML snippet, or a binary file, like a PDF or image? If it's a file, where does it reside on the server? What is the file's MIME type?

Descriptive Metadata

If it's an article, what's the headline? Does the CMS view an article body as being separate from headings and paragraphs, or are all these items seen as one big lump of XML?

Gathering metadata can be very tricky. Let's take a look at a seemingly trivial issue: handling metadata about authors of articles. At first glance, we could say that all of our articles should contain elements for author name and email address, and leave it at that. However, we may later decide that we want site visitors to search or browse articles by author. In this case, it would make more sense to have a centralized list of authors, each with his or her own unique ID. This would eliminate the possibility of our having Tom Myer and Thomas Myer as "separate" authors just because the name was entered differently in individual articles.

Having a separate author listing would also allow us to easily set bylines for each author, in case someone decided they wanted to publish pieces under a pen name. It would also allow us to track author information across content types. We'd know, for instance, if a particular author has penned articles, written reviews, or uploaded files. Of course, agreeing on this approach means that we need to do other work later on, such as building administrative interfaces for author listings.

Once you've figured out the metadata required for a given content type, you can move on to the next content type. Eventually, you'll have a clear picture of all the content types you want your site to support.

What's the point of all this activity? Well, just think of metadata as one of the three pillars of your XML-powered CMS. (The other two are site functionality and site design. In many ways, metadata affect both and, thus, the user's experience of your site.) *Every piece of metadata could potentially drive some kind of site beha-*

vior, but each piece of metadata also must be managed by the administration tools you set up.

Site Behavior

Site behavior should always be based on (and driven by) metadata. For example, if you're collecting keywords for all of your articles, you should be able to build a keyword-driven search engine for your site. If you're not collecting keyword information and want a keyword-driven search engine, you'd better back up and figure out how to add that to your content types.

Typical site behavior for a CMS-powered Website includes browsing by content categories, browsing by author, searching on titles and keywords, dynamic news sidebars, and more. Additionally, many XML- and database-powered sites feature homepages that boast dynamically updated content, such as Top Ten Downloads, latest news headlines, and so on.

CMS Administration

Our CMS will need to have an administrative component for each content type. It will also have to administer pieces of information that have nothing to do with content types, such as which users are authorized to log in to the CMS, and the privileges each of them has.

It goes without saying that your administrative interface has to be secure, otherwise, anyone could click to your CMS and start deleting content, making unauthorized changes to existing content, or adding new content that you may not want to have on your site.

In cases in which more than one person or department is involved with publishing content via the CMS, you'll need to consider workflow. A workflow is simply a set of rules that allow you to define who does what, when, and how. For example, your workflow might stipulate that a user with writer privileges may create an article, but that only a production editor can approve that content for publication on the site.

In many cases, CMS workflows emulate actual workflows that exist in publication and marketing departments. Because we're dealing with XML, we have a great opportunity to build a workflow system that's modular and flexible enough to take into account different requirements.

Defining your Content Types

We want to publish articles and news stories on our site. We definitely want to keep track of authors and site administrators, and we also want to build a search engine. We will also need to keep a record of all the copy on each of our site's pages, as well as binary files such as images and PDFs. That's a lot of work! For now, let's just step through the process of defining an article.

You may be asking, "Why are we messing around with content types at all?" It does seem like a silly thing for a developer to be doing, but it's actually the most vital task in building an XML-powered site. Whenever I build an XML-powered application, I try to define the content types first, because I find that all the other elements cascade from there. Because we've already spent some time discussing the structure of XML documents, and gathering requirements for the documents that will reside in our system, let's jump right in and start to define our article content type.

Articles

The articles in our CMS will be the mainstay of our site. In addition to the article text, each of our articles will be endowed with the following pieces of metadata:

❏ A unique identifier

❏ A headline

❏ A short description

❏ An author

❏ A keyword listing

❏ A publication date, which records when an article went live

❏ Its status

Our article content type requires a root element that contains all the others; we can use `<article>` as that element. This not only makes sense from a "keep it simple" standpoint, but it is semantically appropriate, too.

Furthermore, because we need to identify each article in our system uniquely with an ID of some sort, it makes sense to add an `id` attribute to the root element that will contain this value. A unique identifier will ensure that no mistakes occur when we try to edit, delete, or view an existing article.

Now, each of our articles will have an author, so we need to reserve a spot for that information. There are literally dozens of ways to do this, but we'll take the simplest approach for now:

```
<article id="123">
  <author>Tom Myer</author>
</article>
```

Looking for the DTD?

In Chapter 3, we'll discuss document type definitions (DTDs)—the traditional means to structure the rules for an XML file—in detail. For now, I think it makes more sense to continue our discussion in the direction we've already chosen.

Our article will need a headline, a short description, a publication date, and some keywords. The `<headline>` is very simple—it can have its own element nested under the `<article>` element. Likewise, the `<description>` and `<pubdate>` elements will be nested under `<article>`.

The keyword listing can be handled in one of two ways. You could create under `<article>` a `<keywords>` element that itself was able to contain numerous `<keyword>` items:

```
<article id="123">
  <author>Tom Myer</author>
  <headline>Creating an XML-powered CMS</headline>
  <description>This article will show you how to create an
    XML-powered content management system</description>
  <pubdate>2004-01-20</pubdate>
  <keywords>
    <keyword>XML</keyword>
    <keyword>CMS</keyword>
  </keywords>
</article>
```

This approach will satisfy the structure nuts out there, but it turns out to be too complicated for the way we will eventually use these keywords. It turns out that all you really need is to list your keywords in a single `<keywords>` element, separated by spaces:

```
<article id="123">
  <author>Tom Myer</author>
  <headline>Creating an XML-powered CMS</headline>
  <description>This article will show you how to create an
    XML-powered content management system</description>
  <pubdate>2004-01-20</pubdate>
  <keywords>XML CMS</keywords>
</article>
```

Since individual keywords won't really have any importance in our system, this way of storing them works just fine.

Let's take a look at our growing XML document:

```
<article id="123">
  <author>Tom Myer</author>
  <headline>Creating an XML-powered CMS</headline>
  <description>This article will show you how to create an
    XML-powered content management system</description>
  <pubdate>2004-01-20</pubdate>
  <keywords>XML CMS</keywords>
</article>
```

We also need to track status information on the article. Because we don't need very robust workflows in this application, we can keep our status list very short, to "in progress" and "live."

Any article that is "in progress" will not be displayed on the live Website. It's a piece of content that's being worked on internally. Any article that is "live" will be displayed.

The easiest way to keep track of this information is to add a `<status>` element to our document:

```
<status>in progress</status>
```

However, you probably already see that status is very similar to keyword listings in that it has the potential to belong to many different content types. As such, it makes sense to centralize this information. We'll address this issue later, but for now, we'll continue to store status information in each article.

Now, we have to do something about the article's body. As most of our content will be displayed in a Web browser, it makes sense to use as many tags as possible that a browser like IE or Firefox can already understand. So HTML will form the basis of our article body's code. But for the purposes of our article storage system, we want to treat all of the HTML tags and text that make up the document body as a simple text string, rather than having to handle every single HTML tag that could appear in the article body. The best way to do this is to use a **CDATA section** within our XML document. XML parsers ignore tags, comments, and other XML syntax within a CDATA section—it simply passes the code through as a text string, without trying to interpret it. Here's what this looks like:

```
<body><![CDATA[
  <h1>Creating an XML-powered CMS</h1>
  <p>Here is all of our paragraph information. . .</p>
]]></body>
```

Well, we're done with articles! They now look like this:

```
<article id="123">
  <author>Tom Myer</author>
  <headline>Creating an XML-powered CMS</headline>
  <description>This article will show you how to create an
    XML-powered content management system</description>
  <pubdate>2004-01-20</pubdate>
  <status>live</status>
  <keywords>XML CMS</keywords>
  <body><![CDATA[
    <h1>Creating an XML-powered CMS</h1>
    <p>In this article…</p>
  ]]></body>
</article>
```

Gathering Requirements for Content Display

We now understand our article content type, which defines most of the content we'll display on the site. Now, let's talk about our requirements for displaying content.

❑ The display side of our site will only display articles and other content that have a status of "live."

❑ The search engine will retrieve content by keywords, titles, and descriptions, and only display those pieces that have a status of live.

❑ The Website will display a list of author names by which site visitors can browse content, but it will only display those authors who have live articles posted on the site.

Gathering Requirements for the Administrative Tool

Let's talk briefly about the administrative tool. Here are some of the project's administration requirements:

❑ All CMS users must log into the administrative tool. All passwords set for administrators will be encrypted before they're stored.

❑ Each content type will have its own page through which users may list, add, edit, and delete individual pieces of content.

❑ The same is true for authors and administrators. If you view an author listing, the CMS will display all pieces of content authored by that person.

❑ The CMS will provide an easy method to update status, keyword, and other details for each piece of content on the site. Administrators will be able to group this information by status or content type.

Great—this is enough detail to get us started!

Summary

In this first chapter, we've discussed basic XML concepts, talked about the importance of the requirements gathering process, and performed an analysis to come up with content types and application requirements for our XML-powered CMS.

In the next chapter, we're going to delve deeper into XML, covering such topics as basic XSLT and XPath. We'll get our hands dirty with a little XSLT and start thinking about how we should display articles on our CMS-powered Website.

XML in Practice

The last chapter introduced some basic concepts in XML and saw us start our CMS project. In this chapter, we're going to dig a little deeper into XML as we talk about namespaces, XHTML, XSLT, and CSS. In the process, we'll have take a couple of opportunities to make XML *do* something.

Meet the Family

In Chapter 1, we learned a few things about how XML is structured and what you can do with it. My goal for that chapter was to show you how flexible XML really is.

In this chapter, I'd like to zoom out a little and introduce you to some of the wacky siblings that make up the XML "Family of Technologies." Although I'm going to list a number of tools and technologies here, we'll cover only a few in this chapter. We'll explore some of the others in later chapters, but some will not be covered at all (sorry, but this would be a very long and boring book if we gave equal space to everything).

XSLT

XSLT stands for Extensible Stylesheet Language Transformations. It is both a style sheet specification and a kind of programming language that allows you to transform an XML document into the format of your choice: stripped

ASCII text, HTML, RTF, and even other dialects of XML. In this chapter, you'll be introduced to XSLT concepts; later in the book, we'll explore these in more depth. XSLT uses XPath and several other technologies to do its work.

XPath

XPath is a language for locating and processing nodes in an XML document. Because each XML document is, by definition, a hierarchical structure, it becomes possible to navigate this structure in a logical, formal way (i.e. by following a path).

DTD and XML Schema

A document type definition (DTD) is a set of rules that governs the order in which your elements can be used, and the kind of information each can contain. XML Schema is a newer standard with capabilities that extend far beyond those of DTDs. While a DTD can provide only general control over element ordering and containment, schemas are a lot more specific. They can, for example, allow elements to appear only a certain number of times, or require that elements contain specific types of data such as dates and numbers.

Both technologies allow you to set rules for the contents of your XML documents. If you need to share your XML documents with another group, or you must rely on receiving well-formed XML from someone else, these technologies can help ensure that your particular set of rules is properly followed. We will explore both of these technologies with loving attention in Chapter 3.

XML Namespaces

The ability of XML to allow you to define your own elements provides flexibility and scope. But it also creates the strong possibility that, when combining XML content from different sources, you'll experience clashes between code in which the same element names serve very different purposes. For example, if you're running a bookstore, your use of `<title>` tags in XML may be used to track book titles. A mortgage broker would use `<title>` in a different way—perhaps to track the title on a deed. A dentist or doctor might use `<title>` to track patients' formal titles (Mr., Ms., Mrs., or Dr.) on their medical records. Try to combine all three types of information into one system (or even one document), and you'll quickly see how problems can arise.

XML namespaces attempt to keep different semantic usages of the same XML elements separate and unambiguous. In our example, each person could define their own namespace and then prepend the name of their namespace to specific tags: `<book:title>` is different from `<broker:title>` and `<medrec:title>`. Namespaces, by the way, are one of the technologies that make XSLT and XSD work.

XHTML

XHTML stands for Extensible Hypertext Markup Language. Technically speaking, it's a reformulation of HTML 4.01 as an application of XML, and is not part of the XML family of technologies. To save your brain from complete meltdown, it might be simplest to think of XHTML as a standard for HTML markup tags that follow all the well-formedness rules of XML we covered earlier.

What's the point of that, you might ask? Well, there are tons and tons and *tons* of Websites out there that already use HTML. No one in their right mind could reasonably expect them all to switch to XML overnight. But we *can* expect that some of these pages—and a large percentage of the new pages that are being coded as you read this—will make the transition thanks to XHTML.

As you can see, the XML family of technologies is a pretty big group—those XML family reunions are undoubtedly interesting! It's also important to note that these technologies are open standards-based, which means that any new XML technologies (or proposed changes to existing ones) must follow a public process set down by the W3C (the World Wide Web Consortium[1]) in order to gain acceptance in the community.

Although this means that some ideas take quite a while to reach fruition, and tend to be built by committee, it also means that no single vendor is in total control of XML. And this, as Martha Stewart might say, is a good thing.

A Closer Look at XHTML

Imagine you're at a cocktail party and somebody asks, "Okay, what's XHTML *really*?" You needed to tell them something (besides, "Hey, I'm trying to have a relaxing cocktail here!"). So, what do you say? Not sure? That's what I thought.

Because this is a book about XML and not XHTML, and because there are plenty of terrific books out there on XHTML, I don't want to get into too much detail about the technology here. However, I do feel that a basic knowledge of XHTML

---

[1] http://www.w3.org

will serve you well, and will help to reinforce the concepts we've already introduced.

So, back to our cocktail party. Here are some answers that you might give in that
situation:

❑ XHTML stands for Extensible HyperText Markup Language.

❑ XHTML is designed to replace HTML.

❑ XHTML uses the HTML 4.01 tag set, but is written using the XML syntax
rules.

❑ XHTML is a stricter, cleaner version of HTML.

Why do we need XHTML? Well, put bluntly, the Web has reached a point at
which just about anything will fly when it comes to HTML documents. Take a
look at the following snippet:

```
<html><title>My example</title>
<h1>Hello</h1>
```

Believe it or not, that snippet will render without a problem in most Web
browsers. And so will this:

```
<p><b><i>Hello</b>
```

So will this:

```
Hello
```

I don't want to start some kind of crusade about HTML structure, but hey,
enough is enough! Web pages represent structured information, so please, let's
at least maintain some semblance of structure! At its most basic, XHTML was
designed to form a kind of bridge between the loosy-goosy world of HTML and
the more rigid structure of XML.

Remember that list of statements about XHTML we saw a moment ago? Well,
here's another way to think about XHTML:

❑ XHTML consists of all HTML 4.01 elements combined with the syntax of
XML.

Simple! But, exactly what does this mean? Well, if you recall what we said in Chapter 1 about well-formed XML documents, you can make some very good guesses:

1. XHTML documents must contain a root element that contains all other elements. (In most cases, the `html` element!)

2. XHTML elements must be properly nested.

   ```
   <p>This is a <b>sentence.</b></p>
   ```

3. All XHTML elements must have closing tags (even empty ones).

   ```
   <br />
   <td></td>
   ```

note

Don't Slash Backwards Compatibility

Older browsers, such as Netscape 4, which do not recognize XML syntax, will become confused by self-closing tags like `<br/>`. By simply adding a space before the slash (`<br />`), you can ensure that these browsers will ignore the slash and interpret the tag correctly.

4. All XHTML attribute values must be placed between quotes.

   ```
   <input type="button" name="submit" value="click to finish" />
   ```

5. All XHTML element and attribute names must be written in lowercase.

   ```
   <tr valign="top">
   ```

6. Each XHTML document must have a DOCTYPE declaration at the top.

   ```
   <!DOCTYPE html PUBLIC "-//W3C//DTD XHTML 1.0 Transitional//EN"
       "http://www.w3.org/TR/xhtml1/DTD/xhtml1-transitional.dtd">
   <html xmlns="http://www.w3.org/1999/xhtml">
   ```

There are three XHTML DOCTYPES:

Strict
   Use this with CSS to minimize presentational clutter. In fact, the Strict DOCTYPE expressly prohibits the use of HTML's presentation tags.

```
<!DOCTYPE html
    PUBLIC "-//W3C//DTD XHTML 1.0 Strict//EN"
    "http://www.w3.org/TR/xhtml1/DTD/xhtml1-strict.dtd">
```

Transitional

Use this to take advantage of HTML's presentational features and/or when you're supporting non-CSS browsers.

```
<!DOCTYPE html
    PUBLIC "-//W3C//DTD XHTML 1.0 Transitional//EN"
    "http://www.w3.org/TR/xhtml1/DTD/xhtml1-transitional.dtd">
```

Frameset

Use this when you want to use frames to partition the screen.

```
<!DOCTYPE html
    PUBLIC "-//W3C//DTD XHTML 1.0 Frameset//EN"
    "http://www.w3.org/TR/xhtml1/DTD/xhtml1-frameset.dtd">
```

A Minimalist XHTML Example

Here's a very simple document that illustrates the rules above:

```
<!DOCTYPE html PUBLIC "-//W3C//DTD XHTML 1.0 Transitional//EN"
    "http://www.w3.org/TR/xhtml1/DTD/xhtml1-transitional.dtd">
<html xmlns="http://www.w3.org/1999/xhtml">
<head>
<title>A very simple XHTML document</title>
<meta http-equiv="content-type"
    content="text/html; charset=iso-8859-1" />
</head>
<body>
<p>a simple paragraph that contains a properly formatted<br />
break and some <b><i>properly nested</i></b> formatting.</p>
<div><img src="myphoto.jpg" alt="notice that all my quotes are in
place for attribute values" /></div>
</body>
</html>
```

That's more than enough information about XHTML for the moment. Let's move on to discuss namespaces and XSLT.

XML Namespaces

XML Namespaces were invented to rectify a common problem: the collision of documents using identical element names for different data.

Let's revisit our namespace example from this chapter's introduction. Imagine you were running a bookstore and had an inventory file (called `inventory.xml`, naturally), in which you used a `title` element to store book titles. Let's also say that—unlikely though it sounds—your XML document becomes mixed in with a mortgage broker's master record file. In this file, the mortgage broker has used `title` to store information about a property's legal title.

A human being could probably figure out that one `title` has nothing to do with the other, but an application that tried to sort it out would go nuts. We need to have a way to distinguish between the two different semantic universes in which these identical terms exist.

Let's get even more ambiguous: imagine you had an `inventory.xml` file in your bookstore that used the `title` element to store book titles, and a separate `sales.xml` file that used the `title` element to store the same information, but in a completely different context. Your inventory file stores information about books on the shelf, but the sales file stores information about books that have been bought by customers.

In either situation, regardless of the chasm that lies between the contexts of these identical terms, we need a way to properly label each context.

Namespaces to the rescue! XML namespaces allow you to create a unique namespace based on a URI (Uniform Resource Identifier), give that namespace a prefix, and apply that prefix to XML document elements.

Declaring Namespaces

To use and declare a namespace, we must first tie the namespace to a URI. Notice that I didn't say URL—a specific location that you can reach (although a URI can be a URL). A URI is simply a unique identifier that distinguishes one thing (say, an XML document standard) from another. URIs can take the following forms:

URL   Uniform Resource Locator: a specific protocol, machine address, and file path (e.g. `http://www.tripledogdaremedia.com/index.php`).

URN   Uniform Resource Name: a persistent name that doesn't point to an actual location for the resource, but still identifies it uniquely. For example, all published books have an ISBN. The ISBN uniquely identifies the book, but nowhere in the ISBN is there any indication as to which shelf it sits on in any particular bookstore. However, armed with the ISBN, you could walk into the store, ask an employee to search for you, and they could take you right to the book (provided, of course, that it was in stock).

The following are examples of good URIs:

```
http://www.tripledogdaremedia.com/XML/Namespaces/1
urn:bookstore-inventory-namespace
```

We want to use our namespace throughout our XML documents, though, and the last thing we want to do is type out an entire URI every time we need to distinguish one context from another. So, we define a prefix to represent our namespace to ease the strain on our typing fingers:

```
inv="urn:bookstore-inventory-namespace"
```

But, wait—we're not done yet! We need a way to tell the XML parser that we're creating a namespace. The agreed way to do that is to prefix the namespace declaration with `xmlns:`, like this:

```
xmlns:inv="urn:bookstore-inventory-namespace"
```

At this point, we have something useful. If we needed to, we could add our prefix to appropriate elements to disambiguate (I love that term!) any potentially ambiguous usage, like this:

```
<inv:title>Build Your Own XML-Powered Web Site</inv:title>
<title>Title Deed to the house on 123 Main St., YourTown</title>
```

Namespaces make it very clear that `<inv:title>` is very different from `<title>`.

But, where do we put our namespace declaration?

Placing Namespace Declarations in your XML Documents

In most cases, placing your namespace declarations will be rather easy. They're commonly located in the root element of a document, like so:

```
<inventory xmlns:inv="urn:bookstore-inventory-namespace">
...
</inventory>
```

Please note, however, that namespaces have scope. Namespaces affect the element in which they are declared, as well as all the child elements of that element. In fact, as you'll see when we discuss XSLT later, we'll use the `xsl` prefix in the very element in which we define the XSL namespace:

```
<xsl:stylesheet
    xmlns:xsl="http://www.w3.org/1999/XSL/Transform"
    xmlns="http://www.w3.org/1999/xhtml"
    version="1.0">
```

Any namespace declaration that's placed in a document's root element becomes available to all elements in that document. However, if you want to limit your namespace scope to a certain part of a document, feel free to do so—remembering, of course, that this can get pretty tricky. My advice is to declare your namespaces in the document's root element, then use the prefixes when you need them.

Using Default Namespaces

It would become pretty tiresome to have to type a prefix for every single element in a document. Fortunately, you can declare a default namespace that doesn't contain a prefix. This namespace will apply to all elements that don't contain prefixes.

Let's take another look at a typical opening `<xsl:stylesheet>` tag for an XSLT file:

```
<xsl:stylesheet
    xmlns:xsl="http://www.w3.org/1999/XSL/Transform"
    xmlns="http://www.w3.org/1999/xhtml"
    version="1.0">
```

Notice the non-prefixed namespace: `xmlns="http://www.w3.org/1999/xhtml"` In an XSLT file, this namespace governs all elements that aren't specifically prefixed as XSLT elements, identifying them as XHTML tags. On the other side of the coin, all XSLT elements must be given the `xsl:` prefix.

Using CSS to Display XML In a Browser

The most powerful tools available for displaying XML in a browser are XSLT and Cascading Style Sheets (CSS). Because XSLT can be quite a tricky undertaking for newbies, I've decided to let you practice with CSS first!

The first step in working with CSS is to create a basic XML file:

File: **letter.xml (excerpt)**

```
<?xml version="1.0"?>
<letter>
  <to>Mom</to>
  <from>Tom</from>
  <message>Happy Mother's Day</message>
</letter>
```

As XML documents go, this one could be made a lot simpler, but there's no point in making things too simple. This document contains a root element (`letter`) that contains three other elements (`to`, `from`, and `message`), each of which contains text.

Now, we need to add a style sheet declaration that will point to the CSS document we'll create. To associate a CSS style sheet with an XML file, use the `<?xml-stylesheet?>`directive:

File: **letter-css.xml (excerpt)**

```
<?xml-stylesheet type="text/css" href="letter.css"?>
```

Finally, we write our CSS file, making sure that we provide a style for each element in our XML file:

File: **letter.css**

```
letter {
  display: block;
  margin: 10px;
  padding: 5px;
  width: 300px;
  height: 100px;
  border: 1px solid #00000;
  overflow: auto;
  background-color: #cccccc;
  font: 12px Arial;
}
```

```
to, from {
  display: block;
  font-weight: bold;
}
message {
  display: block;
  font: 11px Arial;
}
```

When you display your XML document, you should see something similar to Figure 2.1.

Figure 2.1. Viewing the CSS results in Internet Explorer.

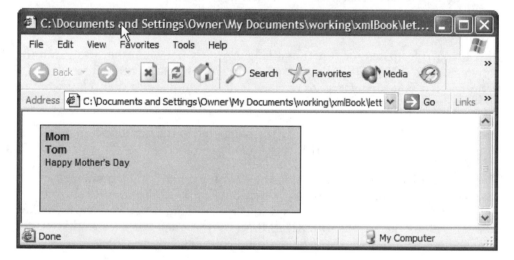

As you can see, CSS did a marvelous job of rendering a nicely shaded box around the entire letter, setting fonts, and even displaying things like margins and padding. What it didn't allow us to do, however, was add text to the output. For instance, we could use a "To:" in front of whatever text was in the to element. If you want to have that kind of power, you'll need to use XSLT.[2]

---

[2]Strictly speaking, the CSS standard does allow for this sort of thing with the content property, which can produce generated text before and after document elements. Many browsers do not support this property, however, and even those that do don't provide anywhere near the flexibility of XSLT.

Getting to Know XSLT

XSLT, as I mentioned earlier in the chapter, stands for Extensible Stylesheet Language Transformations. Think of it as a tool that you can use to transform your XML documents into other documents. Here are some of the possibilities:

❑ Transform XML into HTML or raw ASCII text.

❑ Transform XML into other dialects of XML.

❑ Pull out all the passages tagged as Spanish, or French, or German to create foreign-language versions of your XML document.

Not bad—and we've barely scratched the surface!

XSLT is a rules-based, or functional language. It's not like other programming languages (e.g. PHP or JSP) that are procedural or object-oriented. Instead, XSLT requires that you supply a series of rules (called "templates") that tell it what to do when it encounters the various elements of an XML document.

For instance, upon identifying an XML `<para>` tag in the input document, a rule could instruct XSLT to convert it into an HTML `<p>` tag.

Because XSLT can be a little bewildering even for veteran programmers, the best way to tackle it is to walk through a series of examples. That way, I can give you the practical information you'll need to get started, and you can learn the key concepts along the way. As with XHTML, countless books, articles, and Websites are devoted to XSLT; use these to continue your education.

Your First XSLT Exercise

Let's get started with XSLT. For our first exercise, we'll reuse the very simple Letter to Mother example we saw in the CSS section. We'll also create a very basic Extensible Stylesheet Language (XSL) file to transform that XML. Keeping both these elements simple will give us the opportunity to step through the major concepts involved.

First, let's create the XSL file. This file will contain all the instructions we'll need in order to transform the XML elements into raw text.

In what will become a recurring theme in the world of XML, XSL files are in fact XML files in their own right. They must therefore follow the rules that apply to all XML documents: an XSL file must contain a root element, all attribute values must be quoted, and so on.

All XSL documents begin with a `stylesheet` element This element contains information that the XSLT processor needs to do its job:

File: **letter2text.xsl (excerpt)**

```
<xsl:stylesheet version="1.0"
    xmlns:xsl="http://www.w3.org/1999/XSL/Transform">
```

The `version` attribute is required. In most cases, you'd use `1.0`, as this is the most widely supported version at the time of this writing.

The `xmlns:xsl` attribute is used to declare an XML namespace with the prefix `xsl`. For your stylesheet transformation to work at all, you must declare an XML namespace for the URI `http://www.w3.org/1999/XSL/Transform` in your opening `<stylesheet>` tag. In our example, we will use an `xsl` prefix on all the stylesheet-related tags in our XSL documents to associate them with this namespace. You'll find this is common practice when working with XSLT.

The next element will be the `output` element, which is used to define the type of output you want from the XSL file. For this first example, we'll use `text` as our `method`:

File: **letter2text.xsl (excerpt)**

```
<xsl:output method="text"/>
```

Other possible values for the `method` attribute include `html` and `xml`, but we'll cover those a little later.

Now we come to the heart of XSLT—the `template` and `apply-templates` elements. Together, these two elements make the transformations happen.

Put simply, the XSLT processor (for our immediate purposes, the browser) starts reading the input document, looking for elements that match any of the `template` elements in our style sheet. When one is found, the contents of the corresponding `template` element tells the processor what to output before continuing its search. Where a template contains an `apply-templates` element, the XSLT processor will search for XML elements contained *within* the current element and apply templates associated with them.

There are some exceptions and additional complications that we'll see as we move forward, but for now, that's really all there is to it.

The first thing we want to do is match the `letter` element that contains the rest of our document. This is fairly straightforward:

File: **letter2text.xsl (excerpt)**

```
<xsl:template match="/letter">
  <xsl:apply-templates select="*"/>
</xsl:template>
```

This very simple batch of XSLT simply states: "when you encounter a `letter` element at the root of the document, apply any templates associated with the elements it contains." Let's break this down.

The `<xsl:template>` tag is used to create a template, with the `match` attribute indicating which element(s) it should match. The value of this attribute is an XPath expression (we'll learn more about XPath later). In this case, the `/letter` value indicates that the template should match the `letter` elements at the root of the document. Were the value simply `letter`, the template would match `letter` elements throughout the document.

Now, this `<xsl:template>` tag contains only an `<xsl:apply-templates>` tag, which means that it doesn't actually output anything itself. Rather, the `<xsl:apply-templates>` tag sends the processor looking for other elements with matching templates.

By default, `apply-templates` will match not only elements, but text and even whitespace between the elements as well. XSLT processors have a set of default, or **implicit templates**, one of which simply outputs any text or whitespace it encounters. Since we want to ignore any text or whitespace that appears between the tags inside `<letter>`, we use the `select` attribute of `apply-templates` to tell the processor to look for child elements only in its search. We do this with another XPath expression: `*` means "all child elements of the current element."

Now, we've got our processor looking for elements inside `letter`, so we'd better give it some templates to match them!

File: **letter2text.xsl (excerpt)**

```
<xsl:template match="to">
  TO: <xsl:apply-templates/>
</xsl:template>
<xsl:template match="from">
  FROM: <xsl:apply-templates/>
</xsl:template>
<xsl:template match="message">
```

```
   MESSAGE: <xsl:apply-templates/>
  </xsl:template>
```

Each of these templates matches one of the elements we expect to find inside the letter element: to, from, and message. In each case, we output a text label (e.g. TO:) and then use apply-templates to output the contents of the tag (remember, in the absence of a select attribute that says otherwise, apply-templates will output any text contained in the tags automatically).

The last thing we have to do in the XSL file is close off the stylesheet element that began the file:

```
</xsl:stylesheet>
```

Our style sheet now looks like this:

File: **letter2text.xsl (excerpt)**

```
<xsl:stylesheet version="1.0"
   xmlns:xsl="http://www.w3.org/1999/XSL/Transform">
  <xsl:output method="text"/>
  <xsl:template match="/letter">
    <xsl:apply-templates select="*"/>
  </xsl:template>
  <xsl:template match="to">
    TO: <xsl:apply-templates/>
  </xsl:template>
  <xsl:template match="from">
    FROM: <xsl:apply-templates/>
  </xsl:template>
  <xsl:template match="message">
    MESSAGE: <xsl:apply-templates/>
  </xsl:template>
</xsl:stylesheet>
```

While the logic of this style sheet is complete and correct, there's a slight formatting issue left to be tackled. Left this way, the output would look something like this:

```
    TO: Mom
    FROM: Tom
    MESSAGE: Happy Mother's Day
```

There's an extraneous line break at the top of the file, and each of the lines begins with some unwanted whitespace. The line break and whitespace is actually coming from the way we've formatted the code in the style sheet. Each of our three main templates begins with a line break and then some whitespace before the label, which is being carried through to the output.

But wait—what about the line break and whitespace that *ends* each template? Why isn't *that* getting carried through to the output? Well by default, the XSLT standard[3] mandates that whenever there is *only* whitespace (including line breaks) between two tags, the whitespace should be ignored. But when there is text between two tags (e.g. TO:), then the whitespace in and around that text should be passed along to the output.

IMPORTANT

Avoid Whitespace Insanity

The vast majority of XML books and tutorials out there completely ignore these whitespace treatment issues. And while it's true that whitespace doesn't matter a lot of the time when you're dealing exclusively with XML documents (as opposed to formatted text output), it's likely to sneak up on you and bite you in the butt eventually. Best to get a good grasp of it now, rather than waiting for insanity to set in when you least expect it.

The <xsl:text> tag is useful for controlling the effects of whitespace in our style sheets. All it does is output the text it contains, even if it is just whitespace. Here's the adjusted version of our style sheet, with <xsl:text> tags used to isolate text we want to output:

File: **letter2text.xsl**

```
<xsl:stylesheet version="1.0"
    xmlns:xsl="http://www.w3.org/1999/XSL/Transform">
  <xsl:output method="text"/>
  <xsl:template match="/letter">
    <xsl:apply-templates select="*"/>
  </xsl:template>
  <xsl:template match="to">
    <xsl:text>TO: </xsl:text>
    <xsl:apply-templates/>
    <xsl:text>
</xsl:text>
  </xsl:template>
  <xsl:template match="from">
    <xsl:text>FROM: </xsl:text>
    <xsl:apply-templates/>
    <xsl:text>
</xsl:text>
```

---

[3] http://www.w3.org/TR/xslt#strip

```
  </xsl:template>
  <xsl:template match="message">
    <xsl:text>MESSAGE: </xsl:text>
    <xsl:apply-templates/>
    <xsl:text>
</xsl:text>
  </xsl:template>
</xsl:stylesheet>
```

Notice how each template now outputs its label (e.g. TO:) followed by a single space, then finishes off with a line break. All the other whitespace in the style sheet is ignored, since it isn't mixed with text. This gives us the fine control over formatting that we need when outputting a plain text file.

Are we done yet? Not quite. We have to go back and add to our XML document a **style sheet declaration** that will point to our XSL file, just like we did for the CSS example. Simply open the XML document and insert the following line before the opening <letter> element:

File: **letter-text.xml (excerpt)**

```
<?xml-stylesheet type="text/xsl" href="letter2text.xsl"
    version="1.0"?>
```

Now, our XML document looks like this:

File: **letter-text.xml**

```
<?xml version="1.0"?>
<?xml-stylesheet type="text/xsl" href="letter2text.xsl"
    version="1.0"?>
<letter>
  <to>Mom</to>
  <from>Tom</from>
  <message>Happy Mother's Day</message>
</letter>
```

When you view the XML document in Firefox,[4] you should see something similar to the result pictured in Figure 2.2.

---

[4]You can try viewing this in Internet Explorer as well, but you won't see the careful text formatting we applied in our style sheet. Internet Explorer interprets the result as HTML code, even when the style sheet clearly specifies that it will output text. As a result, whitespace is collapsed and our whole document appears on one line.

Figure 2.2. Viewing XSL results in Firefox.

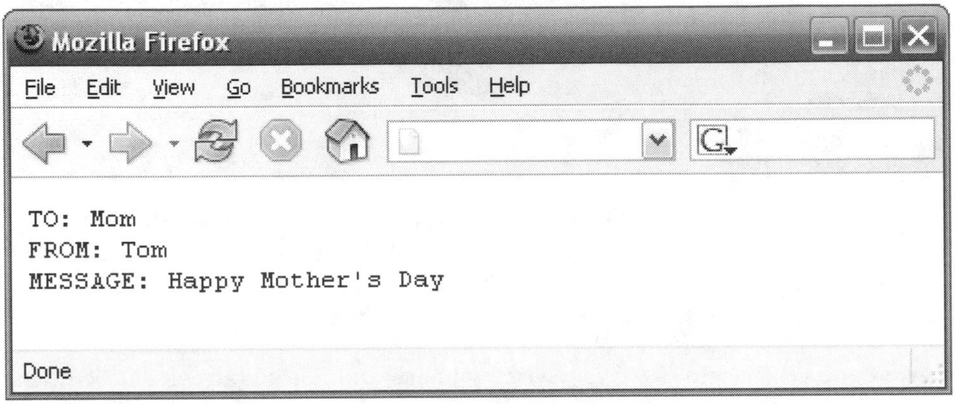

If you're curious, go ahead and view the source of this document. You'll notice that you won't see the output of the transformation (technically referred to as the **result tree**), but you *can* see the XML document source.

note

What About my Favorite Browser?

If you don't use Firefox on a regular basis, you might be a little miffed that I've started out with an example that works only in Mozilla-based browsers.

First of all, if you prefer Internet Explorer, the situation will improve with the next example, which conforms to Internet Explorer's assumption that the result of a transformation must be HTML, not plain text as it was in this example.

As for the other browsers in popular use, including Safari and Opera, these do not yet support XSLT. For this reason, it is not yet practical to rely on browser support for XSLT in a real-world website. As we'll learn in Chapter 7, it is far more sensible to use XSLT on the server side, where it is safe from browser incompatibilities.

For now, however, the solid XSLT capabilities built into Firefox (and to a lesser degree, Internet Explorer) provide a convenient means to learn what XSLT is capable of.

Transforming XML into HTML

That wasn't so bad, was it? You successfully transformed a simple XML document into flat ASCII text, and even added a few extra tidbits to the output.

Now, it's time to make things a little more complex. Let's transform the XML document into HTML. Here's the great part—you won't have to touch the original XML document (aside from pointing it at a new style sheet, that is). All you'll need to do is create a new XSL file:

File: **letter2html.xsl**

```
<xsl:stylesheet version="1.0"
    xmlns:xsl="http://www.w3.org/1999/XSL/Transform">
  <xsl:output method="html"/>
  <xsl:template match="/letter">
    <html>
      <head><title>Letter</title></head>
      <body><xsl:apply-templates/></body>
    </html>
  </xsl:template>
  <xsl:template match="to">
    <b>TO: </b><xsl:apply-templates/><br/>
  </xsl:template>
  <xsl:template match="from">
    <b>FROM: </b><xsl:apply-templates/><br/>
  </xsl:template>
  <xsl:template match="message">
    <b>MESSAGE: </b><xsl:apply-templates/><br/>
  </xsl:template>
</xsl:stylesheet>
```

Right away, you'll notice that the style sheet's output element now specifies an output method of html. Additionally, our first template now outputs the basic tags to produce the framework of an HTML document, and doesn't bother suppressing the whitespace in the source document with a select attribute.

Other than that, these instructions don't differ much from our text-only style sheet. In fact, the only other changes we've made have been to tag the label for each line to be bold, and end each line with an HTML line break (<br/>). We no longer need the <xsl:text> tags, since our HTML <b> and <br/> tags perform the same function.[5]

All we have to do now is edit our XML file to make sure that the <?xml-stylesheet?> instruction references our new style sheet (letter-html.xml in the code archive), and we're ready to display the results in a Web browser.

---

[5]Note the space following each label, which is inside the <b> tag so that it won't be ignored by the processor.

You should see something similar to Figure 2.3.

Figure 2.3. Viewing XSL Results in Internet Explorer.

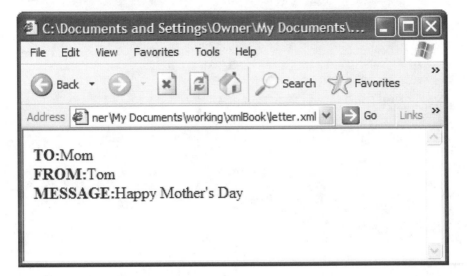

Using XSLT to Transform XML into other XML

What happens if you need to transform your own XML document into an XML document that meets the needs of another organization or person? For instance, what if our letter document, which uses `<to>`, `<from>`, and `<message>` tags inside a `<letter>` tag, needed to have different names, say `<recipient>`, `<sender>`, and `<body>`?

Not to worry—XSLT will save the day! And, as with the two previous examples, we don't even need to worry about changing the source XML document. All we have to do is create a new XSL file, and we're set.

As before, we'll open with the standard `stylesheet` element, but, this time, we'll choose `xml` as our output method. We're also going to instruct XSLT to indent the resulting XML:

File: **letter2xml.xsl (excerpt)**

```
<xsl:stylesheet version="1.0"
    xmlns:xsl="http://www.w3.org/1999/XSL/Transform">
  <xsl:output method="xml" indent="yes"/>
```

The `<template>` elements are structured as before, but this time they output the new XML elements:

File: **letter2xml.xsl (excerpt)**

```
<xsl:template match="/letter">
  <letter><xsl:apply-templates/></letter>
</xsl:template>
<xsl:template match="to">
  <recipient><xsl:apply-templates/></recipient>
</xsl:template>
<xsl:template match="from">
  <sender><xsl:apply-templates/></sender>
</xsl:template>
<xsl:template match="message">
  <body><xsl:apply-templates/></body>
</xsl:template>
</xsl:stylesheet>
```

Now, all you have to do is edit your XML document to point to the style sheet, and you'll be able to view your new XML in any Web browser, right? Wrong! You see, Web browsers only supply collapsible tree formatting for XML documents without style sheets. XML documents that result from a style sheet transformation are displayed without any styling at all, or at best are treated as HTML—not at all the desired result.

Where the browser *can* be useful for viewing XML output is when that XML is an XHTML document—which browsers obviously can display. There are several things that need to be added to your style sheet to signal to the browser that the document is more than a plain XML file, though. The first is the XHTML namespace:

File: **letter2xhtml.xsl (excerpt)**

```
<xsl:stylesheet version="1.0"
    xmlns:xsl="http://www.w3.org/1999/XSL/Transform"
    xmlns="http://www.w3.org/1999/xhtml">
```

Here we have declared a default namespace for tags without prefixes in the style sheet. Thus tags like `<html>` and `<b>` will be correctly identified as XHTML tags.

Next up, we can flesh out the `output` element to more fully describe the output document type:

File: **letter2xhtml.xsl (excerpt)**

```
<xsl:output method="xml" indent="yes" omit-xml-declaration="yes"
    media-type="application/xhtml+xml" encoding="iso-8859-1"
    doctype-public="-//W3C//DTD XHTML 1.0 Transitional//EN"
    doctype-system=
    "http://www.w3.org/TR/xhtml1/DTD/xhtml1-transitional.dtd"/>
```

In addition to the `method` and `indent` attributes, we have specified a number of new attributes here:

omit-xml-declaration This tells the processor not to add a `<?xml?>` declaration to the top of the output document. Internet Explorer for Windows displays XHTML documents in Quirks Mode when this declaration is present, so by omitting it we can ensure that this browser will display it in the more desirable Standards Compliance mode.

media-type Though not required by current browsers, setting this attribute to `application/xhtml+xml` offers another way for the browser to identify the output as an XHTML document, rather than plain XML.

encoding Sets the character encoding of the output document, controlling which characters are escaped as character references (`&xnn;`).

doctype-public
doctype-system Together, these two attributes provide the values needed to generate the DOCTYPE declaration for the output document. In this example, we've specified values for an XHTML 1.0 Transitional document, but you could also specify an XHTML 1.0 Strict document if that's what you need:

```
<xsl:output method="xml" indent="yes" omit-xml-declaration="yes"
    media-type="application/xhtml+xml" encoding="iso-8859-1"
    doctype-public="-//W3C//DTD XHTML 1.0 Strict//EN"
    doctype-system=
    "http://www.w3.org/TR/xhtml1/DTD/xhtml1-strict.dtd"/>
```

The rest of the style sheet is as it was for the HTML output example we saw above. Here's the complete style sheet so you don't have to go searching:

File: **letter2xhtml.xsl**

```
<xsl:stylesheet version="1.0"
    xmlns:xsl="http://www.w3.org/1999/XSL/Transform"
```

```
    xmlns="http://www.w3.org/1999/xhtml">

<xsl:output method="xml" indent="yes" omit-xml-declaration="yes"
    media-type="application/xhtml+xml" encoding="iso-8859-1"
    doctype-public="-//W3C//DTD XHTML 1.0 Transitional//EN"
    doctype-system=
    "http://www.w3.org/TR/xhtml1/DTD/xhtml1-transitional.dtd"/>

<xsl:template match="/letter">
  <html>
    <head><title>Letter</title></head>
    <body><xsl:apply-templates/></body>
  </html>
</xsl:template>

<xsl:template match="to">
  <b>TO: </b><xsl:apply-templates/><br/>
</xsl:template>

<xsl:template match="from">
  <b>FROM: </b><xsl:apply-templates/><br/>
</xsl:template>

<xsl:template match="message">
  <b>MESSAGE: </b><xsl:apply-templates/><br/>
</xsl:template>
</xsl:stylesheet>
```

Point the `<?xml-stylesheet?>` processing instruction in your XML document at this style sheet and then load it in Firefox or Internet Explorer. You should see the output displayed as an XHTML document.

So yes, if the XML you are generating happens to be XHTML, a browser can display it just fine. Otherwise, what we need to display XML output is some kind of standalone XSLT processor that we can run instead of a Web browser... but, guess what? We've run out of space to talk about XSLT in this chapter. We'll pick up this discussion in Chapter 4.

Our CMS Project

In Chapter 1, we did quite a bit of work to analyze the article content type. Now, we need to identify exactly what we need for our news items, binary files, and Web copy. We must also manage and track site administrators using XML. By the time we get to the end of this chapter, we'll be roughly two-thirds the way through the requirements-gathering phase. Don't worry, though—time spent in this part of the process will pay off in a big way when we start development.

News

Compared to our article content type, news will be fairly straightforward. We will need to track these pieces of information:

❏ Unique identifier

❏ Headline

❏ Author

❏ Short description

❏ Publication date

❏ Status

❏ Keywords

❏ URL for more information

Everything else should look just like the article content type, except that we won't allow HTML tags inside our description. Here's what a typical news item would look like:

```
<news id="123">
  <headline>New XML application being built</headline>
  <author>Tom Myer</author>
  <description>A new XML application is now finally being released
    by …</description>
  <pubdate>2004-01-20</pubdate>
  <status>live</status>
  <keywords>XML</keywords>
  <url>http://www.yahoo.com/</url>
</news>
```

From a programmatic standpoint, we will only display news pieces with a "live" status.

Web Copy

Many of our site's Web pages, including the homepage, will display copy of some form, be it the contact details for our company, or a description of the services we can provide. If we built a CMS that didn't allow us to manage this copy, we wouldn't have a proper CMS, would we?

The easiest way to keep track of copy is to treat each piece a little like an article. In fact, Web copy has many of the same characteristics as your standard articles, except that we generally don't need to track authors. An XML document that tracks a piece of Web copy will look like this:

```
<webcopy id="123">
  <navigationlabel>XML CMS</navigationlabel>
  <headline>XML-powered CMS Solutions</headline>
  <description>Learn about our XML-powered CMS products.
  </description>
  <pubdate>2004-01-20</pubdate>
  <status>live</status>
  <keywords>XML CMS</keywords>
  <body><![CDATA[
    <h1>Creating an XML-powered CMS</h1>
    <p>Are you tired of waiting around for your "IT Guy" or
      expensive designer to update your web site? Well, those
      days will be long forgotten if you buy our XML-powered CMS!
      With this revolutionary new tool, you can make quick and
      easy updates to your own web site! Forget all the hassles!
      It slices, it dices!</p>
  ]]></body>
</webcopy>
```

The `<keywords>` and `<status>` elements will work in much the same way as they do for articles and news pieces.

Administrators

Our final content type isn't really a content type—it's more of a supporting type. We will need to keep track of each administrator on the site, as these are the folks who can log in and make changes to advertisement copy, articles, news pieces, and binary files.

We will need to record each administrator's name, username, password (encrypted, of course), and email address. For the moment, we won't worry about exactly how the password is encrypted—we'll talk about that later.

File: **admin.xml**

```xml
<?xml version="1.0" encoding="iso-8859-1"?>
<admins>
  <admin id="1">
    <name>Joe</name>
    <username>joe</username>
    <password>$1$064.HQ..$x912OhlIlHFylTPJmJR/k/</password>
    <email>joe@myerman.com</email>
  </admin>
  <admin id="2">
    <name>Bill</name>
    <username>bill</username>
    <password>$1$Ep5.7h4.$R6iGqy.Wj2Dz8SAE9WG3lO</password>
    <email>bill@myerman.com</email>
  </admin>
  <admin id="3">
    <name>Tom</name>
    <username>tom</username>
    <password>$1$Cl/.j3..$QcjxGtxqYxOVNp3QanGnPO</password>
    <email>tom@myerman.com</email>
  </admin>
</admins>
```

As with each article/news item/binary file/advertisement copy item, each administrator will need a unique ID—otherwise, the system may not know who's trying to log in.

Summary

We covered a lot in this chapter—I'm glad you're still with me! In Chapter 3, we're going to dig around inside DTDs and XML Schemas. And, in the CMS section, we'll take a look at an alternative approach to handling status, keyword, and author listings—I think you'll really like the way we change things around. After that, you should have enough of a working knowledge of XML (and its wacky family) to really start development.

3

DTDs for Consistency

So far, we've created some very simple XML documents and learned what they're made of. We've also walked through some very simple examples in which we've transformed XML into something else, be it text, HTML, or different XML. Now, it's time to learn how to make your XML documents consistent.

Consistency in XML

Ralph Waldo Emerson, the great American thinker and essayist, once said, "A foolish consistency is the hobgoblin of little minds." Well, foolish or not, in the world of XML, we like consistency. In fact, in many contexts, consistency can be a very beautiful thing.

Remember that XML allows you to create any kind of language you want. We've already seen some varying examples in this book: from a letter to mom, to articles and news stories. In many cases, as long as you follow the rules of well-formedness, just about anything goes in XML.

However, there will come a time when you need your XML document to follow some rules—to pass a validity test—and those times will require that your XML data be consistently formatted. For example, our CMS should not allow a piece of data that's supposed to be in the admin information file to show up in a content file. What we need is a way to enforce that kind of rule.

In XML, there are two ways to set up consistency rules: DTDs and XML Schema. A DTD (document type definition) is a tried and true (if not old-fashioned) way of achieving consistency. It has a peculiar, non-XML syntax that many XML newcomers find rather limiting, but which evokes a comfortable, hometown charm among the old-school XML programmers. XML Schema is newer, faster, better, and so on; it does a lot more, and is written like any other XML document, but many find it just as esoteric as DTDs.

Information on DTDs and XML Schema could fill thick volumes if we gave it a chance. Each of these technologies contains lots of hidden nooks and crannies crammed with rules, exceptions, notations, and side stories. But, remember why we're here: we must learn as much as we need to know, then apply that knowledge as we build an XML-powered Website.

Fun with Terminology

Speaking of side stories, did you know that DTD actually stands for two things? It stands not just for document type definition, but also document type declaration. The *declaration* consists of the lines of code that make up the *definition*. Since the distinction is a tenuous one, we'll just call them both "DTD" and move on!

This chapter will focus on DTDs, as you're still a beginner, and providing information on XML Schema would be overkill. However, I will take a few minutes to explain XML Schema at a high level, and provide some comparisons with DTDs.

Just a warning before we start this chapter: consistency in XML is probably the hardest aspect we've covered so far, because DTDs can be pretty esoteric things. However, I think you'll find it worth your while, since using a DTD will prevent many problems down the road.

What's the Big Deal About Consistency?

Okay, before we get started, let's ask a very obvious question: "Why, oh why, are we sitting here on a lovely Saturday afternoon talking about the importance of consistency in XML documents? Why aren't we out in the park with our loyal dog Rover, a picnic basket, and our wonderful significant other?"

Well, you've actually asked two questions there. I can't answer the second one, because I really don't want to get into your personal life right now. As for the first question, many possible answers spring to mind:

1. There will be a pop quiz later, so you'd better know your stuff.

2. Your boss told you to learn it.

3. You need to share your XML document with another company/department/organization, and they expect your information in a certain format.

4. Your application requires that the XML documents given to it pass certain tests.

Although answers 1 and 2 can loom large in one's life, answers 3 and 4 are more solid reasons to understand the importance of consistency in XML documents. Using a system to ensure consistency allows your XML documents to interact with all kinds of applications, contexts, and business systems—not just your own. In layman's terms, using a DTD with your XML documents makes them easier to share with the outside world.

DTDs

The way DTDs work is relatively simple. If you supply a DTD along with your XML file, then the XML parser will compare the content of the document with the rules that are set out in the DTD. If the document doesn't conform to the rules specified by the DTD, the parser raises an error and indicates where the processing failed.

DTDs are such strange creatures that the best way to describe them is to just jump right in and start writing them, so that's exactly what we're going to do. A DTD might look something like this:

```
<!DOCTYPE letter [
  <!ELEMENT letter (to,from,message)>
  <!ELEMENT to (#PCDATA)>
  <!ELEMENT from (#PCDATA)>
  <!ELEMENT message (#PCDATA)>
]>
```

Those of you who are paying attention should have noticed some remarkable similarities between this DTD and the Letter to Mother example that we worked on in Chapter 2. In fact, if you look closely, each line of the DTD provides a clue as to how our letter should be structured.

The first line of the DTD, which begins with <!DOCTYPE, indicates that our document type is letter. Any document we create on the basis of this DTD must therefore have a letter as its root element, or the document won't be valid.

The rest of the DTD is devoted to explaining two things:

1.   The proper order of elements in the XML document.

2.   The proper content of elements in the XML document.

In the next few sections, I'll walk you through the most important parts of element declarations. Then, we'll work on attribute and entity declarations. Once we have all that under our belts, we'll get our hands dirty building some sample XML files with DTDs.

Element Declarations

Let's have a look at the next line of the DTD above: the one that comes after the DOCTYPE.

```
<!ELEMENT letter (to,from,message)>
```

This is called an **element declaration**. You can declare elements in any order you want, but they must all be declared in the DTD. To keep things simple, though, and to mirror the order in which elements appear in the actual XML file, I'd suggest that you do what we've done here: declare your root element first.

A DTD element declaration consists of a tag name and a definition in parentheses. These parentheses can contain rules for any of:

❏   Plain text

❏   A single child element

❏   A sequence of elements

In this case, we want the `letter` element to contain, in order, the elements `to`, `from`, and `message`. As you can see, the sequence of child elements is comma-delimited.

In fact, to be more precise, the sequence not only specifies the order in which the elements should appear, but also, how many of each element should appear. In this case, the element declaration specifies that one of each element must appear in the sequence. If our file contained two `from` elements, for example, it would be as invalid as if it listed the `message` element before `to`.

Naturally, there will come a time when you'll need to specify more than just one of each element. How will you do that? With a neat little system of notation, defined in Table 3.1, which may remind you of UNIX regular expressions.

Table 3.1. XML Element Declaration Notation

Symbol	Meaning
?	Element can appear only once, if at all. `<!ELEMENT letter (to,from,message,sig?)>` (one optional `sig`)
+	Element must appear at least once. `<!ELEMENT letter (to,from,message,sig+)>` (one or more `sig`s)
*	Element can appear as many times as necessary, or none at all. `<!ELEMENT letter (to,from,message,sig*)>` (zero or more `sig`s)
|	Defines a choice between elements. `<!ELEMENT letter (to,from,message,sig|ps)>` (end `letter` with either `sig` or `ps`)
()	Defines the grouping of elements. `<!ELEMENT letter ((to,from,message)|#PCDATA)>` (`letter` has `to`, `from`, and `message` or just text)

With this notation as a backdrop, you can get pretty creative:

Require at least two instances of an element.

```
<!ELEMENT chapter (title,para,para+)>
```

(at least two `para`s)

Apply element count modifiers to element groups.

```
<!ELEMENT chapter ((title,para+)+)>
```

(one or more `titles`, each followed by one or more `paras`)

Allow an element to contain an element or plain text.

```
<!ELEMENT title (subtitle|#PCDATA)>
```

(`title` contains a `subtitle` or plain text)

Require exactly three instances of an element.

```
<!ELEMENT instruction (step,step,step)>
```

(exactly three `steps`)

Elements that Contain only Text

Let's keep looking at our original DTD. After the `letter` declaration, we see these three declarations:

```
<!ELEMENT to (#PCDATA)>
<!ELEMENT from (#PCDATA)>
<!ELEMENT message (#PCDATA)>
```

Here, we see #PCDATA used to define the contents of our elements. #PCDATA stands for parsed character data, and refers to anything other than XML elements. So whenever you see this notation in a DTD, you know that the element must contain only text.

Mixed Content

What if you want to have something like this in your XML document?

```
<paragraph>This is a paragraph in which items are <b>bolded</b>,
  <i>italicized</i>, and even <u>underlined</u>. Some items are
  even deemed <highpriority>high priority</highpriority>.
</paragraph>
```

You'd probably think that you needed to declare the paragraph element as containing a sequence of #PCDATA and other elements, like this:

```
<!ELEMENT paragraph (#PCDATA,b,i,u,highpriority)>  <!-- wrong! -->
```

You might think that, but you'd be wrong! The proper way to declare that an element can contain mixed content is to separate its elements using the | symbol and add a * at the end of the element declaration:

```
<!ELEMENT paragraph (#PCDATA|b|i|u|highpriority)*> <!-- right! -->
```

This notation allows the paragraph element to contain any combination of plain text and b, i, u, and highpriority elements. Note that with mixed content like this, you have no control over the number or order of the elements that are used.

Empty Elements

What about elements such as the hr and br, which in HTML contain no content at all? These are called empty elements, and are declared in a DTD as follows:

```
<!ELEMENT hr EMPTY>
<!ELEMENT br EMPTY>
```

So far, most of this makes good sense. Let's talk about attribute declarations next.

Attribute Declarations

Remember attributes? They're the extra bits of information that hang around inside the opening tags of XML elements. Fortunately, attributes can be controlled by DTDs, using what's called an attribute declaration.

An attribute declaration is structured differently than an element declaration. For one thing, we define it with !ATTLIST instead of |!ELEMENT. Also, we must include in the declaration the name of the element that contains the attribute(s), followed by a list of the attributes and their possible values.

For example, let's say we had an XML element that contained a number of attributes:

```
<actor actorid="HF1234" gender="male" type="superstar">
  Harrison Ford</actor>
```

The element and attribute declarations for that element might look like this:

```
<!ELEMENT actor (#PCDATA)>
<!ATTLIST actor
  actorid ID #REQUIRED
  gender (male|female) #REQUIRED
  type CDATA #IMPLIED>
```

The easiest attribute to understand is type—it contains CDATA, or character data. Basically, this attribute can contain any string of characters or numbers.

Acceptable values for this attribute might be "superstar", "leading man", or even "dinosaur." As developers, we can't exert much control over what is placed in an attribute of type `CDATA`.

Do you see `#IMPLIED` right after `CDATA`? In DTD-speak, this means that the attribute is optional. Don't ask why they didn't use `#OPTIONAL`—this legacy has been passed down from the days of SGML, XML's more complex predecessor.

Let's take a look at the `gender` attribute's definition. This attribute is `#REQUIRED`, so a value for it has to be supplied with every `actor` element. Instead of allowing any arbitrary text, however, the DTD limits the values to either `male` or `female`.

If, in our document, an `actor` element fails to contain a `gender` attribute, or contains a `gender` attribute with values other than `male` or `female`, then our document would be deemed invalid.

Let's look at the most complex attribute value in our example, then we'll stop talking about attribute and element declarations. The `actorid` attribute has been designated an ID. In DTD-speak, an ID attribute must contain a unique value, which is handy for product codes, database keys, and other identifying factors.

In our example, we want the `actorid` attribute to uniquely identify each actor in the list. The `ID` type set for the `actorid` attribute ensures that our XML document is valid if and only if a unique `actorid` is assigned to each actor.

Some other rules that you need to follow for IDs include:

❑ ID values must start with a letter or underscore.

❑ There can only be one ID attribute assigned to an element.

Incidentally, if you want to declare an attribute that must contain a *reference* to a unique ID that is assigned to an element somewhere in the document, you can declare it with the `IDREF` attribute type. We won't have any use for this attribute type in this book, however.

Entity Declarations

Back in Chapter 1, we talked a little bit about entities. An entity is a piece of XML code that can be used (and reused) in a document with an **entity reference**. For example, the entity reference `&lt;` is used to represent the < character, an XML built-in entity.

XML supports a number of built-in entities (among them <, >, &quote; and &) that don't ever need to be declared inside a DTD. With entity declarations, you can define your own entities—something that I think you'll find very useful in your XML career.

There are different types of entities, including general, parameter, and external. Let's go over each very quickly.

General entities are basically used as substitutes for commonly-used segments of XML code. For example, here is an entity declaration that holds the copyright information for a company:

```
<!ENTITY copyright "&#xA9; 2004 by Triple Dog Dare Media">
```

Now that we've declared this entity, we could use it in our documents like so:

```
<footer>&copyright;</footer>
```

When the parser sees &copyright;, an entity reference, it looks for its entity declaration and substitutes the text we've declared as the entity.

There are a couple of restrictions on entity declarations:

❑ Circular references are not allowed. The following is a no-no:

```
<!ENTITY entity1 "&entity2; is a real pain to deal with!">
<!ENTITY entity2 "Or so &entity1; would like you to believe!">
```

❑ We can't reference a general entity anywhere but in the XML document proper. For entities that you can use in a DTD, you need parameter entities.

Parameter entities are both defined and referenced within DTDs. They're generally used to keep DTDs organized and to reduce the typing required to write them. Parameter entity names start with the % sign. Here's an example of a parameter entity, and its use in a DTD:

```
<!ENTITY % acceptable "(#PCDATA|b|i|u|citation|dialog)*">
<!ELEMENT paragraph %acceptable;>
<!ELEMENT intro %acceptable;>
<!ELEMENT sidebar %acceptable;>
<!ELEMENT note %acceptable;>
```

What this says is that each of the elements paragraph, intro, sidebar, and note can contain regular text as well as b, i,u, citation, and dialog elements. Not only does the use of a parameter entity reduce typing, it also simplifies maintenance of the DTD. If, in the future, you wanted to add another element (`sidebar`) as an acceptable child of those elements, you'd only have to update the `%acceptable;` entity:

```
<!ENTITY % acceptable "(#PCDATA|b|i|u|citation|dialog|sidebar)">
```

External entities point to external information that can be copied into your XML document at runtime. For example, you could include a stock ticker, inventory list, or other file, using an external entity.

```
<!ENTITY favquotes SYSTEM "http://www.example.com/favstocks.xml">
```

In this case, we're using the `SYSTEM` keyword to indicate that the entity is really a file that resides on a server. You'd use the entity in your XML documents as follows:

```
<section>
  <heading>Current Favorite Stock Picks</heading>
  &favquotes;
</section>
```

External DTDs

The DTD example we saw at the start of this chapter appeared within the DOCTYPE declaration at the top of the XML document. This is okay for experimentation purposes, but with many projects, you'll likely have dozens—or even hundreds—of files that must conform to the same DTD. In these cases, it's much smarter to put the DTD in a separate file, then reference it from your XML documents.

An external DTD is usually a file with a file extension of `.dtd`—for example, `letter.dtd`. This external DTD contains the same notational rules set forth for an internal DTD.

To reference this external DTD, you need to add two things to your XML document. First, you must edit the XML declaration to include the attribute `standalone="no"`:

```
<?xml version="1.0" standalone="no"?>
```

This tells a validating parser to validate the XML document against a separate DTD file. You must then add a `DOCTYPE` declaration that points to the external DTD, like this:

```
<!DOCTYPE letter SYSTEM "letter.dtd">
```

This will search for the `letter.dtd` file in the same directory as the XML file. If the DTD lives on a Web server, you might point to that instead:

```
<!DOCTYPE letter SYSTEM
    "http://www.example.com/xml/dtd/letter.dtd">
```

A 10,000-Foot View of XML Schema

The XML Schema standard fulfills the same requirements as DTDs: it allows you to control the structure and content of an XML document. But, if it serves the same purpose as DTDs, why would we use XML Schema?

Well, DTDs have a few disadvantages:

1. DTD notation has little to do with XML syntax, and therefore cannot be parsed or validated the way an XML document can.

2. All DTD declarations are global, so you can't define two different elements with the same name, even if they appear in different contexts.

3. DTDs cannot strictly control the type of information a given element or attribute can contain.

XML Schema is written in XML, so it can be parsed by an XML parser. XML Schema allows you, through the use of XML namespaces, to define different elements with the same name. Finally, XML Schema provides very fine control over the kinds of data contained in an element or attribute.

Now, for some major drawbacks: if you thought that DTDs were esoteric, then you won't be pleased by the complexity introduced by XML Schema. Most of the criticism aimed at XML Schema is focused on its complexity and length. In fact, at first glance, a schema's verbosity will remind you of your motor-mouth friend who hogs the airspace at any gathering.

We won't get much of a chance to work with XML Schema in this book, but there are many fine books available on the subject.

Getting Our Hands Dirty

Okay, now you know a lot more about DTDs than you did before. If you're thinking that all this talk of consistency in XML seems fairly esoteric, you're not alone. But stick with me—we're about to embark on the practical examples that will illustrate exactly how these concepts fit into the overall XML picture.

Let's start out by creating a sample document and using a DTD to validate it. For this exercise, we'll be working with Macromedia Dreamweaver MX, as it includes a built-in XML validator.

Our First Case: A Corporate Memo

You work for Amalgamated International, LLC. The big boss comes into your office because he heard a rumor that you're an XML wizard. This is really great news, because he's just come back from a conference where he learned that XML is a terrific way to get your internal corporate memos under control.

He instructs you to figure out how to get all the corporate memos into XML, and yes, they do need to be validated, because they will be used later by an application that's capable of searching through the memos.

The first thing you do is you take a look at the dozens of corporate memos you and your colleagues have received in the past few months. After a day or two of close examination, a pattern emerges.

Just by looking at them, you can see that all memos have the following elements:

❏ Date

❏ Sender

❏ Recipient list

❏ Priority

❏ Subject line

❏ One or more paragraphs

❏ Signature block

❏ Preparer's initials

You're sure that there's more to it than that, so you decide to gather more information. When you talk to your department's administrative assistant, he fills in the rest of the picture:

❏ There is almost always some kind of departmental code assigned to the file. This code is not always printed on the physical memos, but is always used as part of the filename. These codes help designate the memo's department of origin (accounting, finance, marketing, etc.).

❑ There is almost always a blind copy list on each memo—in other words, a list of recipients who, though they received it, are not listed anywhere on the memo as having received it.

❑ Many memos also have an expiration date. At Amalgamated, if a given memo has no expiration date, the information on the memo is deemed good for 180 days. Most memos contain information with lifetimes of less then six months, so most employees never see this kind of information. Other memos—those concerning HR policies, for instance—may have expiration dates that are years away.

With this information in hand, you begin to create a DTD for XML-based memos.

Although your first impulse might be to run out and create a sample XML memo document, please resist that urge for now. There's nothing wrong with this approach—indeed, it does provide useful modeling techniques. However, right now, we want to work with DTDs, then apply what we know to the building of the XML document.

So, the first thing you need to do is declare a DOCTYPE. Because these memos are internal to the company, and there may be a need for a separate external memo DOCTYPE, you decide to use `internalmemo` as your root element name:

File: **internalmemo-standalone.xml** (excerpt)

```
<?xml version="1.0"?>
<!DOCTYPE internalmemo [
```

Now, it's time to define your elements. The first element—the root element—is `internalmemo`. This element will contain all the other elements, which hold date, sender, recipient, subject line, and all other information. Because these represent a lot of elements, it would be useful to split your document into two logical partitions: `header` and `body`. The `header` will contain recipient, subject line, date, and other information. The `body` will contain the actual text of the memo.

Here is the element declaration for our root element:

File: **internalmemo-standalone.xml** (excerpt)

```
<!ELEMENT internalmemo (header,body)>
```

In DTD syntax, the above declaration states that our `internalmemo` element must contain one `header` element and one `body` element. Next, we will indicate which elements these will contain.

Here's what the `header` will contain:

File: **internalmemo-standalone.xml (excerpt)**

```
<!ELEMENT header (date,sender,recipients,blind-recipients?,
    subject)>
```

In DTD syntax, the above declaration states that the `header` element must contain single `date`, `sender`, and `recipients` elements, an optional `blind-recipients` element, and then a `subject` element.

Here is the `body`:

File: **internalmemo-standalone.xml (excerpt)**

```
<!ELEMENT body (para+,sig)>
```

In DTD syntax, the above declaration states that the `body` element must contain one or more `para` elements, followed by a single `sig` element.

Most of the other elements will contain plain text, except the `para` elements, in which we will allow bold and italic text formatting.

File: **internalmemo-standalone.xml (excerpt)**

```
<!ELEMENT date (#PCDATA)>
<!ELEMENT sender (#PCDATA)>
<!ELEMENT recipients (#PCDATA)>
<!ELEMENT blind-recipients (#PCDATA)>
<!ELEMENT subject (#PCDATA)>
<!ELEMENT sig (#PCDATA)>
<!ELEMENT para (#PCDATA|b|i)*>
<!ELEMENT b (#PCDATA)>
<!ELEMENT i (#PCDATA)>
```

That was simple enough. However, when we glance at the requirements, we can see that we haven't even begun to handle priority levels, preparer's initials, expiration dates, and department of origin.

What's the best way to handle these pieces of information? We could certainly add them as elements in the `head` section of our memos, but that wouldn't make much sense. Those pieces of information are hardly ever displayed on a document—they are used only for administrative purposes.

In any case, we want to be able to control the data that document creators put in for values such as priority. It wouldn't make much sense for them to enter "alligator" or "Disney World" when our application is going to be looking for "low", "medium" and "high."

The best way to store these pieces of information is to add them as attributes to the root element. To do that, we need to add an attribute declaration to our DTD:

File: **internalmemo-standalone.xml** (excerpt)

```
<!ATTLIST internalmemo
  priority (low|medium|high) #REQUIRED
  initials CDATA #REQUIRED
  expiredate CDATA #REQUIRED
  origin (marketing|accounting|finance|hq|sales|ops) #REQUIRED>
]>
```

So, what does a valid internal memo document look like? I'm glad you asked:

File: **internalmemo-standalone.xml**

```
<?xml version="1.0"?>
<!DOCTYPE internalmemo [
<!ELEMENT internalmemo (header,body)>
<!ELEMENT header (date,sender,recipients,blind-recipients?,
    subject)>
<!ELEMENT body (para+,sig)>
<!ELEMENT date (#PCDATA)>
<!ELEMENT sender (#PCDATA)>
<!ELEMENT recipients (#PCDATA)>
<!ELEMENT blind-recipients (#PCDATA)>
<!ELEMENT subject (#PCDATA)>
<!ELEMENT sig (#PCDATA)>
<!ELEMENT para (#PCDATA|b|i)*>
<!ELEMENT b (#PCDATA)>
<!ELEMENT i (#PCDATA)>
<!ATTLIST internalmemo
  priority (low|medium|high) #REQUIRED
  initials CDATA #REQUIRED
  expiredate CDATA #REQUIRED
  origin (marketing|accounting|finance|hq|sales|ops) #REQUIRED>
]>
<internalmemo priority="high" initials="hjd"
    expiredate="01/01/2008" origin="marketing">
  <header>
    <date>01/05/2004</date>
```

```
    <sender>Thomas Myer</sender>
    <recipients>Marketing Department</recipients>
    <subject>Sell more stuff</subject>
  </header>
  <body>
    <para>This is a <i>simple</i> memo from the marketing
department: sell <b>more</b> stuff!</para>
    <sig>Thomas Myer</sig>
  </body>
</internalmemo>
```

Validating Our First Case

Now that we have a DTD and XML document, it's time to validate. Fortunately, Macromedia Dreamweaver MX has a built-in validation tool that we can use during development (in "real life" we would use a built-in validator that's part of our application). If you don't already own Dreamweaver, you can get a trial copy.[1]

All we have to do is open our XML document (which contains a DTD) in Dreamweaver, then choose File > Check Page > Validate as XML. The result should look a lot like Figure 3.1.

Figure 3.1. Validating our first case with Dreamweaver MX.

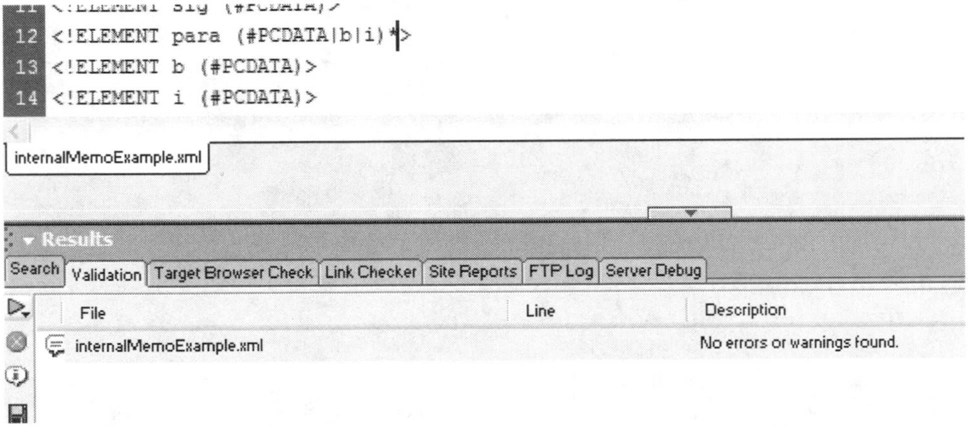

---

[1] http://www.macromedia.com/go/trydreamweaver

Do you see how, under Results, it reads No errors or warnings found.? That's what you want to see.[2]

What happens if some things are out of place? For instance, what if, as a priority, you wrote "Extremely Urgent"? What would happen then? In that case, you'd see an error message like the one in Figure 3.2 below.

Figure 3.2. Error resulting from a bad attribute value.

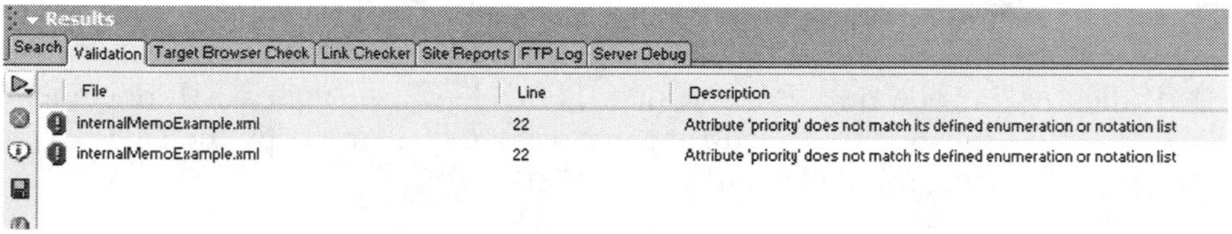

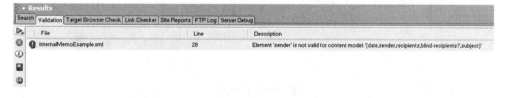

Notice that Dreamweaver MX tells you where the problem lies (with a specific line number) and provides a description of the problem. In this case, the validator is saying that the value of the priority attribute in your XML document doesn't match any of the possibilities defined in the DTD.

What if you decided to put the `<sender>` tag before the `<date>` tag? The validator catches that too, as you can see in Figure 3.3.

Figure 3.3. Error resulting from a misplaced element.

Again, the validator gives you a line number and a description that can lead you to resolve the problem. All you need to do is put the `sender` element back in the prescribed order, and the document will validate once more.

---

[2]In Dreamweaver MX 2004, the results list for a valid document is simply empty, and the status bar beneath the list reads Complete.

Second Case: Using an External DTD for Memos

Our first case was simple enough—an internal memo DTD and XML file. In that case, we embedded the DTD right into the file. This is a practical thing to do when you're only dealing with a small number of files for each DTD, but in Amalgamated's case, they'll be dealing with tens (if not hundreds) of thousands of memos.

There's no way that you want to have to maintain all those copies of the DTD separately. Instead, you want to have a single DTD that is included in all of your XML files. What you do is copy your DTD code out of your XML document and save it in a separate file called `internalmemo.dtd`. Don't copy the DOCTYPE line, or the last line that closes off the brackets!

When you're finished, your DTD file should look like this:

File: **internalmemo.dtd**

```
<!ELEMENT internalmemo (header,body)>
<!ELEMENT header (date,sender,recipients,blind-recipients?,
    subject)>
<!ELEMENT body (para+,sig)>
<!ELEMENT date (#PCDATA)>
<!ELEMENT sender (#PCDATA)>
<!ELEMENT recipients (#PCDATA)>
<!ELEMENT blind-recipients (#PCDATA)>
<!ELEMENT subject (#PCDATA)>
<!ELEMENT sig (#PCDATA)>
<!ELEMENT para (#PCDATA|b|i)*>
<!ELEMENT b (#PCDATA)>
<!ELEMENT i (#PCDATA)>
<!ATTLIST internalmemo
  priority (low|medium|high) #REQUIRED
  initials CDATA #REQUIRED
  expiredate CDATA #REQUIRED
  origin (marketing|accounting|finance|hq|sales|ops) #REQUIRED>
```

Next, place a link to that external DTD in your XML document, like this:

File: **internalmemo.xml (excerpt)**

```
<!DOCTYPE internalmemo SYSTEM "internalmemo.dtd">
```

You also need to change your XML document declaration (the first line of our XML document) to look like this:

File: **internalmemo.xml (excerpt)**

```
<?xml version="1.0" standalone="no"?>
```

If you've done everything right, your file should validate when you use Dreamweaver's built-in validator. You now have a reusable DTD that you can apply to other internal memos.

Our CMS Project

In Chapter 2, we added a few more content types to our CMS project. We now understand articles, news stories, binary files, and Web copy, and are well on our way to completing the requirements-gathering phase of the project—we can start coding soon!

However, and this is a big "however," we've also run into something of a problem. If you recall, we are tracking author, status, keyword, and other vital information in separate files. That is, each individual article, news story, binary file, and Web copy file keeps track of its own keywords, status, author, and dates.

For most of this information, which will rarely be used except in connection with the particular document, this isn't a problem, but author information is something of a special case. If we wanted to display all documents for a certain author, we would have to dig through all of our files to find all the matches. This isn't a big deal when our site is small, but the task grows more unmanageable with each passing day.

Never fear—I have a proposal that will solve this problem. In fact, the rest of this chapter will be devoted to tackling this issue. With any luck, it will also give you some insights into the ways in which you can analyze requirements and come up with more architecturally sound XML designs.

Reworking the Way we Track Author Information

Let's take a quick look at our article. I've reprinted what we came up with at the end of Chapter 1 below for easy reference:

```
<article id="123">
  <author>Tom Myer</author>
  <headline>Creating an XML-powered CMS</headline>
  <description>This article will show you how to create an
    XML-powered content management system</description>
  <pubdate>2004-01-20</pubdate>
```

```
<status>live</status>
<keywords>XML CMS</keywords>
<body><![CDATA[
  <h1>Creating an XML-powered CMS</h1>
  <p>In this article...</p>
]]></body>
</article>
```

So far, it's been very convenient to track our author information using the `author` element. However, doing it this way presents two problems, one of which we've already mentioned: eventually, we will have hundreds of articles on the site, and it would put a lot of strain on our application to dig through each one in order to display a list of articles by author.

The other problem is a little less obvious. What happens if, in one article, my name is listed as "Tom Myer," and in another, it's "Thomas Myer"? Or if, in one article, someone misspells my name as "Tom Meyer" (this happens a lot). To our application, these three names are different, and articles will thus be listed under three different authors.

To solve this problem, we should create a separate author listing (`authors.xml`), then use an `authorid` to reference that information in our articles. Once we have this figured out, we can get rid of the `author` element in all the other content types, and replace them with an `authorid` elements.

Handling our authors this way also allows us to track other information about authors, such as their email addresses, their bylines (in case they want to publish under pseudonyms), and other such information.

Here's a sample of what that code would look like:

File: **authors.xml**

```
<authors>
  <author id="1">
    <name>Thomas Myer</name>
    <byline>myerman</byline>
    <email>tom@tripledogdaremedia.com</email>
  </author>
</authors>
```

Instead of a separate `author` element, we would add an `authorid` element to our articles, like this:

```
<article id="123">
  <authorid>1</authorid>
  ...
```

Now we've solved the problem of **redundancy**—in other words, we've centralized our author information instead of having it spread across many different files. All we need to do is use this author ID in our articles, news stories, and all other content we add to our CMS; this ID is used to look up the author and retrieve the information we need.

Assign DTDs to our Project Documents?

The big question remains: do we take the time and effort to create DTDs or schemas for each of our content types? The answer is, as with most things technical, "it depends."

To be completely honest, most articles, news stories, and such will be submitted to the site through our administrative tool. This tool will have the necessary forms that will restrict data entry to certain fields. In other words, our administrative tool will do most of the work of validating our content. You could, therefore, suggest that a DTD would be completely superfluous, and you'd be right.

However, I think it would be good practice to develop a DTD for our article content type—after all, this is one of the most important document types we have in our system, and it has to be done right.

Here's a first shot at our article DTD:

```
<!ELEMENT article (authorid,headline,description,pubdate,status,
    keywords,body)>
<!ATTLIST article
  id CDATA #REQUIRED>
<!ELEMENT authorid (#PCDATA)>
<!ELEMENT headline (#PCDATA)>
<!ELEMENT description (#PCDATA)>
<!ELEMENT pubdate (#PCDATA)>
<!ELEMENT status (#PCDATA)>
<!ELEMENT keywords (#PCDATA)>
<!ELEMENT body (#PCDATA)>
```

Although we have declared our body element to contain character data, our article bodies will indeed be formatted using HTML tags. Because this HTML content will be wrapped in a CDATA block, those tags will be ignored by any XML processor reading an article file. We can use a CDATA block to hold any kind of text, as the XML parser will ignore any XML syntax that might appear in it. We therefore don't need to worry about the intricacies of HTML markup in this DTD.

If you asked ten XML folks whether they agreed with this approach, you'd get ten different opinions and alternative approaches. For now, we've created something that will work—and work quickly.

If you'd like more practice with DTDs, you can go back to Chapter 2 and look at the XML formats we created for our other content types, like Web copy and news items. Try writing DTDs for these as well. If you ever need to check the documents stored in your CMS for validity, you can use these DTDs to do it.

Summary

Wow! In three chapters we've covered basic XML, some XSLT and CSS, and, now, the basics of DTDs. Plus, we've nailed down most of the requirements for our CMS project. I think we're in pretty good shape to start looking more deeply at the rest of our project. Along the way, we'll pick up a few more XSLT and XML tricks.

Displaying XML in a Browser

In Chapter 2, we went over some basic XSLT and CSS using a very simple XML document. In this chapter, we're going to revisit some of those concepts with a more complex document. Once we've taken care of that, we'll return to our CMS project and start building the display pages for our site.

A Word on XPath

We've already been exposed to XSLT to a small degree. We used it to transform an XML letter to mother into something that could be displayed in a browser window. In this chapter, we're going to use a much more complex document as our starting point, and we'll learn how to use XPath.

Understanding XPath is the key to making effective use of XSLT. XPath is used in a variety of applications and technologies, however, XSLT is where its power and versatility really shine.

For all intents and purposes, XPath is a query language. It allows us to declaratively specify a "path" to an element or group of elements in an XML document. It uses a simple notation that is very similar to directory paths (hence the name XPath). You've already seen XPath in action within XSLT through some of the earlier examples.

When we put together a template, we normally use XPath to establish a match. For example, we can always handle the root of an XML document like this:

```
<xsl:template match="/">
```

With XPath, you can select all elements that have a particular tag name. For example, this template will match all the `<title>` tags in the document:

```
<xsl:template match="title">
```

Or, you could match certain elements depending on their location within an XML file. To match `<title>` tags that have a `<memo>` tag as their parent, you would use this expression:

```
<xsl:template match="memo/title">
```

As you can see, the basic XPath syntax looks a lot like a file path on your computer. That's because XML documents and your computer's file system are both hierarchical in nature. But you can go a step further and set conditions on which elements are matched within your specified path. These conditions are called **predicates**, and appear within square brackets following the element name you wish to set conditions for.

This example contains a predicate to make sure that it matches only `<title>` tags whose `priority` attribute is set to `hot`:

```
<xsl:template match="title[@priority='hot']">
```

The @ symbol identifies `priority` in this example as an attribute name, not a tag name.

XPath also has a number of useful functions built in. For example, if you need to grab the first or last element of a series, you can use XPath to do so. This template will match the first `<para>` tag within each `<memo>` tag:

```
<xsl:template match="memo/para[first()]">
```

This template will match the first `<para>` tag within the last `<memo>` tag:

```
<xsl:template match="memo[last()]/para[first()]">
```

Although most practical applications are relatively simple, XPath can get quite twisty when it needs to be. The XPath Recommendation[1] is quite a useful reference to these areas of complexity.

I've been giving you examples within an XSLT context, but XPath is used in a lot of different places, including PHP 5's new SimpleXML API. We'll get into SimpleXML a little later.

A Practical XSLT Application

Instead of using a simple letter to mother, let's use something a bit more complex: a book chapter. Book chapters provide an excellent opportunity to understand the arbitrary complexity of most XML documents.

If you were to look at a typical book chapter (like this one), you'd probably only think of it as a flow of information. From the perspective of an XML document designer, however, a book chapter can be intimidatingly complex. Chapters can have titles and sections, and those sections can have titles. There are paragraphs throughout—some belong to the chapter (for example, introductory paragraphs), but others belong to sections. Sections can contain subsections. Paragraphs can contain text in italics, bold text, and other inline markup. In fact, one could even have different *types* of paragraphs, like notes, warnings, and tips. We mustn't forget that chapters can also hold non-textual content, in the form of images, graphs, and other visual materials. There are lots of possibilities for displaying these kinds of information.

Here's what a very short chapter might look like:

File: **chapter.xml**

```
<?xml version="1.0"?>
<?xml-stylesheet type="text/xsl" href="chapter2html.xsl"?>
<chapter id="example">
  <title>XML Example</title>
  <para type="intro">This is an introductory paragraph. It doesn't
    belong to any of the sections.</para>
  <section>
    <title>Main Section</title>
    <para type="intro">This is the <b>first</b> paragraph of the
      first section.</para>
    <para>Second paragraph.</para>
    <para type="note">This is a note!</para>
```

---
[1] http://www.w3.org/TR/xpath

```
    <para type="warning">Don't even think about turning the page
      yet!</para>
    <section>
      <title>Subsection</title>
      <para type="intro">Looks like we started another section
        here!</para>
    </section>
  </section>
  <section>
    <title>Another Section</title>
    <para type="intro">And the chapter continues...</para>
  </section>
</chapter>
```

This sample file could go on and on, but I think you get the idea. Now it's time to try to parse this document and make sense of it. We'll perform some simple tasks first, then extend our knowledge as we go.

A First Attempt at Formatting

Now, let's create the corresponding XSL file, `chapter2html.xsl`. This file will contain all the instructions we will use to transform the XML elements in the chapter file we have just seen into XHTML. As we saw in Chapter 2, an XSL file that generates XHTML should begin as follows:

File: **chapter2xhtml.xsl (excerpt)**

```
<xsl:stylesheet version="1.0"
  xmlns:xsl="http://www.w3.org/1999/XSL/Transform"
  xmlns="http://www.w3.org/1999/xhtml">

  <xsl:output method="xml" indent="yes" omit-xml-declaration="yes"
    media-type="application/xhtml+xml" encoding="iso-8859-1"
    doctype-public="-//W3C//DTD XHTML 1.0 Transitional//EN"
    doctype-system=
    "http://www.w3.org/TR/xhtml1/DTD/xhtml1-transitional.dtd"/>
```

Now, let's start matching elements. The first thing we want to do is to match the root of our document. We can use this template to output the basic tags required to produce an XHTML document:

File: **chapter2xhtml.xsl (excerpt)**

```
<xsl:template match="/">
  <html>
    <head>
```

```
    <title>A Book Chapter</title>
    <meta http-equiv="content-type"
        content="application/xhtml+xml; charset=iso-8859-1"/>
  </head>
  <body>
    <xsl:apply-templates/>
  </body>
 </html>
</xsl:template>
```

Remember that, in XPath notation, / by itself stands for the root of your document, so we can rest assured that this template will only match once for each document that this style sheet transforms.

The `apply-templates` element then goes looking for other elements to match, so let's write some templates for those that it is likely to find. At this stage there's nothing we really want to output for the `chapter` element that we haven't already written out for the document root above, so we'll let the XSLT processor handle that with its default behavior for now. Let's instead concentrate on the elements inside the chapter:

File: **chapter2html.xsl (excerpt)**

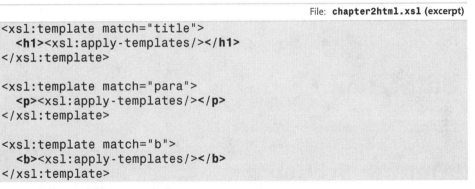

```
<xsl:template match="title">
  <h1><xsl:apply-templates/></h1>
</xsl:template>

<xsl:template match="para">
  <p><xsl:apply-templates/></p>
</xsl:template>

<xsl:template match="b">
  <b><xsl:apply-templates/></b>
</xsl:template>
```

Nothing could be simpler, right? We've matched all of our elements and for each we have output HTML tags as needed. Viewed in a browser, our output will look something like that shown in Figure 4.1.

Figure 4.1. Viewing the chapter example in Firefox.

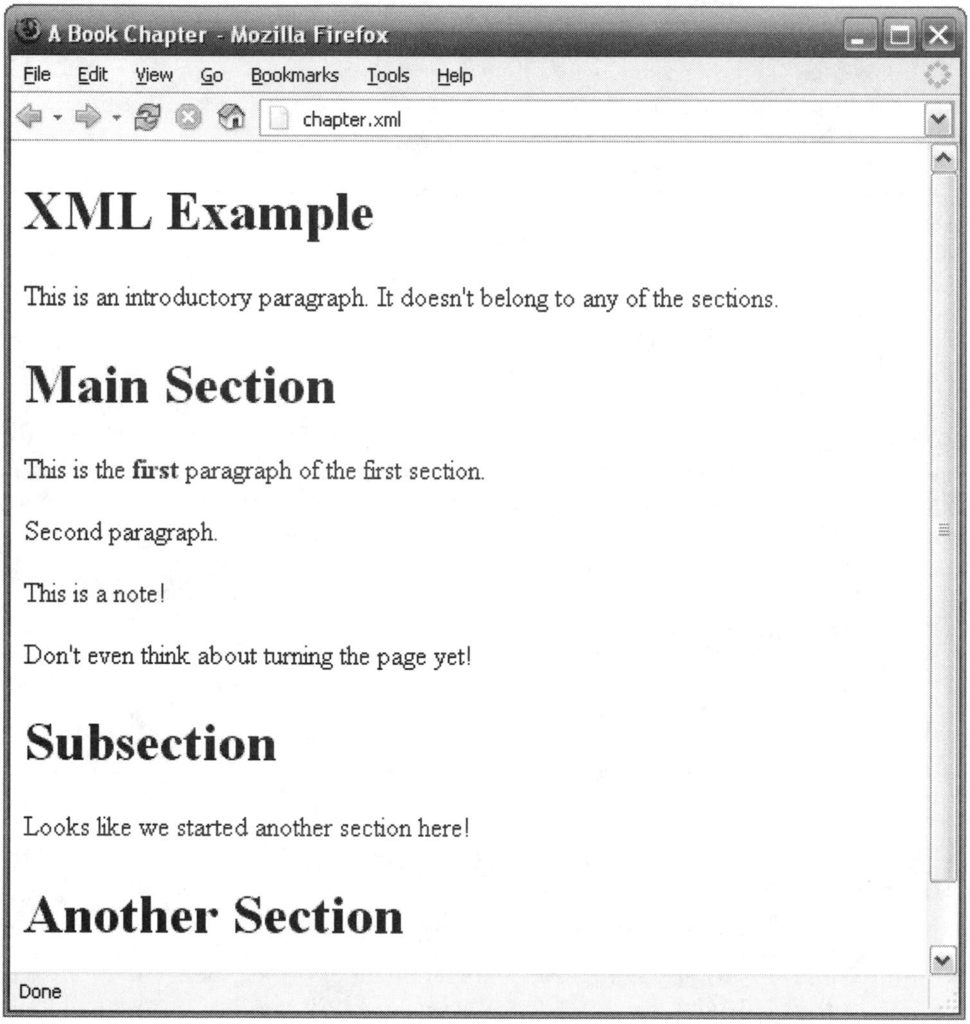

Looks pretty good, doesn't it? But, isn't there something missing? Of course there is. In our XSLT file, we are treating all `para` and `title` elements the same, regardless of where they appear in the XML document. That ain't right!

Using XPath to Discern Element Context

The `title` element near the top of the document is the chapter title, and should be handled differently from the `title` elements in the different nested sections. Likewise, `para` elements that denote warnings or introductions should be handled differently from other paragraphs.

Let's handle the `title` elements first. Chapter titles should be formatted with `<h1>` tags. Other `title` elements, which serve as nested section titles, should use incrementally smaller headings (`<h2>`, `<h3>`, and so on) in accordance with their level of nesting.

To distinguish between these different `title` types, you can use XPath notation. To pick out `title` elements that are children of the `chapter` tag, we can use the XPath expression `chapter/title`. To pick out `title` elements in top-level sections, we can use `chapter/section/title`, and so forth.

So here's an effective set of templates to handle the titles in our document:

File: **chapter2html.xsl (excerpt)**

```
<xsl:template match="chapter/title">
  <h1><xsl:apply-templates/></h1>
</xsl:template>

<xsl:template match="chapter/section/title">
  <h2><xsl:apply-templates/></h2>
</xsl:template>

<xsl:template match="chapter/section/section/title">
  <h3><xsl:apply-templates/></h3>
</xsl:template>

<xsl:template match="chapter/section/section/section/title">
  <h4><xsl:apply-templates/></h4>
</xsl:template>
```

Figure 4.2 shows how this code displays in the browser.

Figure 4.2. Viewing the chapter example with XPath. (Part 1)

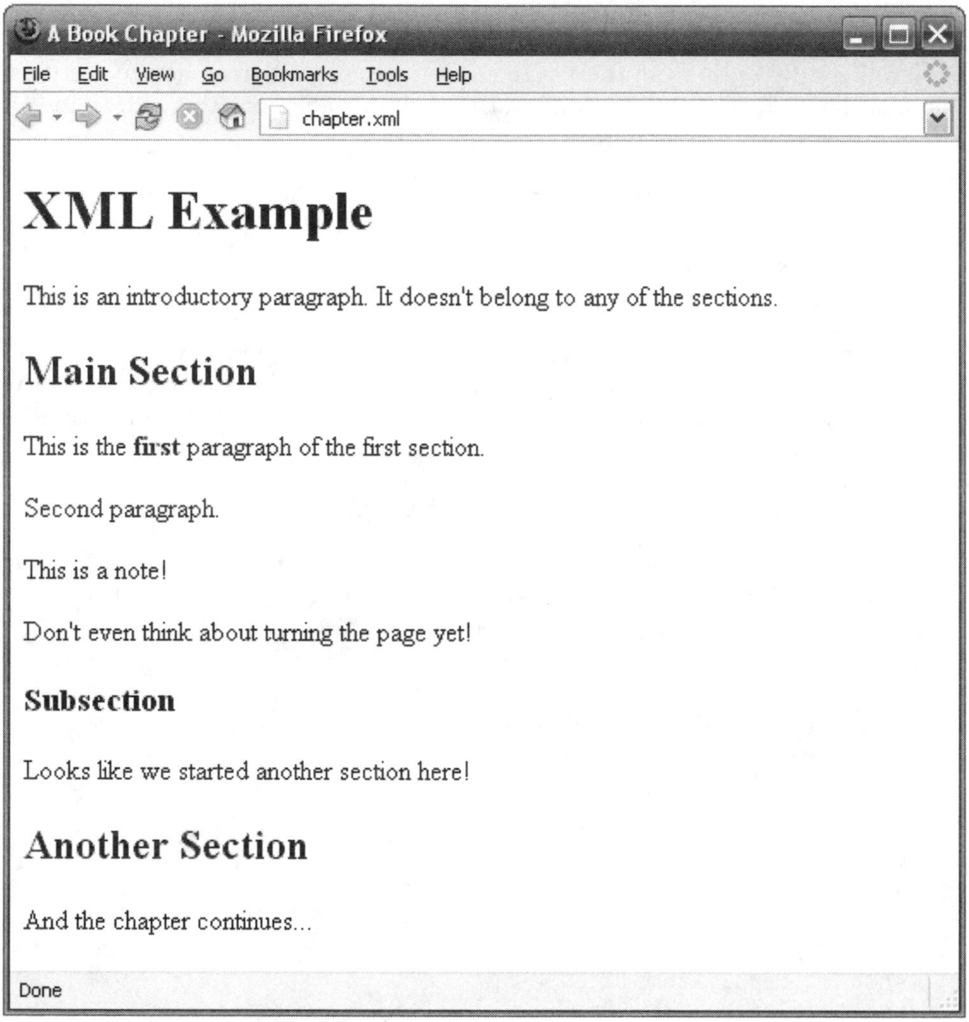

We're getting closer!

Matching Attribute Values with XPath

What about the paragraphs? Unlike the titles, they are not distinguishable by their placement in the document alone. Instead, the document uses the `type` attribute to distinguish normal paragraphs from introductions, tips, and warnings.

Luckily, XPath lets us specify matches based on attribute values, too. In XPath, we use a predicate (a condition in square brackets) to match an attribute value. To isolate `intro` paragraphs, for example, we would use the XPath expression `para[@type='intro']`.

We should definitely take advantage of this ability and distinguish each of our paragraph types visually. Let's italicize all introductory paragraphs, and put gray boxes around notes and warnings. We can also make sure that warnings are displayed in red text.

Now, we've already seen a template that can take care of normal paragraphs, which have no `type` attribute:

File: **chapter2html.xsl** (excerpt)

```
<xsl:template match="para">
  <p><xsl:apply-templates/></p>
</xsl:template>
```

Our template for introductory paragraphs is quite similar:

File: **chapter2html.xsl** (excerpt)

```
<xsl:template match="para[@type='intro']" priority="1">
  <p><i><xsl:apply-templates/></i></p>
</xsl:template>
```

Note the `priority` attribute on this template. Since an introductory paragraph would match both XPath expressions, `para` and `para[@type='intro']`, we need to give some indication as to which of the two templates should be used. By default, XSL templates have a priority between -0.5 and 0.5, depending on the XPath expression in the `match` attribute. To make sure our introductory paragraphs will use this second template, we therefore assign a priority of 1. Normal paragraphs will continue to use the first template, since they don't match the higher-priority second template.

With what we've just learned in mind, here are the templates for warnings and notes. Notice that we've added a `style` attribute to the opening `<p>` tag in each template to provide the desired style information for these paragraph types.[2]

---

[2]In a practical application, you should instead put these style properties in a CSS file and `<link>` it to the HTML document. These templates would then use `class` attributes on the `<p>` tags to invoke the appropriate formatting.

File: **chapter2html.xsl** (excerpt)

```
<xsl:template match="para[@type='warning']" priority="1">
  <p style="background-color: #cccccc; border: thin solid;
      width:300px; color:#ff0000;">
    <xsl:apply-templates/>
  </p>
</xsl:template>

<xsl:template match="para[@type='note']" priority="1">
  <p style="background-color: #cccccc; border: thin solid;
      width:300px;">
    <b><xsl:apply-templates/></b>
  </p>
</xsl:template>
```

Figure 4.3 shows the end result displayed in Firefox.

Using `value-of` to Extract Information

You'll notice the page title is the rather nondescript phrase, "A Book Chapter". How can we modify our template to display the actual chapter title in this spot instead?

When you need to pull a simple piece of information out of the XML document without messing around with templates to process the element(s) that house it, you can use a `value-of` element to grab what you want with an XPath expression:

File: **chapter2html.xsl** (excerpt)

```
<xsl:template match="/">
  <html>
    <head>
      <title><xsl:value-of select="/chapter/title"/></title>
      <meta http-equiv="content-type"
          content="application/xhtml+xml; charset=iso-8859-1"/>
    </head>
    <body>
      <xsl:apply-templates/>
    </body>
  </html>
</xsl:template>
```

As you can see, the `select` attribute is an XPath expression that searches for the value of the `title` within the `chapter`. With `value-of`, we can print that value out. Now our file displays something like the results shown in Figure 4.4. Notice the title bar of the browser window, which now contains the title of the chapter.

Figure 4.3. Viewing the chapter example with XPath. (Part 2)

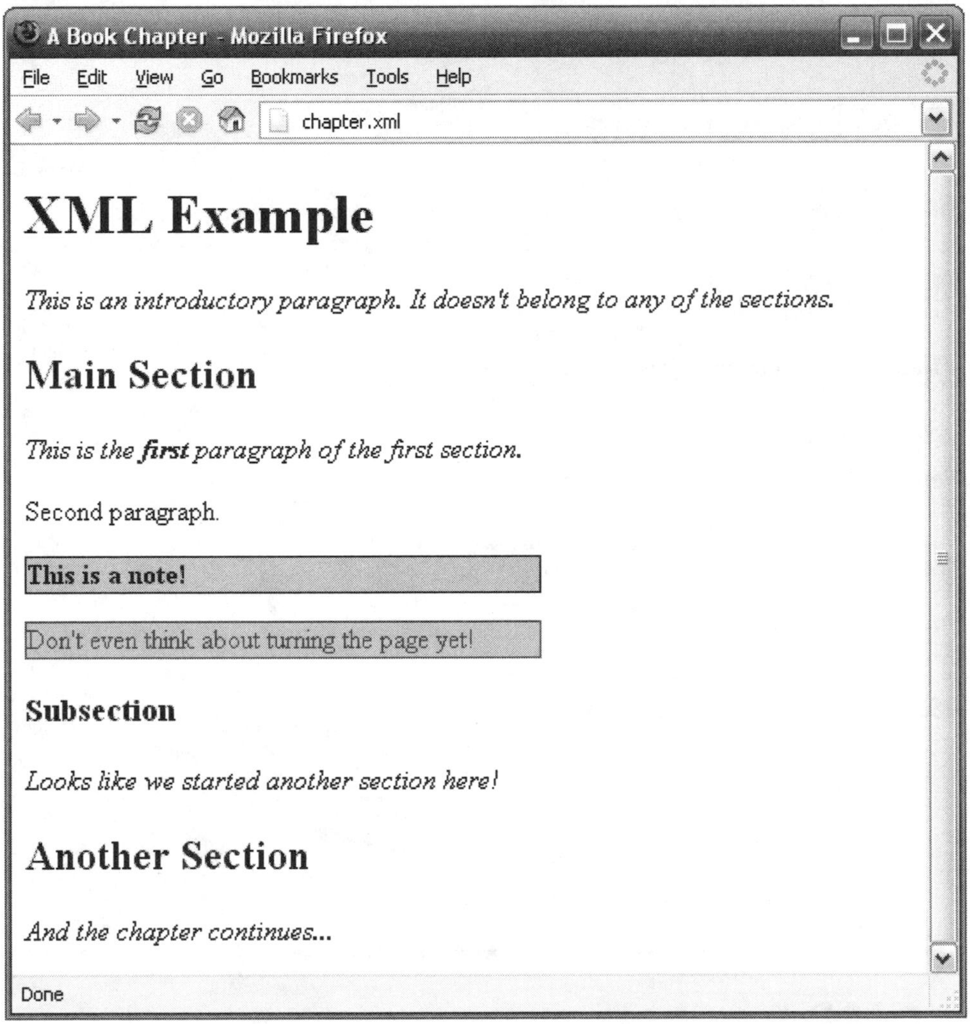

Figure 4.4. Viewing the chapter example with XPath. (Part 3)

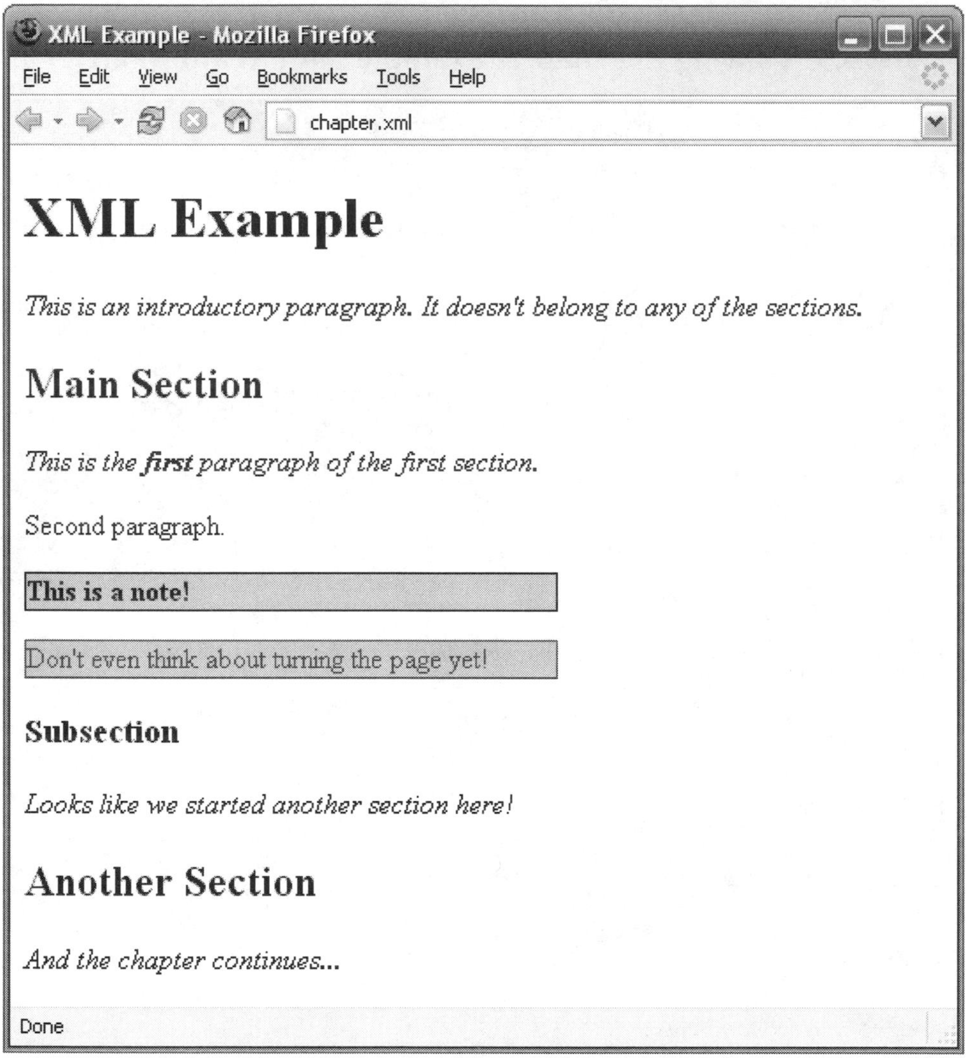

Our CMS Project

In the preceding chapters, we gathered requirements for our XML files, administration tool, and display components. In this chapter, I'd like to spend some time building the display pages for our project—the homepage, other internal pages, news sidebars, search widgets, and more.

Before we do that, though, let's recap the list of requirements we gathered for the display pages:

❑ The display side of our Website will only display articles and other content that has a status of "live."

❑ The search engine will retrieve articles by keywords, headlines, and descriptions, and only display those pieces that have a status of "live."

❑ The Website will display a list of authors by which site visitors can browse, but it only displays those authors who have live articles posted on the site.

Why Start with the Display Side?

You may be asking yourself, "Why is Tom starting with the display side? We haven't even built the admin tool for all the content it will display."

That's a good question. I decided to start with the display side because:

❑ It's much simpler than the admin tool, and gives us a chance to build some straightforward XML tools with PHP without having to get bogged down in detail.

❑ It means that we have to work from our requirements. Remember, we took the time to specify what each file would look like; now, all we have to do is work from these specs. As long as we continue to work from our specifications, everything will work together once it's done.

So, let's get started with our display pages. We'll begin with an include file that we can use on all of our pages.

Creating a Common Include File

Because our Website will entail some complex interaction between PHP and XML, it's a good idea to store your most needed functions and variables in a separate file, then include that file in all your other pages.

We're going to create this include file and start to add some information to it:

File: **common.inc.php**

```php
<?php
session_start();

$fileDir = $_SERVER['DOCUMENT_ROOT'] . '/xml/';
?>
```

This file will eventually contain many necessary variables that we'll use later in the project.

Before we go on to create a rudimentary homepage, let's create an include file that contains a search widget.

Creating a Search Widget Include File

All of our public display pages will offer a search widget, so it's a good idea to create a file that contains the needed form elements:

File: **search.inc.php**

```html
<form id="searchWidget" method="post" action="doSearch.php">
  Search site:
  <input name="term" type="text" id="term" />
  <input name="search" type="submit" id="search" value="Search" />
</form>
```

As with our common include file, we'll be using the PHP include command to include this form on all of our pages. In this case, we do so because it lowers maintenance costs: we only have to edit the form once to affect the whole site.

Notice that the action is set to a file called doSearch.php. We will work on that file soon—it's the file that will process XML and return search results to site visitors.

Building the Homepage

The most important page on the site is the homepage. That's where most of your visitors will likely begin, so you'll want to display as much information as you possibly can to interest them in going further.

From a structural point of view, the pages of our site will consist of three <div> tags: a page header, a navigation menu, and the content area.

The header will hold global navigation elements. Like our search widget file, this navigation will be an include file—after all, we want to reuse these elements on other pages of the site.

For the homepage of our site, the navigation menu will contain our search widget and a list of current news items. In the main content area, we'll display our homepage copy along with links to articles and other content on the site.

We'll go through these sections one at a time. But, before we do, let's take a quick look at the appearance of our site's homepage—it's shown in Figure 4.5.

Figure 4.5. The appearance of the homepage.

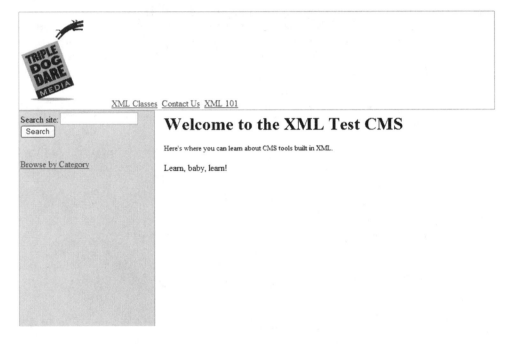

Building the Top Navigation Include File

Our top navigation will be placed in an include file. It will contain an image of the site's logo (hot-linked to the homepage for easy navigation), and a list of links that take users to each of the pages on the site.

This include file will make use of PHP 5's new SimpleXML functions. The great thing about the SimpleXML API is that it greatly simplifies the way you interact with, and extract information from, an XML document. Although a detailed look at SimpleXML will have to wait until Chapter 7, we'll cover the basics here.

Simply put, the `simplexml_load_file` function loads our entire XML document into a hierarchy of objects, which allows us to grab elements using PHP's familiar arrow notation. Imagine, for example, that you had this very simple XML document:

```
<person>
  <name>Tom</name>
  <age>33</age>
</person>
```

After loading this XML document into a variable called $person, you would be able to examine the name element with $person->name. Likewise, you would be able to examine the age element with $person->age. If you're familiar with object oriented programming in PHP, you'll get the hang of it very quickly.

An even easier way to access XML elements with SimpleXML is to use an XPath query. You can pass a SimpleXML object just about any XPath statement, and it will retrieve the elements you need.

We'll get into a lot more detail later on, but for right now you can rest assured that at least one part of your job has been made easier!

Let's take a look at the code that will build the navigation bar at the top of the page. Then, we'll walk through it:

File: **navtop.inc.php**

```php
<div id="navTop">
<a href="index.php"><img src="images/logo.gif" border="0"
    width="160" height="170" alt="Triple Dog Dare Media" /></a>
<?php
include_once 'common.inc.php';

$handle = opendir($fileDir);
while (($file = readdir($handle)) !== FALSE) {
  if (is_dir($fileDir . $file)) continue;
  if (!eregi("^webcopy.*\.xml$", $file)) continue;

  $webcopy = simplexml_load_file($fileDir . $file);
  if (count($webcopy->xpath('/webcopy[status="live"]'))) {
    $id = htmlentities($webcopy['id']);
    $label = htmlentities($webcopy->navigationlabel);
    echo "<a href=\"innerpage.php?id={$id}\">{$label}</a> ";
```

```
    }
}
?>
</div>
```

Our first task is fairly simple: open the xml directory and find every XML file whose name begins with webcopy:

File: **navtop.inc.php (excerpt)**

```
$handle = opendir($fileDir);
while (($file = readdir($handle)) !== FALSE) {
  if (is_dir($fileDir . $file)) continue;
  if (!eregi("^webcopy.*\.xml$", $file)) continue;
```

Remember, $fileDir is a variable set by common.inc.php to let this and other scripts on our site know where to find the XML files.

Regular Expressions

This code uses a **regular expression** to match the required file name pattern. For the lowdown on regular expressions in PHP, see Kevin Yank's book *Build Your Own Database Driven Website Using PHP & MySQL* (SitePoint), or refer to the PHP Manual.[3]

With our Web copy XML files in hand, we'll load every such file using SimpleXML. Although this may seem like an expensive way to do things, you'll find that SimpleXML is extremely fast. We simply use the simplexml_load_file function to load the contents of each file into memory:

File: **navtop.inc.php (excerpt)**

```
 $webcopy = simplexml_load_file($fileDir . $file);
```

Once we have the desired file loaded into the $webcopy variable, we can start to look at the XML document it contains. In this case, we're only interested in the files whose status is "live," so we use SimpleXML to check that the status element does indeed contain a text value of live:

File: **navtop.inc.php (excerpt)**

```
  if (count($webcopy->xpath('/webcopy[status="live"]'))) {
```

---

[3] http://www.php.net/regex

Here, we're using SimpleXML's `xpath` method to check if the `webcopy` element at the root of the document contains a `status` element with a value of `live`. The method returns an array of elements that match the criteria specified; in this case that array will either contain a reference to the `webcopy` element in the file (if the `status` is `live`), or it will be empty. We use PHP's `count` function to check.

If the file passes the test, we pull out the value of the `webcopy` element's `id` attribute and the value contained in the nested `navigationlabel` element.

File: **navtop.inc.php (excerpt)**

```php
$id = htmlentities($webcopy['id']);
$label = htmlentities($webcopy->navigationlabel);
```

As you can see, attributes are referenced as elements in an array (`$webcopy['id']`), while nested elements are referenced as object properties (`$webcopy->navigationlabel`).

With these values in hand, we can print out appropriate links for our page navigation:

File: **navtop.inc.php (excerpt)**

```php
echo "<a href=\"webcopy.php?id={$id}\">{$label}</a>
```

Let's move on to the rest of the homepage.

Building the Bottom Half of the Homepage

Remember when I said that our homepage would be made up of three `<div>` tags? Well, we've just taken care of the first—the page header. Let's now talk about the remaining two `div`s that sit beneath the first.

The file for our homepage will be called `index.php`. This file includes both the `common.inc.php` and `navtop.inc.php` files as needed. It then goes on to produce the secondary navigation and content `div`s (`navSide` and `mainContent`, respectively).

File: **index.php**

```php
<?php
include_once 'common.inc.php';
$file = $fileDir . 'homepage.xml';
$homePage = simplexml_load_file($file);
?>
<!DOCTYPE html PUBLIC "-//W3C//DTD XHTML 1.0 Transitional//EN"
```

```
      "http://www.w3.org/TR/xhtml1/DTD/xhtml1-transitional.dtd">
<html xmlns="http://www.w3.org/1999/xhtml">
<head>
  <title><?php echo htmlentities($homePage->headline); ?></title>
  <meta http-equiv="Content-Type"
      content="text/html; charset=iso-8859-1" />
  <link rel="stylesheet" href="xmlcms.css" type="text/css" />
</head>
<body>
<?php
include 'navtop.inc.php';
?>
<div id="navSide">
  <?php
  include 'search.inc.php';
  include 'news.inc.php';
  ?>
</div>
<div id="mainContent">
  <?php
  echo '<h1>' . htmlentities($homePage->headline) . '</h1>';
  echo '<p><small>' . htmlentities($homePage->description) .
      '</small></p>';
  echo $homePage->body;
  ?>
</div>
</body>
</html>
```

It looks really simple, doesn't it? In this file, we're using a variety of includes and PHP functions to do a lot of the dirty work for us. We'll also use this approach when we want to build the other display pages for articles, Web copy, and the like.

The only part that is somewhat complicated is the first few lines:

File: **index.php** (excerpt)

```
<?php
include_once 'common.inc.php';
$file = $fileDir . 'homepage.xml';
$homePage = simplexml_load_file($file);
?>
…
<title><?php echo htmlentities((string)$homePage->headline);
  ?></title>
```

In this code, we open the file called `homepage.xml` in the `xml` directory, and then `echo` out the contents of the `headline` element as the page title.

For the left-side navigation `div`, we will use two includes:

File: **index.php (excerpt)**

```
<div id="navSide">
  <?php
  include 'search.inc.php';
  include 'news.inc.php';
  ?>
</div>
```

The first include is the search widget that we built earlier on. The second should produce a listing of live news items, but we haven't built that yet.

For the most part, our news include file will be very similar in structure to the code we used in `navtop.inc.php`. All we're doing is extracting news items that have a `status` of `live`:

File: **news.inc.php (excerpt)**

```
<?php
include_once 'common.inc.php';

$handle = opendir($fileDir);
echo '<p>';
while (($file = readdir($handle)) !== FALSE) {
  if (is_dir($fileDir . $file)) continue;
  if (!eregi('^news.*\.xml$', $file)) continue;

  $news = simplexml_load_file($fileDir . $file);
  if (count($news->xpath('/news[status="live"]'))) {
    $id = htmlentities($news['id']);
    $label = htmlentities($news->headline);
    echo "<a href=\"innerpage.php?id={$id}\">{$label}</a><br />";
  }
}
echo '</p>';

?>
```

Now that we've completed the left side of the homepage, it's time to pull together the right side of the page. This area will display the headline and body copy that's stored for the homepage in a file called `homepage.xml`. Since we've already loaded this file to obtain the page title, we can continue using the `$homePage` variable to pull out the values we need:

File: **index.php (excerpt)**

```
<div id="mainContent">
  <?php
  echo '<h1>' . htmlentities($homePage->headline) . '</h1>';
  echo '<p><small>' . htmlentities($homePage->description) .
      '</small></p>';
  echo $homePage->body;
  ?>
</div>
</body>
</html>
```

Writing the Style Sheet

This isn't a book about CSS page layout, so I won't dwell on the details of the site's style sheet. For the sake of completeness, however, here's the code, which ensures our pages are laid out the way we intended:

File: **xmlcms.css**

```
body {
  color: #000;
  background: #fff;
  font-family: Helvetica, Arial, sans-serif;
  margin: 0;
  padding: 0;
}
#navTop {
  margin: 12px 12px 0 12px;
  border: 1px solid #999;
  padding: 2px;
}
#navSide {
  position: absolute;
  width: 250px;
  min-height: 400px;
  left: 12px;
  background-color: #ccc;
  border: 1px solid #999;
  margin-top: -1px;
  padding: 2px;
}
#mainContent {
```

```
  margin: 8px 8px 8px 280px;
}
```

Creating an Inner Page

We have the homepage all roughed out. Now, we need to build another template that will handle the display of the rest of the site's content. We'll get this work started now, and come back to it later as necessary.

For now, all we have to do is make a copy of index.php and call it inner-page.php—this will maintain the same includes and layout as our homepage. We'll make a few minor changes to this new template, in particular, to the code that is used to extract information from the correct file in the xml directory.

An id variable will be passed in the query string, which will correspond to the filename of the XML file that contains the associated content. So the ID webcopy3 will correspond to a file named webcopy3.xml in the xml directory.

Since we're using input from the browser (the id variable) as a filename in our script, we must be sure to check that the value passed is not a security risk. Otherwise, we could find our script turned against us as a clever hacker submits a value that points to some sensitive file on the system. For our purposes, a regular expression that verifies that the variable contains an alphanumeric string (only numbers and letters) will suffice.

With these considerations in mind, here's the code that loads the XML file associated with the supplied ID:

File: **innerpage.php** (excerpt)

```
<?php
include_once 'common.inc.php';
if (!isset($_GET['id']) or !eregi('^[a-z0-9]+$', $_GET['id']))
  return;
$file = $fileDir . $_GET['id'] . '.xml';
$inner = simplexml_load_file($file);
?>
```

With the file loaded, we must pull out the values inside for display in the template. In this instance, we're using a single template file to display two different types of content: news items (news123.xml) and Web copy (webcopy123.xml). If you refer back to Chapter 2, where we defined these XML formats, you'll see that the Web copy has navigationlabel and body elements that news items do not. We'll have to detect these to make sure our template displays the right thing.

The best way to do this with the SimpleXML API is to use an XPath query. For example, we want to use the `navigationlabel` element for the page title, but if no such element exists we want to fall back on the `headline` element. Here's the code:

File: **innerpage.php (excerpt)**

```
<title>
<?php
if (count($inner->xpath('navigationlabel'))) {
  echo htmlentities($inner->navigationlabel);
} elseif (count($inner->xpath('headline'))) {
  echo htmlentities($inner->headline);
}
?>
</title>
```

With all this in mind, you should be in a position to understand the complete template at a glance.

File: **innerpage.php**

```
<?php
include_once 'common.inc.php';
if (!isset($_GET['id']) or !eregi('^[a-z0-9]+$', $_GET['id']))
  return;
$file = $fileDir . $_GET['id'] . '.xml';
$inner = simplexml_load_file($file);
?>
<!DOCTYPE html PUBLIC "-//W3C//DTD XHTML 1.0 Transitional//EN"
    "http://www.w3.org/TR/xhtml1/DTD/xhtml1-transitional.dtd">
<html xmlns="http://www.w3.org/1999/xhtml">
<head>
<title>
<?php
if (count($inner->xpath('navigationlabel'))) {
  echo htmlentities($inner->navigationlabel);
} elseif (count($inner->xpath('headline'))) {
  echo htmlentities($inner->headline);
}
?>
</title>
<meta http-equiv="content-type"
    content="text/html; charset=iso-8859-1" />
<link rel="stylesheet" href="xmlcms.css" type="text/css" />
</head>
<body>
```

```php
<?php
include 'navtop.inc.php';
?>
<div id="navSide">
  <?php
  include 'search.inc.php';
  include 'news.inc.php';
  ?>
</div>
<div id="mainContent">
  <?php
  echo '<h1>' . htmlentities($inner->headline) . '</h1>';
  echo '<p><small>' . htmlentities($inner->description) .
      '</small></p>';
  if (count($inner->xpath('body'))) {
    echo $inner->body;
  }
  ?>
</div>
</body>
</html>
```

That's really all we need at the moment—we have the foundations of a Website working already! We don't have much formatting yet, nor a working search engine, but the display side is coming together quite nicely.

What does our sample site look like so far? Well, since we haven't created any XML documents yet, yours might not work at all. On my system, however, I've inserted a number of files, which I've supplied for you in the code archive for this chapter, and the site looks like that shown in Figure 4.6.

Over the next few chapters, we'll create XML documents with an administration tool, and the project will really start to come together.

Summary

In this chapter, we got a closer look at XSLT as we roughed out the display pages we'll need for our project. In Chapter 5, we'll look even more closely at XSLT, as we learn some of the more programmatic aspects of the language, such as loops, variables, and branches. We'll also fill in the elements we'll need for the display side, such as a working search engine, some formatting rules, and other details.

Figure 4.6. Displaying the CMS project so far.

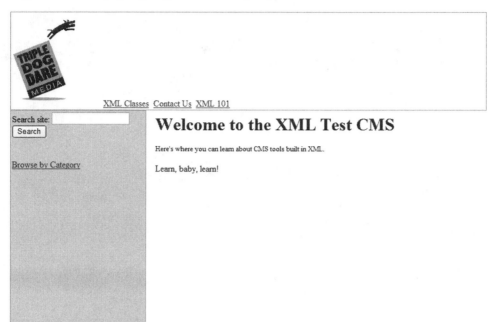

5

XSLT in Detail

In Chapter 2 and Chapter 4, you got some exposure to XSLT, and learned some basic tips for displaying XML in a Web browser. Now it's time to uncover some of XSLT's more advanced syntax. The goal of this chapter is to help you get a better understanding of the power of XSLT. Once we've taken care of that, we'll return to our CMS project and start applying XSLT rules to the display pages we built in the last chapter. First, though, let's take another look at XPath.

XPath

You've already been exposed to XPath in our work with XSLT so far, but in keeping with the theme of this chapter, let's stop and take a closer look at it now.

Without XPath, you really can't control XSLT (or other XML technologies) with any kind of granularity. To draw an analogy, trying to use XSLT without a knowledge of XPath is like trying to understand databases without knowing Structured Query Language (SQL). Just like SQL, XPath is a query language, but its syntax is more closely related to file paths.

For example, if you were working on a UNIX machine and I told you to open up the following file, you'd know to look in your current working directory:

```
File.xml
```

Imagine I told you to look here:

`../File.xml`

In this case, you'd know to look in the directory "above" your current working directory. What if I gave you this location?

`/home/File.xml`

You'd go all the way to the root of your directory hierarchy, and look in the `home` directory for the appropriate file. Experienced users know instinctively that some of these file path notations could point to the same file, or they could point to three completely different files, depending on the current working directory.

XPath works in much the same way. You can always grab the root element of a document using this expression:

`/*`

As in file paths, the slash (`/`) represents the root of the document structure, and the asterisk (`*`) is a wildcard that will match any XML element that occurs at that location. Since XML documents must have a single root element, this expression will match that one element, whatever it may be.

XPath also lets you seek out and find all elements with a particular name in the document:

`//title`

The double-slash (`//`) notation in XPath means "this element or any of its descendants, named…" When it occurs at the start of the XPath expression, "this element" implicitly refers to the root of the document. The particular expression shown here will therefore locate any `title` elements anywhere in the document.

Rather than looking for elements throughout the document, you could match only certain elements, depending on their context:

`memo/title`

This expression matches `title` elements that are children of a `memo` element that is a child of the current element. Adding double-slashes in various places can loosen up the requirements of this expression. For example, `memo//title` would match `title` elements occurring anywhere inside memo, the memo element, not only its children. `//memo/title` would match `title` elements that were children of a memo element found anywhere in the document, not a child of the current element. And for the ultimate in flexibility, //memo//title would match title elements located anywhere inside a memo element found anywhere in the document.

As with file paths, you can use the . and .. notation as well. Predictably, . is shorthand for "the current node" and .. is shorthand for "the parent of the current node".

If XPath were just good at retrieving nodes based on paths, that would be terrific. As we first saw in Chapter 4, XPath also allows us to be more discriminating with our searches. For example, we may want to retrieve only those elements for which a certain attribute value is set:

```
title[@priority='hot']
```

This expression grabs title elements that are children of the current element, but only those that have a priority attribute set to hot. The **predicate** (the portion of the expression in square brackets) acts as a filter, restricting the results to those that satisfy certain criteria. In this case, the @ symbol in front of priority indicates that we're referring to an attribute, not an element name.

What if you want to retrieve all title nodes for which any priority attribute value is set? You'd use this expression:

```
title[@priority]
```

You can use similar notation to find elements that have a certain value. For example, let's say that in a slightly different schema, we're storing the priority as a text value within a tag, not as an attribute. If we wanted to retrieve all the title elements that have a priority element containing a value of hot, here's how we'd do it:

```
title[priority='hot']
```

Let's continue to mix and match. Here's how you'd pick out all the date child elements of title elements anywhere in the document that have a priority attribute with a value of hot:

```
//title[@priority='hot']/date
```

XPath also provides selectors that can operate on logical node positions. For example, to retrieve the first and last `title` elements of any `memo` elements respectively, you'd use:

```
memo/title[first()]
```

```
memo/title[last()]
```

You could also select the first `title` elements of any `memo` elements using an index selector:

```
memo/title[1]
```

This is actually shorthand for the following:

```
memo/title[position()=1]
```

In other cases, you might need to select multiple branches within the same document. Here's an example that shows how you might pick out memo titles and authors at the same time:

```
memo/title|memo/author
```

As you can see, the XPath query language is powerful and flexible—it allows you to retrieve just about any combination of nodes from an XML document, which can make all the difference when you're working with XSLT and other XML technologies.

Programmatic Aspects of XSLT

In this section, we're going to cover sorting, counting, numbering, conditional processing, and looping in XSLT. The goal is to give you a solid background in some of the more programmatic aspects of XSLT. Yes, there *is* more to XSLT than just displaying stuff in a browser!

Sorting

Sometimes, you may want to change the order of the nodes in your XML document. In fact, if you're using some kind of software process to create a file (such as an inventory readout), it's likely that the nodes will be output in the same order in which they were written to the file.

XSLT's sort element can be a big help here. It allows you to sort nodes in alphabetical or numerical order, as well as in ascending (a, b, c) or descending (z, y, x) order.

Let's take a look at a hypothetical XML file, which contains a list of products in a catalog. As you can see from the example below, the product listing is not in any discernible order.

File: **productlisting.xml**

```
<?xml version="1.0" encoding="iso-8859-1"?>
<catalog>
  <product sku="212993">Lamp</product>
  <product sku="488839">Folder</product>
  <product sku="198102">Stapler</product>
  <product sku="91882">Notebook</product>
  <product sku="873638">Inbox</product>
  <product sku="192839">Desk</product>
  <product sku="66553">Pen</product>
  <product sku="38289">Calculator</product>
</catalog>
```

Sorting Alphabetically

You can sort this product list in ascending alphabetical order by adding an <xsl:sort> tag as a child of the <xsl:apply-templates> tag used to select the product elements.

File: **sort.xsl (excerpt)**

```
<xsl:template match="catalog">
  <h1>Alphabetical List of Products</h1>
  <xsl:apply-templates select="product">
    <xsl:sort/>
  </xsl:apply-templates>
</xsl:template>

<xsl:template match="product">
  <p><xsl:apply-templates/></p>
</xsl:template>
```

Figure 5.1 shows the file displayed in a Web browser. As you can see, the product elements have been sorted by their contents before being processed by the corresponding template.

Figure 5.1. Alphabetical sort of product listing example.

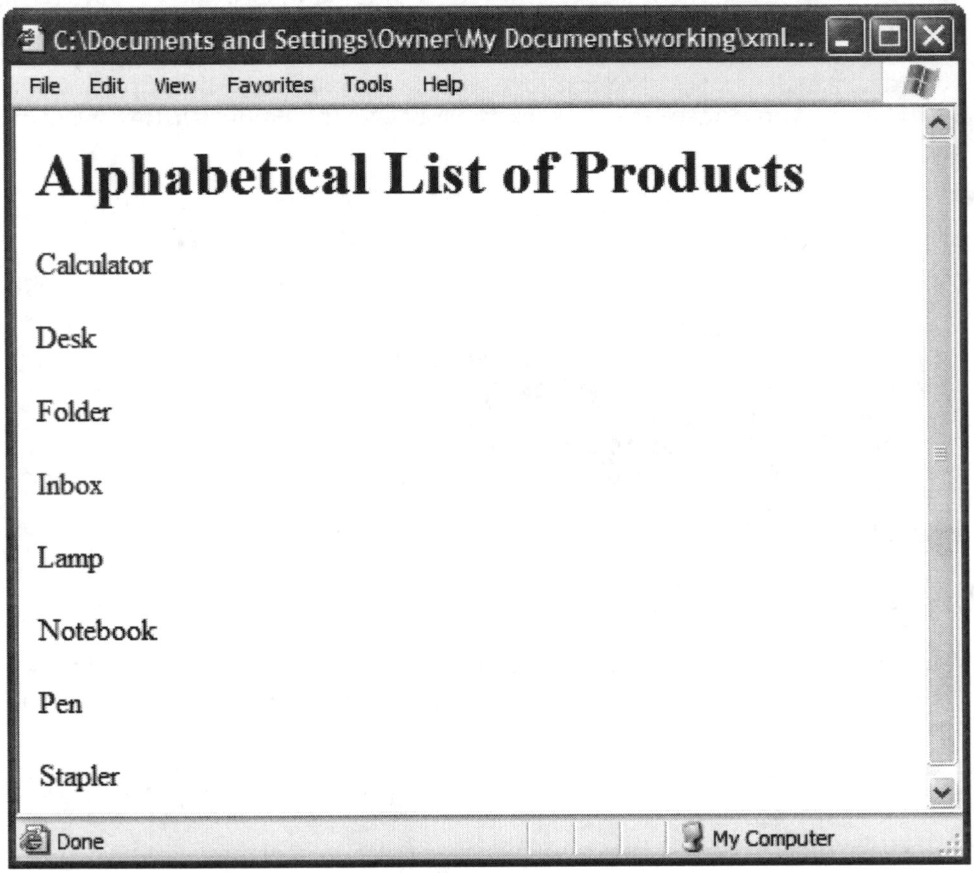

Reversing the Sort

What if you wanted to sort the list in reverse order? Easy! Just add an `order` attribute to the sort instruction:

File: **sort-descending.xsl (excerpt)**

```
<xsl:template match="catalog">
  <h1>Alphabetical List of Products</h1>
  <xsl:apply-templates select="product">
    <xsl:sort order="descending"/>
  </xsl:apply-templates>
</xsl:template>
```

The reverse listing is shown in Figure 5.2.

Figure 5.2. Reversing the sort on our product listing.

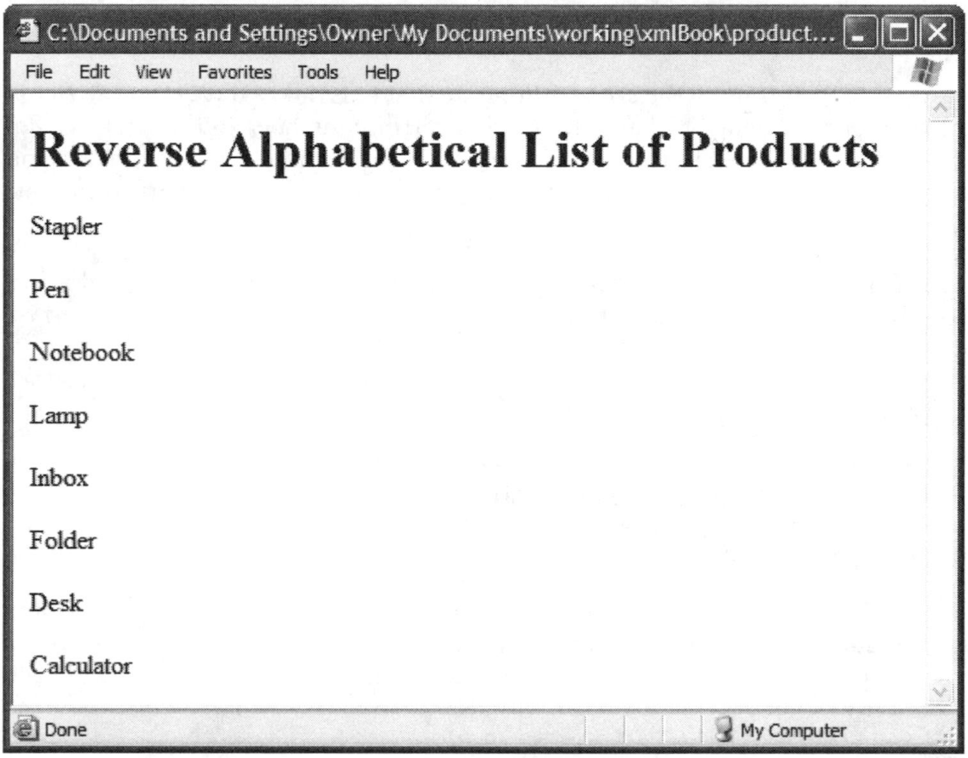

Sorting by the Numbers

Now that we have a handle on sorting alphabetically, let's take a look at sorting numerically. What we want to do is sort the list of products by the value of their sku attribute.

Here's the listing again:

File: **productlisting.xml**

```
<?xml version="1.0" encoding="iso-8859-1"?>
<catalog>
  <product sku="212993">Lamp</product>
  <product sku="488839">Folder</product>
  <product sku="198102">Stapler</product>
```

```
  <product sku="91882">Notebook</product>
  <product sku="873638">Inbox</product>
  <product sku="192839">Desk</product>
  <product sku="66553">Pen</product>
  <product sku="38289">Calculator</product>
</catalog>
```

If we want to sort using the `sku` attribute, we first must add a `data-type` attribute to the `sort` element, so that it knows it's sorting numbers and not text values (the default). There are three valid values for this attribute: `text`, `number`, and `qname`. For now, we'll concentrate on `number`, because it will allow us to sort the lists on the numeric SKUs.[1]

We also have to tell XSLT what to look at when performing the sort. To do this, we use the `select` attribute of the `sort` element.

File: **sort-sku.xsl (excerpt)**

```
<xsl:template match="catalog">
  <h1>Product Listing</h1>
  <xsl:apply-templates select="product">
    <xsl:sort select="@sku" data-type="number"/>
  </xsl:apply-templates>
</xsl:template>
```

What's happening here is that for each element to be sorted, the `select` attribute of the `sort` element provides an XPath expression that locates the data to be used in performing the sort. In this case, `@sku` points to the `sku` attribute of each `product` element.

Figure 5.3 shows the results of this XSLT processing.

What happens if we want to display the SKU as well as the product name? We can simply modify the template for our `product` elements to output the value using a `value-of`.

File: **sort-sku-show.xsl (excerpt)**

```
<xsl:template match="product">
  <p><xsl:value-of select="@sku"/> - <xsl:apply-templates/></p>
</xsl:template>
```

Figure 5.4 shows the new display.

---

[1]SKU stands for Stock Keeping Unit, which is simply a unique numeric ID for a product for sale.

Figure 5.3. Sorting by numbers.

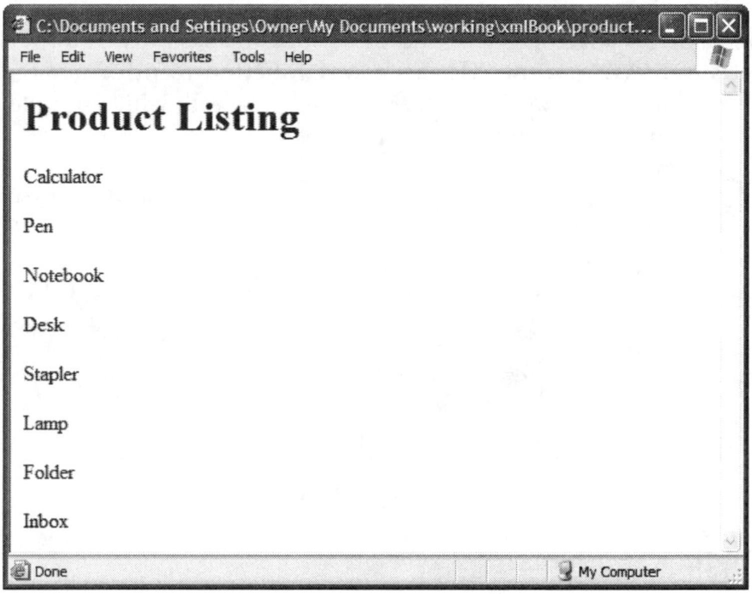

Figure 5.4. Sorting by numbers. (Part 2)

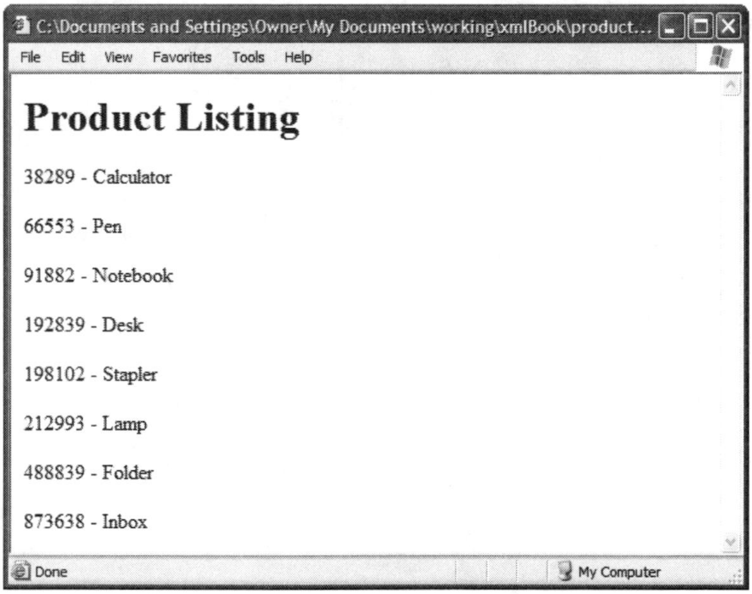

Counting

Sorting the product listing by SKU is good, but it might be nice to provide a total count of products as well. We can use XPath's count function to print out the number of elements matched by a particular expression. In the following example, I've added a count of elements to the SKU sort example:

File: **sort-count.xsl (excerpt)**

```
<xsl:template match="catalog">
  <h1>Product Listing</h1>
  <p><em>Total products: <xsl:value-of select="count(product)"/>
    </em></p>
  <xsl:apply-templates select="product">
    <xsl:sort select="@sku" data-type="number"/>
  </xsl:apply-templates>
</xsl:template>
```

Figure 5.5 shows how this appears in a Web browser.

Figure 5.5. Counting products.

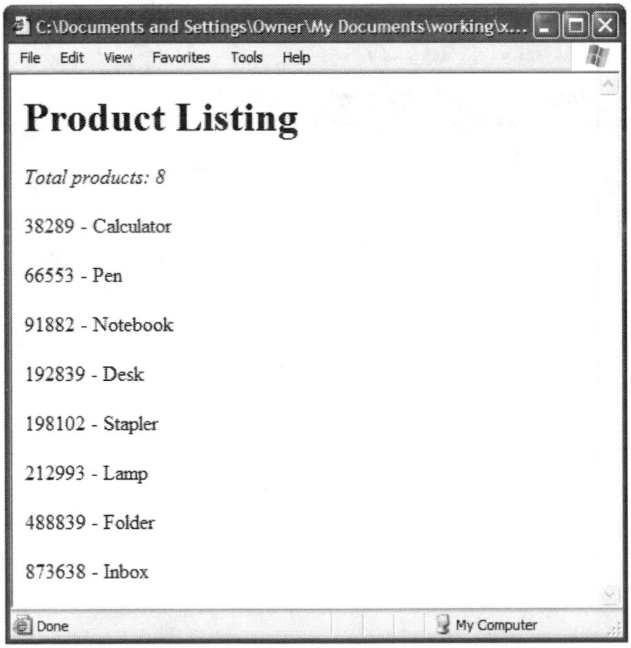

Numbering

If you need to add numbered lists to your XSLT output, use the `<xsl:number>` tag. In this example, we'll use it to print a number next to each product in the list.

Let's see the example first. Then, we'll step through it to see how it's done.

File: **number.xsl (excerpt)**

```
<xsl:template match="catalog">
  <h1>Product Listing</h1>
  <p><em>Total products: <xsl:value-of select="count(product)"/>
    </em></p>
  <xsl:apply-templates select="product"/>
</xsl:template>

<xsl:template match="product">
  <p><xsl:number format="1. "/><xsl:apply-templates/>
    (<xsl:value-of select="@sku"/>)</p>
</xsl:template>
```

Notice that this style sheet is almost the same as our last one, except that, here, we aren't sorting the results. Furthermore, in the second template, we've added a `number` element. This tells XSLT to output a number, based on the `format` attribute, counting up for each element in a series of nodes matched by this template.

The `format` attribute lets you create numbering schemes using integers, integers with leading zeros, upper- and lowercase letters, and upper- and lowercase Roman numerals. Simply supply a value that indicates how you'd like the first number in the series to look, and XSLT will take it from there. In this example, the value `1.` indicates that we want an integer number followed by a period (`.`) and then a space. In this context, `1` is a special character that tells XSLT that we want it to write out integers. Table 5.1 provides a summary of these special characters.

Table 5.1. `format` Attribute Numbering Codes

Code	Results	Code	Results
1	1 2 3 4 ...	A	A B C D E F...
01	01 02 03 04 ...	i	i ii iii iv v ...
a	a b c d e f ...	I	I II III IV V ...

By default, the number generated for each element is based on the original position of the node in the XML file. Thus, if we were to sort our output in any way, the numbers would be mixed up. Figure 5.6 shows what happens when we use the number element; Figure 5.7 shows what happens when we sort the data at the same time.

Figure 5.6. Numbering your output.

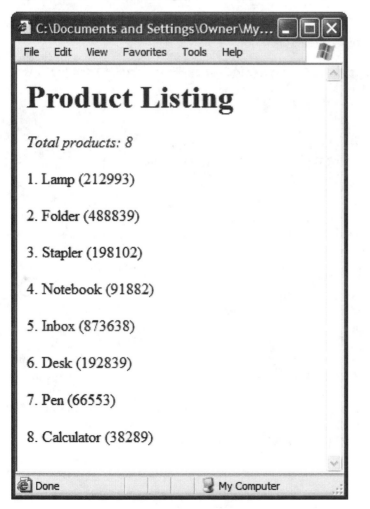

File: **number-position.xsl (excerpt)**

```
<xsl:template match="catalog">
  <h1>Product Listing</h1>
  <p><em>Total products:
    <xsl:value-of select="count(product)"/></em></p>
  <xsl:apply-templates select="product">
    <xsl:sort/>
  </xsl:apply-templates>
</xsl:template>
```

Figure 5.7. Numbering with a sort.

So, how can you perform a sort and have the numbers appear in the right order—based on the resulting sort, not the source XML? This can be done with the help of the XSLT `position` function. The `number` element supports a `value` attribute with which you can control the number that is displayed. `position` gives the position of the current element within the current (sorted) group of elements, so it's exactly the number we want:

File: **number-position.xsl (excerpt)**

```
<xsl:template match="product">
  <p><xsl:number format="1. " value="position()"/>
    <xsl:apply-templates/> (<xsl:value-of select="@sku"/>)</p>
</xsl:template>
```

The resulting list is shown in Figure 5.8.

A Complex Affair

You may be wondering why numbering and positioning has to be so complicated. You may ask why you can't just use an HTML ordered list:

```
<xsl:template match="catalog">
  <h1>Product Listing</h1>
  <p><em>Total products: <xsl:value-of select="count(product)"/>
    </em></p>
  <ol>
    <xsl:apply-templates select="product">
      <xsl:sort/>
    </xsl:apply-templates>
  </ol>
</xsl:template>

<xsl:template match="product">
  <li><xsl:apply-templates/> (<xsl:value-of select="@sku"/>)</li>
</xsl:template>
```

HTML's `<ol>` tag is a great way to make numbering work, and works regardless of the sort, since the numbering is performed by the browser. However, something like that won't help if you're outputting plain text. XSLT numbering provides a more general solution, which will work even when HTML output isn't an option.

Figure 5.8. The right way to sort and number output.

Conditional Processing

Most programming languages allow us to perform some kind of conditional processing. In other words, they let us test if something is true or false, then perform an appropriate action. Although it's not a fully-fledged programming language, XSLT does provide basic conditional processing tools.

`<xsl:if>`

Continuing with our product listing example, let's imagine that we only want to display those products whose SKU is greater than 100,000. How would this work in a style sheet?

The answer is to use the `<xsl:if>` tag. This instruction allows you to set a test, and then do something based on the results. In the following style sheet, we use this technique to print out those products that have an SKU above 100,000.

File: **conditional.xsl (excerpt)**

```
<xsl:template match="catalog">
  <h1>Product Listing</h1>
  <ol>
    <xsl:apply-templates select="product">
      <xsl:sort/>
    </xsl:apply-templates>
  </ol>
</xsl:template>

<xsl:template match="product">
  <xsl:if test="@sku &gt; 100000">
    <li><xsl:apply-templates/>
      (<xsl:value-of select="@sku"/>)</li>
  </xsl:if>
</xsl:template>
```

Notice first that we wrap the entire output in an HTML ordered list. Second, notice that we use `<xsl:if>` to perform our test in the second `template` block:

File: **conditional.xsl (excerpt)**

```
<xsl:if test="@sku &gt; 100000">
```

Every `if` element must have a corresponding `test` attribute. In this particular case, we're testing the value of the `sku` attribute (`@sku` in XPath notation). If it's over 100,000, we print the product node. `&gt;`, as you'll know from HTML, is the escaped form of `>`, the greater-than symbol.

Escaping Less-Than and Greater-Than

Since the less-than (<) and greater-than (>) symbols are used to start and end tags in XML, you must escape these characters when you use them in some other capacity. This includes using them as operators in XPath expressions.

Thus, if you want to perform a "less than" test, you must escape the < operator as <:

```
<xsl:if test="@sku &lt; 100000">
```

If you forget to escape a special character like this, chances are you'll be facing an error message when you try to process a file using the style sheet.

Figure 5.9 shows how the output displays in a Web browser.

Figure 5.9. Conditional processing using <xsl:if>.

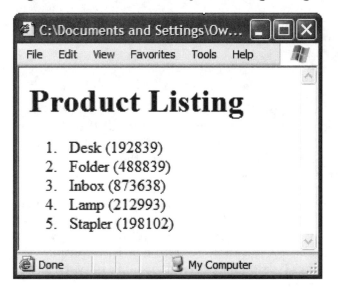

<xsl:choose>

What's the difference between <xsl:if> and <xsl:choose>? The if element only allows you to test one condition at a time, whereas a choose element can have multiple branches, each of which responds to a different condition.

Let's keep working on our product example. In the last section, we used an if element to print out any product that had an SKU over 100,000. This time, we're going to use choose to format the different products depending on their SKU values.

File: **conditional2.xsl (excerpt)**

```
<xsl:template match="product">
  <xsl:choose>
    <xsl:when test="@sku &gt; 100000">
      <li><strong><xsl:apply-templates/>
        (<xsl:value-of select="@sku"/>)</strong></li>
    </xsl:when>
    <xsl:when test="@sku &gt; 50000">
      <li><em><xsl:apply-templates/>
        (<xsl:value-of select="@sku"/>)</em></li>
    </xsl:when>
    <xsl:otherwise>
      <li><xsl:apply-templates/>
        (<xsl:value-of select="@sku"/>)</li>
    </xsl:otherwise>
  </xsl:choose>
</xsl:template>
```

As you can see, the <xsl:when> tag plays host to a number of <xsl:when> tags, and optionally a <xsl:otherwise> tag. The test attributes of the whens are checked in order, and the first one that is found to be true determines which when branch is executed. If none of the tests works out, then the contents of the optional branch are processed instead.

Our two when branches in this case are fairly straightforward. In the first branch, we check to see if the SKU is greater than 100,000. If it is, then we print out the product's name and its SKU in bold (<strong>). In the second branch, we test to see if the value of the SKU is greater than 50,000. If it is, we display the product's name and SKU in italics (<em>). The otherwise handles any remaining products, displaying them normally.

Figure 5.10 shows the results.

Figure 5.10. Conditional processing using xsl:choose.

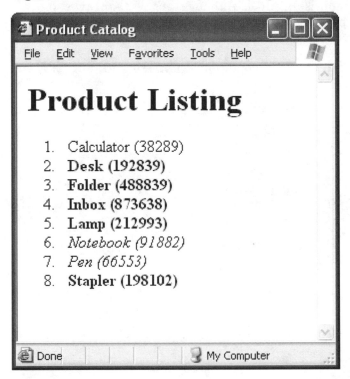

Looping Through XML Data

With `<xsl:for-each>`, you can loop through a set of XML elements, processing each element as you specify. This looping construct is very useful when you need to repeat a process or function multiple times, and it can be a great time-saver over writing a template to do the job. In the example below, we'll use `for-each` instead of `apply-templates` to print out the products in our catalog.

File: **foreach.xsl (excerpt)**

```
<xsl:template match="catalog">
  <h1>Product Listing</h1>
  <ol>
    <xsl:for-each select="product">
      <li><xsl:apply-templates/></li>
    </xsl:for-each>
  </ol>
</xsl:template>
```

As you can see, the `for-each` loop construct allows us to process XML data quickly, and in a very concise manner. Although `apply-templates` provide greater flexibility and is generally easier to maintain and extend, sometimes the simplicity of a `for-each` is exactly what you need.

As with templates, you can even add conditional processing to print only the product nodes that have certain SKUs:

File: **foreach-conditional.xsl (excerpt)**

```
<xsl:template match="catalog">
  <h1>Product Listing</h1>
  <ol>
    <xsl:for-each select="product">
      <xsl:if test="@sku &gt; 100000">
        <li><xsl:apply-templates/></li>
      </xsl:if>
    </xsl:for-each>
  </ol>
</xsl:template>
```

Another way to achieve this would be to use a predicate in the XPath query in the `for-each`:

File: **foreach-conditional2.xsl (excerpt)**

```
<xsl:template match="catalog">
  <h1>Product Listing</h1>
  <ol>
    <xsl:for-each select="product[@sku &gt; 100000]">
      <li><xsl:value-of select="."/></li>
    </xsl:for-each>
  </ol>
</xsl:template>
```

Some might argue that this alternative method is more elegant, pithy, and compact, while others might prefer the programmatic structure of an `if` nested inside the `for-each` loop.

Our CMS Project

In the last chapter, we took a giant leap forward with our CMS, building most of the public pages we'll need to make our site work. In this chapter, we're going to finish the search engine and start adding some formatting rules to our documents.

Finishing our Search Engine

In the last chapter, we created a very simple search widget. This widget contained the following HTML:

File: search.inc.php (excerpt)

```
<form id="searchWidget" method="post" action="doSearch.php">
  Search Site:
  <input name="term" type="text" id="term" />
  <input name="search" type="submit" id="search" value="Search" />
</form>
```

What we'll do now is create the doSearch.php file, which will contain the code that implements the search. When we originally discussed our requirements for the Website, we said: "The search engine will retrieve content by keywords, titles, and descriptions, and only display those pieces that have a status of live."

So let's start working on doSearch.php. The structure of the page is quite similar to the rest of our site's pages. The heart of the page's code, however, loops through our files looking for the submitted search string in appropriate places:

File: doSearch.php (excerpt)

```
<?php
include_once 'common.inc.php';
$term = $_POST['term'];
?>
<!DOCTYPE html PUBLIC "-//W3C//DTD XHTML 1.0 Transitional//EN"
    "http://www.w3.org/TR/xhtml1/DTD/xhtml1-transitional.dtd">
<html xmlns="http://www.w3.org/1999/xhtml">
<head>
<title>Search Results</title>
<meta http-equiv="content-type"
    content="text/html; charset=iso-8859-1" />
<link rel="stylesheet" href="xmlcms.css" type="text/css" />
</head>
<body>
<?php
include 'navtop.inc.php';
?>
<div id="navSide">
  <?php
  include 'search.inc.php';
  include 'news.inc.php';
  ?>
```

```
</div>
<div id="mainContent">
  <?php
  $handle = opendir($fileDir);
  $items = array();
  while (($file = readdir($handle)) !== FALSE) {
    if (is_dir($fileDir . $file)) continue;
    if (!eregi("^(news|article|webcopy).*\.xml$", $file))
      continue;

    $xmlItem = simplexml_load_file($fileDir . $file);
    if ((stripos($xmlItem->keywords, $term) !== FALSE or
        stripos($xmlItem->headline, $term) !== FALSE or
        stripos($xmlItem->description, $term) !== FALSE) and
        (string)$xmlItem->status == 'live') {
      $item = array();
      $item['id'] = (string)$xmlItem['id'];
      $item['headline'] = (string)$xmlItem->headline;
      $items[] = $item;
    }
  }
```

Though this code is imposing, most of it should be familiar. It simply scans through our xml directory in search of XML files containing news, articles, and Web copy. It loads every such file using SimpleXML and checks the keywords, headline, and description elements to see if they contain the search string ($term). Upon finding a match, we dump information about the file into an array ($items).

A few details of note:

File: **doSearch.php (excerpt)**

```
if (!eregi("^(news|article|webcopy).*\.xml$", $file))
  continue;
```

This regular expression simply checks that the filename begins with news, article, or webcopy, and ends with .xml.

File: **doSearch.php (excerpt)**

```
if ((stripos($xmlItem->keywords, $term) !== FALSE or
    stripos($xmlItem->headline, $term) !== FALSE or
    stripos($xmlItem->description, $term) !== FALSE) and
    (string)$xmlItem->status == 'live') {
```

The `stripos` function used here is new to PHP 5. It performs a case-insensitive search of its first argument for the second argument, and returns false if the value was not found. In this case, we're using it to look for the search term in the various XML element values.

In the last line, we must **cast** the value of the `status` element to a string (`(string)$xmlItem->status`), in order to compare it with the string `'live'`, because SimpleXML actually stores the information as an object. You'll notice we've also cast a couple of other values (such as `$xmlItem['id']`) before storing them in variables. Functions like `stripos` that take only string values perform this conversion automatically, which is why the values of the `keywords`, `headline`, and `description` elements are used directly. Casting values is a fact of life in fully object oriented languages like Java, but in PHP it's a rare necessity.

We run a test to see if the `$items` array has a length greater than zero, and print out the appropriate result: a search results list, or a message stating that no content items were found to match that search term.

File: **doSearch.php** (excerpt)

```php
if (count($items) > 0) {
  echo '<h1>Search Results for ' . htmlentities($term) .
    '</h1>';
  echo '<table border="1" cellspacing="0" cellpadding="3"
      width="85%">';
  echo '<tr valign="top"><th>Content Item</th><th>Content Type
      </th></tr>';
  foreach ($items as $item) {
    echo '<tr valign="top"><td><a href="innerpage.php?id=' .
        $item['id'] . '">';
    echo htmlentities($item['headline']) . '</a></td>';
    echo '<td>';
    echo ereg_replace('[0-9]', '', $item['id']);
    echo '</td></tr>';
  }
  echo '</table>';
} else {
  echo '<h1>Sorry!</h1>';
  echo '<p>No files found with the search term ' .
      htmlentities($term) . '</p>';
}
?>
</div>
</body>
</html>
```

We now have a fast and effective XML-driven search engine for our site, as shown in Figure 5.11.

Figure 5.11. Our new search engine.

Creating an XSLT-Powered Site Map

A search engine can certainly help our site visitors get around, but a site map will show them exactly where specific content is located, and how to get to it.

In this section, we'll build a PHP- and XSLT-powered site map. This will give us first-hand experience with the creation of XML files from PHP, the processing of XML with XSLT from PHP, and the use of dynamic sorting options within XSLT.

Generating a Site Map Dynamically

The first thing we need to do is create a PHP script, which will dynamically generate a site map in memory. It will then process that site map with an XSLT file that we'll create shortly.

Within our PHP file, we'll use PHP 5's SimpleXML functions to create our XML file. First we'll create a timestamp (in the format YYYYMMDDHHMMSS) using

PHP's `date` function, which we use in the `<sitemap>` tag at the root of the site map document:

File: **sitemap.php (excerpt)**

```php
<?php
include_once 'common.inc.php';
$timestamp = date('YmdHis');

$xmlstring = '<?xml version="1.0"?>';
$xmlstring .= '<sitemap created="' . $timestamp . '">';
```

Our next step involves grabbing content from live XML documents in the `xml` directory. As we did previously for the site search engine, we'll use SimpleXML to open each file and pull out the values we need:

File: **sitemap.php (excerpt)**

```php
$handle = opendir($fileDir);
while (($file = readdir($handle)) !== FALSE) {
  if (is_dir($fileDir . $file)) continue;
  if (!eregi("^(news|article|webcopy).*\.xml$", $file)) continue;

  $xmlItem = simplexml_load_file($fileDir . $file);
  if ((string)$xmlItem->status == 'live') {
    $id = (string)$xmlItem['id'];
    $type = ereg_replace('[0-9]', '', $id);
    $created = ereg_replace('[^0-9]', '', $id);
    $xmlstring .= '<content id="' . $id . '">';
    $xmlstring .= '<headline>' .
        htmlspecialchars($xmlItem->headline) . '</headline>';
    $xmlstring .= '<type>' . $type . '</type>';
    $xmlstring .= '<created>' . $date . '</created>';
    $xmlstring .= '</content>';
  }
}
$xmlstring .= '</sitemap>';
```

You'll note that we have made a new assumption here. The ID of each content item is assumed to obey a certain format: it will start with the type of content (e.g. `news`, `article`, `webcopy`)—we assume this in the search engine script as well—and then the item's creation date/time, in the form YYYYMMDDH-HMMSS. We'll shortly use this second value, which can be treated as a single large number, to sort our content items according to their creation date.

Now that we've generated our site map as an XML string, we'll feed it into SimpleXML using `simplexml_load_string`:

File: **sitemap.php** (excerpt)

```
$xml = simplexml_load_string($xmlstring);
```

The last thing we'll do in preparation for displaying our site map will be to set a variable that will determine how the content list will be sorted. For this application, we want the user to be able to sort on the basis of the headline, creation date, or content type of the items on the site. We'll accept the user's choice of sort mode as a variable in the query string, with a default of headline sorting:

File: **sitemap.php** (excerpt)

```
if (isset($_GET['sortby'])) {
  $sortby = $_GET['sortby'];
} else {
  $sortby = 'headline';
}
```

Now we can apply a style sheet to the information in order to display it in the Web browser. In PHP 5, the XSLT functionality has been separated from the XML functions, which allows you to use XSLT regardless of the method used to generate the XML data in the first place. This does, however, mean that you need to make sure that your PHP installation has XSLT support enabled.

XSLT support in PHP is provided by the optional XSL extension.[2] This extension isn't enabled by default; so you'll need to compile it in using *--with-xsl* on Unix-style installations. You'll need to install libxslt[3] on your server before you can do this. On Windows, the process is a bit easier; you simply need to add the php_xsl.dll file to your php.ini file on Windows.

The first thing we need to do is load our style sheet. In PHP, we use the built-in DOMDocument class to do this. We'll learn more about DOMDocument in later chapters, but for now you just need to know how to load an XML file with it:

File: **sitemap.php** (excerpt)

```
$xsl = new DOMDocument;
$xsl->load('xslt/sitemap.xsl');
```

With this loaded, we can use the style sheet with PHP's XSLTProcessor class:

File: **sitemap.php** (excerpt)

```
$proc = new XSLTProcessor;
$proc->importStyleSheet($xsl);
```

---

[2] http://www.php.net/xsl
[3] http://xmlsoft.org/XSLT/

Next, we pass the `$sortby` variable to the style sheet as a parameter. We do this with the `xsltprocessor`'s `setParameter` method. The first argument has to do with namespaces and is almost always left blank; the second sets the name of the parameter as it will be used in the style sheet; the third is the parameter's value. The style sheet will use this parameter to sort the site map according to the user's preference:

File: **sitemap.php (excerpt)**

```
$proc->setParameter('', 'SORTBY', $sortby);
```

Finally, we transform our XML data using the style sheet and send the output to the browser:

File: **sitemap.php (excerpt)**

```
echo $proc->transformToXML($xml);
?>
```

With the processing logic in place, all that's left to do is write the style sheet.

Creating the Style Sheet

The style sheet will be very simple. It will transform `sitemap.xml` into an XHTML display for the browser, presenting the live content on the site as a list of links. The user will be able to sort the display by headline, date of creation, and content type.

In the preamble, we set the output method for XHTML output:

File: **sitemap.xsl (excerpt)**

```
<xsl:stylesheet version="1.0"
    xmlns:xsl="http://www.w3.org/1999/XSL/Transform"
    xmlns="http://www.w3.org/1999/xhtml">

  <xsl:output method="xml" indent="yes" omit-xml-declaration="yes"
      media-type="application/xhtml+xml" encoding="iso-8859-1"
      doctype-public="-//W3C//DTD XHTML 1.0 Transitional//EN"
      doctype-system=
      "http://www.w3.org/TR/xhtml1/DTD/xhtml1-transitional.dtd"/>
```

Now we need to declare the `SORTBY` parameter that our style sheet will accept to indicate how to sort the headlines in the site map. To do this, we use an XSLT `<xsl:param>` tag, like this:

File: **sitemap.xsl** (excerpt)

```
<xsl:param name="SORTBY">headline</xsl:param>
```

As you can see, the tag contains the default value of the parameter (to be used in case our script didn't pass a value for it).

Next, we write a template for the root of the document that generates the static elements of the page. In particular, it includes a number of links to allow users to sort the display. These links pass the query string variable, `sortby`, that the PHP script expects to receive.

File: **sitemap.xsl** (excerpt)

```
<xsl:template match="/">
  <html>
    <head>
      <title>Site Map</title>
      <meta http-equiv="content-type"
          content="application/xhtml+xml; charset=iso-8859-1"/>
    </head>
    <body>
      <h1>Site Map</h1>
      <p>sort: <a href="?sortby=type">type</a> |
        <a href="?sortby=headline">headline</a> |
        <a href="?sortby=date">date</a></p>
      <xsl:apply-templates/>
    </body>
  </html>
</xsl:template>
```

The next template matches the `sitemap` element. It uses an XSLT `sort` element to arrange the list of content according to the user's preference. As we saw in `sort-sku.xsl` earlier in this chapter, this element takes an optional `select` attribute that specifies what value to sort on using an XPath expression. In this case, we use the `SORTBY` parameter's value (referred to in XSLT as `$SORTBY`), which will be passed from the PHP script as either `type`, `headline`, or `date`. In each case, the style sheet will assign an appropriate value to the `sort` element's `select` attribute, to instruct the XSL processor to use the corresponding element within each `content` element to sort the list.

File: **sitemap.xsl** (excerpt)

```
<xsl:template match="sitemap">
  <ul>
    <xsl:choose>
      <xsl:when test="$SORTBY='type'">
```

```
      <xsl:apply-templates>
        <xsl:sort select="type" />
      </xsl:apply-templates>
    </xsl:when>
    <xsl:when test="$SORTBY='date'">
      <xsl:apply-templates>
        <xsl:sort select="created" />
      </xsl:apply-templates>
    </xsl:when>
    <xsl:otherwise>
      <xsl:apply-templates>
        <xsl:sort select="headline" />
      </xsl:apply-templates>
    </xsl:otherwise>
  </xsl:choose>
 </ul>
 <p><small>sorting by: <u><xsl:value-of select="$SORTBY"/></u>
  </small></p>
</xsl:template>
```

The final template, for the `content` elements, simply prints out a link to `inner-page.php` using the `headline` and `type` elements from the dynamically generated XML site map:

File: **sitemap.xsl** (excerpt)

```
<xsl:template match="content">
  <li><a href="innerpage.php?id={@id}">
    <xsl:apply-templates select="headline"/></a>
    (<xsl:value-of select="type"/>)</li>
 </xsl:template>
</xsl:stylesheet>
```

Of particular note here is the way we've included the value of the `id` attribute in the `href` attribute of the link. By surrounding it with braces ({}), you can output the value of any XPath expression in an attribute value, as we've done here.

That's all there is to it! Now all we have to do is add a link to the `sitemap.php` file (preferably in the left navigation area), so your users can view all the live content on the site. The finished site map should look like Figure 5.12.

Figure 5.12. Our new site map.

Summary

We learned a great deal more about XSLT in this chapter, and, in the process, we finished up our search engine and added a site map to the project Website. In the next chapter, we'll learn how to manipulate XML with JavaScript and DHTML.

6

Manipulating XML with JavaScript/DHTML

In this chapter, we're going to learn how to manipulate XML data within your visitors' browsers with JavaScript and DHTML. Along the way, you'll be introduced to the Document Object Model (DOM).

Learning how to work with client-side tools and XML can be a very valuable bridge to success in future projects. Combined with knowledge of server-side XML processing, client-side skills can give you quite an edge in a complex project.

Why Use Client-Side Scripting?

At first glance, it seems pretty silly to process XML data on the client side when such powerful languages as PHP, ASP.NET, Java, and Perl exist to handle processing on the back end. But, if you've been around the world of Web development for any length of time, you'll know that there are circumstances in which it makes sense to handle things on the server side, and other conditions that suit processing on the client side.

Processing data on the client side can help relieve server load and give the visitor a better, more responsive experience of your site. For example, the use of server-side programming to perform a task as simple as sorting a column in a table, or formatting some data, is unnecessary; it also forces the user to wait longer than they should have to for such trivial operations. Client-side processing of XML data can be a big help in situations like this.

Working with the DOM

What is the DOM? It's the **Document Object Model**, a W3C Standard that allows you, the programmer, to put together a document dynamically, and to navigate and manipulate its structure and content.

In this chapter, we're going to spend some time on the DOM. Consider this discussion a precursor to Chapter 7, where we'll get into more detail with PHP's SimpleXML library, and discuss DOM and SAX, two alternate approaches to processing XML documents. There's a lot to cover, so buckle your seat belts and get ready!

Loading Documents into Memory

Earlier, we mentioned that most programming languages that interface with XML use an XML parser to load XML documents into memory. Once they're loaded, information in the documents can be retrieved and manipulated through the **Document Object Model (DOM)**.

You can visualize the DOM's structure as a tree of **nodes**. The root of the tree is a `Document` node, which has one or more child nodes that branch off from this trunk. Each of these child nodes may in turn contain child nodes of their own, and so on.

Every node in the document offers some standardized functionality, described by the DOM standard as the `Node` interface. The DOM standard supports roughly a dozen node types, each of which contains specialized functionality on top of the standard `Node` interface. The `Document` is one such node type. `Element`, `Attr`, and `Text` are others.

There are two useful methods by which we can load a DOM representation of an existing XML document on the client side. The first is to load XML code from an existing file; the second is to create the code as a JavaScript string and load it into the parser that way. A third method involves creating what's called an XML Data Island directly inline with the HTML content, but, as this method works only in Internet Explorer, we won't cover it here.

We'll examine both of the common methods in a moment, but first we need to learn how to instantiate an XML parser.

Using the XML Parser

To manipulate or traverse an XML document in Internet Explorer, we first have to instantiate the Microsoft XMLDOM parser. In Internet Explorer 5.0 and above, we can instantiate the parser using JavaScript:

File: **clientside-ie.html** (excerpt)

```
<script type="text/javascript">
var xml = new ActiveXObject("Microsoft.XMLDOM");
...
</script>
```

Internet Explorer only

Although we will eventually implement a cross-browser solution for manipulating XML data on the client side, let's start with an Internet Explorer-only solution for simplicity.

Once the parser is instantiated, we can load a file into it using a series of commands. In this example, we load a file named menu.xml into the parser.

File: **clientside-ie.html** (excerpt)

```
<script language="JavaScript">
var xml = new ActiveXObject("Microsoft.XMLDOM");
xml.async = false;
xml.load("menu.xml");
...
</script>
```

Why Set xml.async?

Setting the async property of the xml variable to false ensures that the parser will wait until the document is fully loaded before it does anything else.

Here's the XML file we'll use for the examples that follow in this section:

File: **menu.xml**

```
<?xml version="1.0" encoding="iso-8859-1"?>
<menu>
  <meal>
```

```
    <title>Buddha's Delight</title>
    <desc>A feast for the senses!</desc>
    <price>$4.95</price>
  </meal>
</menu>
```

If it's more suitable for your application, you can instead create a string variable to hold the XML data, then feed it directly to the parser. Notice that to do this, you must use the loadXML method instead of the load method:

File: **clientsidestring-ie.html** (excerpt)

```
<script type="text/javascript">
var xmlcode = '<?xml version="1.0" encoding="iso-8859-1"?>';
xmlcode += '<menu><meal>';
xmlcode += '<title>Buddha\'s Delight</title>';
xmlcode += '<desc>A feast for the senses!</desc>';
xmlcode += '<price>$4.95</price>';
xmlcode += '</meal></menu>';

var xml = new ActiveXObject("Microsoft.XMLDOM");
xml.async = false;
xml.loadXML(xmlcode);
…
</script>
```

Accessing Different parts of the Document

Now that we've successfully loaded a DOM representation of an XML document, we can access the information it contains in a variety of ways. In theory, the properties and methods used to do this are specified by the W3C DOM Recommendations[1], but in practice different browsers (especially Internet Explorer) have defined their own interfaces, sometimes rather loosely inspired by the standard.

When the parser loads an XML document, what it gives you in return is a reference to the document itself. From this, you can get a reference to the root element in the document (in our example, the menu element) with the property name documentElement. The children of that element are in turn accessible through the childNodes property.

File: **clientside-ie.html** (excerpt)

```
var nodes = xml.documentElement.childNodes;
```

---

[1] http://www.w3.org/DOM/DOMTR

The `childNodes` property, and thus the `nodes` variable in this example, contains a `NodeList`. In accordance with the DOM standard, you can access the elements of a `NodeList` by passing a numerical index to the `item` method, with 0 corresponding to the first node in the list. In this example, therefore, `nodes.item(0)` would return a reference to the first child element of the `menu` element—the `meal` element.

The DOM standard calls for nodes to support a `textContent` property, which would return all of the text contained by a given element and all of its descendants. Internet Explorer doesn't support this property, but it does support a nonstandard `text` property that does the same thing. We can use this property to print out all of the text contained in the first `meal` element in the document:

File: **clientside-ie.html (excerpt)**

```
document.write(nodes.item(0).text);
```

The result should look something like this:

```
Buddha's Delight A feast for the senses! $4.95
```

What if we wanted to print out only the text in the `title` element of the first meal? To do this, we'd need to modify our JavaScript slightly:

```
var nodes = xml.documentElement.childNodes.item(0).childNodes;
document.write(nodes.item(0).text);
```

When we run the code now, the text "Buddha's Delight" is displayed in the browser window.

NodeLists as Arrays

Internet Explorer (and indeed many other DOM implementations) lets you treat `NodeList`s as arrays to simplify the code you use to work with them. In this example, you could use array syntax to access nodes instead of the `item` method:

```
var nodes = xml.documentElement.childNodes[0].childNodes;
document.write(nodes[0].text);
```

This method of accessing text values within an XML file by numerical index is useful, but it can get a little cumbersome. Fortunately, there is another way to approach the problem.

Accessing XML Elements by Name

You can use the `getElementsByTagName` method to retrieve a list of nodes of a given type from your document. This method retrieves all elements of the specified name that occur under the node on which the method is called. For example, to print "Buddha's Delight" from our sample menu document, you could write the following code:

File: **clientside-bytagname-ie.html** (excerpt)
```
document.write(xml.getElementsByTagName("title").item(0).text);
```

With a larger menu document, you could pick up all the titles and display each as an HTML header with this code:

```
var titles = xml.getElementsByTagName("title");
for (var i = 0; i < titles.length; i++) {
  document.write("<h1>" + titles.item(i).text + "</h1>");
}
```

XSLT Processing with JavaScript

In this section, we'll create a simple XML file and a simple XSLT file. Then, we'll use JavaScript on Internet Explorer to process the two together and print out some results.

Internet Explorer Only

Again, this first example will work only on Internet Explorer! We'll look at cross-browser compatible methods later in this chapter.

Ready to go? Here's the very simple XML file:

File: **test.xml**
```
<?xml version="1.0" encoding="iso-8859-1"?>
<body>
<header>This is a simple headline</header>
<para>Some random text. Notice that in our XML source, we aren't
  pointing to a specific XSLT file.</para>
</body>
```

One thing you should notice right away is that we haven't used a `<?xml-stylesheet>` processing instruction in this file. But, before we get into all that, let's create the style sheet for this XML file.

File: **test.xsl**

```
<xsl:stylesheet version="1.0"
    xmlns:xsl="http://www.w3.org/1999/XSL/Transform"
    xmlns="http://www.w3.org/1999/xhtml">

  <xsl:output method="xml" indent="yes" omit-xml-declaration="yes"
      media-type="application/xhtml+xml" encoding="iso-8859-1"
      doctype-public="-//W3C//DTD XHTML 1.0 Transitional//EN"
      doctype-system=
      "http://www.w3.org/TR/xhtml1/DTD/xhtml1-transitional.dtd"/>

  <xsl:template match="body">
    <html>
      <head>
        <title>Processing XML/XSLT with JavaScript</title>
        <meta http-equiv="content-type"
            content="application/xhtml+xml; charset=iso-8859-1"/>
      </head>
      <body>
        <xsl:apply-templates/>
      </body>
    </html>
  </xsl:template>

  <xsl:template match="header">
    <h1><xsl:apply-templates/></h1>
  </xsl:template>

  <xsl:template match="para">
    <p><xsl:apply-templates/></p>
  </xsl:template>

</xsl:stylesheet>
```

Now, let's build a Web page to perform the transformation. This file will contain mostly JavaScript code that will load the XML and XSLT files into memory, process them, and display the results. Let's take a look at what that looks like. Then, we'll walk through it line by line:

File: **jsTest-ie.html**

```
<!DOCTYPE html PUBLIC "-//W3C//DTD XHTML 1.0 Transitional//EN"
    "http://www.w3.org/TR/xhtml1/DTD/xhtml1-transitional.dtd">
<html xmlns="http://www.w3.org/1999/xhtml">
<head>
<title>Processing XML/XSLT with JavaScript</title>
```

```
<meta http-equiv="Content-Type"
    content="text/html; charset=iso-8859-1" />
<script type="text/javascript">
var xml = new ActiveXObject("Microsoft.XMLDOM");
xml.async = false;
xml.load("test.xml");

var xsl = new ActiveXObject("Microsoft.XMLDOM");
xsl.async = false;
xsl.load("test.xsl");

window.onload = function() {
  document.write(xml.transformNode(xsl));
}
</script>
</head>

<body>
</body>
</html>
```

Inside the `<script>` tag, the code creates an instance of the Microsoft XML parser (XMLDOM) and loads our XML file (`test.xml`) into memory. This part should be extremely familiar to you—we learned to do this earlier, in our introduction to the DOM.

File: **jsTest-ie.html (excerpt)**

```
var xml = new ActiveXObject("Microsoft.XMLDOM");
xml.async = false;
xml.load("test.xml");
```

The second snippet of code creates another instance of XMLDOM and loads our XSLT file (`test.xsl`) into memory. Since XSLT files are formatted as XML, you can load them just as you would any other XML file:

File: **jsTest-ie.html (excerpt)**

```
var xsl = new ActiveXObject("Microsoft.XMLDOM");
xsl.async = false;
xsl.load("test.xsl");
```

The remainder of the code waits until the document finishes loading, then transforms the XML document using the XSL style sheet, and replaces the page with the results of the transformation.

File: **jsTest-ie.html (excerpt)**

```
window.onload = function() {
  document.write(xml.transformNode(xsl));
}
```

Here, we've used Internet Explorer's `transformNode` method, which takes as its argument the object that holds the XSL file. Because we're wrapping this operation inside a call to `document.write`, the entire expression forms a fairly concise command that says, in effect: "take our XSLT and apply it to our XML document, then display the resulting document."

Figure 6.1 shows how our work appears in Internet Explorer.

Figure 6.1. Using JavaScript to transform XML in IE.

Now, try to look at the same file in Firefox. You'll find that it doesn't display at all. If you use the built-in JavaScript Console, you'll see a message like that shown in Figure 6.2.

Figure 6.2. Problems arising with Firefox.

This is because Firefox (and other Mozilla-based browsers) cannot identify the `ActiveXObject` that we're attempting to create on line 10. We need to make some changes to our script so that it works across browsers.

Making our Test Script Cross-Browser Compatible

Now we know that we have to make our little script work in both IE and Mozilla-based browsers like Firefox. Each type of browser handles XML loading in a different fashion, so any script that will work on both will have to do some browser detection and respond accordingly.

The hard way to do this is to learn from scratch how to load XML in Firefox and Internet Explorer, and do all the necessary browser detection yourself. A better way is to open your Web browser, and download the latest copy of the Sarissa[2] JavaScript XML library.[3] The package comes with a number of JavaScript (.js) files, and various documentation files.

Basically, Sarissa makes it possible for you to use a single API to make your JavaScript XML handling work in both types of browser. It's a huge time-saver! It works fairly reliably on Internet Explorer 5.5 and above, Firefox 1.0 and above, Netscape 6 and above, and Mozilla 1.6 and above.[4]

This example uses Sarissa to achieve what we did in the last section:

File: **jsTest-ie2.html (excerpt)**

```
<script type="text/javascript" src="sarissa/sarissa.js"></script>
<script type="text/javascript">
var xml = Sarissa.getDomDocument();
xml.async = false;
xml.load("test.xml");

var xsl = Sarissa.getDomDocument();
xsl.async = false;
xsl.load("test.xsl");

window.onload = function() {
  var xslt = new XSLTProcessor();
  xslt.importStylesheet(xsl);
  var out = xslt.transformToDocument(xml);
  document.write(Sarissa.serialize(out));
};
</script>
```

---

[2] http://sarissa.sourceforge.net/

[3] This book was written and tested with Sarissa 0.9.6, the latest version as of this writing. As the library is still under development, some changes may have been made to the API by the time you read this.

[4] Many of its features also work in Safari browsers, but XSLT transformations, sadly, are not among them.

This code should print the transformed XML to the page for display. Let's look at the differences between this and the Internet Explorer-specific code of the previous example.

First, we must use the `Sarissa` class' `getDomDocument` method to create XML documents in memory:

File: **jsTest-ie2.html (excerpt)**

```
var xml = Sarissa.getDomDocument();
```

We must also use a class called `XSLTProcessor` to perform the style sheet transformation. After creating the object, we load our style sheet's DOM representation using `importStylesheet`:

File: **jsTest-ie2.html (excerpt)**

```
var xslt = new XSLTProcessor();
xslt.importStylesheet(xsl);
```

Now, whereas Internet Explorer lets us transform our document directly to an XML string, most other browsers (and therefore Sarissa) only support transforming to a DOM representation of the output document. We must then use the `Sarissa` class' `serialize` method to convert it to a string for output:

File: **jsTest-ie2.html (excerpt)**

```
var out = xslt.transformToDocument(xml);
document.write(Sarissa.serialize(out));
```

Now, if you test this new script in Internet Explorer, you'll see that it produces the same output as the browser-specific example. Unfortunately, as Figure 6.3 illustrates, we run into a bit of a glitch when we test the script in Firefox and other Mozilla browsers.[5]

What's going on here? If you use JavaScript's `alert` function to display the XML code of the output document, you'll see the code in Figure 6.4. While this is a perfectly valid XHTML document, a namespace prefix of a0 has been used for the XHTML tags, instead of allowing XHTML to be the default namespace in the document. As a result, the built-in CSS style rules that the browser uses to apply basic styling to HTML documents do not match any of the tags, and you get unstyled output.

---

[5]This issue was fixed with the release of Firefox 1.5 (after this book first went to print), where the example should work perfectly. If you need to support users running older browsers like Firefox 1.0, read on for the work-around; otherwise, feel free to skip to the next section.

Figure 6.3. Firefox displaying the XHTML without styling due to a serialization glitch.

Processing XML/XSLT with JavaScript - Mozilla Firefox

File   Edit   View   Go   Bookmarks   Tools   Help

jsTest-ie2.html

Processing XML/XSLT with JavaScript This is a simple headline Some random text. Notice that in our XML source, we aren't pointing to a specific XSLT file.

Done

Figure 6.4. A namespace prefix added to the document.

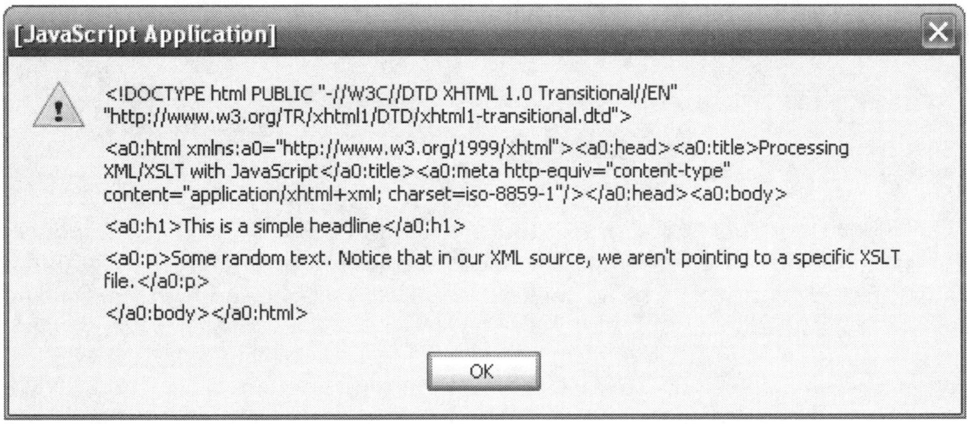

[JavaScript Application]

```
<!DOCTYPE html PUBLIC "-//W3C//DTD XHTML 1.0 Transitional//EN"
"http://www.w3.org/TR/xhtml1/DTD/xhtml1-transitional.dtd">

<a0:html xmlns:a0="http://www.w3.org/1999/xhtml"><a0:head><a0:title>Processing
XML/XSLT with JavaScript</a0:title><a0:meta http-equiv="content-type"
content="application/xhtml+xml; charset=iso-8859-1"/></a0:head><a0:body>

<a0:h1>This is a simple headline</a0:h1>

<a0:p>Some random text. Notice that in our XML source, we aren't pointing to a specific XSLT
file.</a0:p>

</a0:body></a0:html>
```

OK

This namespace prefix is an annoying product of Firefox's built-in XML serialization functionality—there is no practical way to get rid of it, short of removing the namespace declaration at the top of the `test.xsl` style sheet; unfortunately, that trips up the XSLT processor in Internet Explorer, causing the transformation there to fail completely.

The best workaround I can suggest is messy, and requires you to work around a couple more browser limitations, but it works. Since we have the transformed document as a DOM representation in memory, we can use DOM methods to extract the element(s) we require from the transformed document and insert them into our existing document. Here's the code:

File: **jsTest.html (excerpt)**

```
window.onload = function() {
  var xslt = new XSLTProcessor();
  xslt.importStylesheet(xsl);
  var out = xslt.transformToDocument(xml);
  var docBody = document.getElementsByTagName('body').item(0);
  var outBody = out.documentElement.childNodes.item(1);
  // Clear the current document body
  while (docBody.hasChildNodes()) {
    docBody.removeChild(docBody.firstChild);
  }
  // Refill it with the 'out' document body's children
  for (var i = 0; i < outBody.childNodes.length; i++) {
    var node = outBody.childNodes.item(i);
    node = document.importNode(node, true);
    docBody.appendChild(node);
  }
};
```

Let's step through this somewhat convoluted solution, as it contains a couple of method calls with which you are probably not yet familiar.

Once the transformation has occurred, the first thing our script does is obtain DOM references to the body elements of both the currently-displayed document, and the document that resulted from the transformation:

File: **jsTest.html (excerpt)**

```
  var docBody = document.getElementsByTagName('body').item(0);
  var outBody = out.documentElement.childNodes.item(1);
```

You'll notice that while the method we've used to get the displayed document's body is quite straightforward (look for the first body element in the document), we use a more roundabout way of getting the body of the transformation output (getting the second child of the document's root element). A bug or limitation of Internet Explorer's XML support prevents us from accessing tags by name in the result of an XSLT transformation, so this alternative approach is needed.

Our next task is to empty out the body of our displayed document, by deleting all of its child nodes (be they text, elements, or anything else):

File: **jsTest.html (excerpt)**

```
// Clear the current document body
while (docBody.hasChildNodes()) {
  docBody.removeChild(docBody.firstChild);
}
```

The methods and properties used here, though new, are part of the DOM standard and are relatively self-explanatory. hasChildNodes returns true if the element has any child nodes; removeChild removes a child node from the element; and the firstChild property is equivalent to childNodes.item(0).

With the body of the displayed document now empty, we can fill it with nodes from our transformation output document:

File: **jsTest.html (excerpt)**

```
// Refill it with the 'out' document body's children
for (var i = 0; i < outBody.childNodes.length; i++) {
  var node = outBody.childNodes.item(i);
  node = document.importNode(node, true);
  docBody.appendChild(node);
}
```

This code is a little less self-explanatory, but is equally straightforward. The for loop iterates through each of the child nodes of the body of the transformation output document, using the length property of the childNodes collection to get the number of these nodes. We use the importNode method of the currently-displayed document to create copies of each of these nodes (including their contents, as indicated by the true second argument) for use in that document. Those nodes are then added to the currently-displayed document's body element using the appendChild method.

The result of this process is that the contents of the transformed document are added to and displayed as part of the existing page, as shown in Figure 6.5. This solution is effective so long as you didn't need to display the document title, or anything else inside the head element of the transformation output.

Figure 6.5. The XSLT output is correctly displayed in Firefox (at last).

Why not just use similar techniques to replace the entire displayed document, rather than just the contents of the body? A limitation of Internet Explorer's DOM implementation actually prevents this, once again. Internet Explorer uses completely different DOM libraries to work with documents displayed in the browser and to perform XSLT transformations of documents in memory. These two libraries were not designed to work together. The Sarissa library makes a valiant attempt at overcoming this limitation, but the importNode method that is used here to copy nodes from the transformed document to the displayed document will only work on elements that are allowed within the body of an HTML document, thus forcing us to approach the problem as we did.

Thankfully, you'll rarely need to perform an XSLT transformation on the client side to produce a full HTML document for display. More often, you'll use XSLT to generate a small document fragment, in which case the technique shown here of inserting the result using the DOM is completely appropriate, not an inconvenient alternative.

Creating Dynamic Navigation

Now that we understand how to apply style sheets with JavaScript, let's implement something a little more complicated. Let's extract some XML from a file and use it to build a navigation system with JavaScript.

First, let's create a simple file that holds our navigation menu in XML format:

File: **navmenu.xml**

```
<?xml version="1.0" encoding="iso-8859-1"?>
<menu>
  <item label="home" target="index.html"/>
  <item label="services" target="services.html"/>
  <item label="about us" target="aboutus.html"/>
  <item label="contact us" target="contactus.html"/>
  <item label="kb" target="kb.html"/>
</menu>
```

Let's create a very simple JavaScript (using the Sarissa library for cross-browser functionality), which will load this menu file and display it as a very simple list of HTML links.

The first thing we need to do is load the Sarissa libraries:

File: **navmenu.html (excerpt)**

```
<!DOCTYPE html PUBLIC "-//W3C//DTD XHTML 1.0 Transitional//EN"
    "http://www.w3.org/TR/xhtml1/DTD/xhtml1-transitional.dtd">
<html xmlns="http://www.w3.org/1999/xhtml">
<head>
<title>XML Based Menu</title>
<meta http-equiv="Content-Type"
    content="text/html; charset=iso-8859-1" />
<script type="text/javascript" src="sarissa/sarissa.js"></script>
```

Next, we'll create a JavaScript function called `initMenu`. This function loads our `navmenu.xml` file, and pulls all the `item` nodes into the JavaScript `nodes` variable.

File: **navmenu.html (excerpt)**

```
<script type="text/javascript">
function initMenu(xmlFile) {
  var xml = Sarissa.getDomDocument();
  xml.async = false;
  xml.load(xmlFile);

  var nodes = xml.documentElement.childNodes;
```

Now we'll use a `for` loop to look at each `item` in the menu. Since Firefox counts the whitespace between tags as text nodes, we must ensure each time through the `for` loop that we're dealing with an element node. This is accomplished by checking the `nodeType` property to see if it equals `Node.ELEMENT_NODE`.

File: **navmenu.html** (excerpt)

```
for (var i = 0; i <= nodes.length - 1; i++) {
    if (nodes.item(i).nodeType != Node.ELEMENT_NODE) continue;
```

With that done, we can use the `getAttribute` method of the element node to grab the `label` and `target` values as we want:

File: **navmenu.html** (excerpt)

```
    var output = '<a href="' +
        nodes.item(i).getAttribute('target') + '">' +
        nodes.item(i).getAttribute('label') + '</a><br />';
    document.write(output);
  }
}
</script>
</head>
```

Finally, let's make that all-important call to `initMenu` in the body of the document, passing in the name of our menu file.

File: **navmenu.html** (excerpt)

```
<body>
<h1>My Menu</h1>
<script type="text/javascript">
initMenu('navmenu.xml');
</script>
</body>
</html>
```

Figure 6.6 illustrates the results.

An Alternative Approach

If you're already comfortable with JavaScript, you'll know that there's a much better way of doing things than to call `document.write` to print out the items of our menu.

A more elegant approach is to set aside a container element (typically a `div`) with a known ID. We can then write the contents of that element on-the-fly using our JavaScript code.

Figure 6.6. A simple menu.

Here's our new HTML:

File: **navmenu2.html (excerpt)**

```
<body>
<h1>My Menu</h1>
<div id="menudiv"></div>
</body>
</html>
```

Now, we must go back to our `for` loop. We use the `getElementById` method to select our `div`, and write our output to that element's `innerHTML` property.

File: **navmenu2.html (excerpt)**

```
var output = '';
for (var i = 0; i <= nodes.length - 1; i++) {
   if (nodes.item(i).nodeType != Node.ELEMENT_NODE) continue;
   output += '<a href="' + nodes.item(i).getAttribute('target') +
```

```
        '">' + nodes.item(i).getAttribute('label') + '</a><br />';
    }
    document.getElementById('menudiv').innerHTML = output;
}
```

Finally, we set up our `initMenu` function to be run when the rest of the document finishes loading:

File: **navmenu2.html (excerpt)**

```
window.onload = function() {
  initMenu('navmenu.xml');
};
```

Here's our new code in its entirety:

File: **navmenu2.html**

```
<!DOCTYPE html PUBLIC "-//W3C//DTD XHTML 1.0 Transitional//EN"
    "http://www.w3.org/TR/xhtml1/DTD/xhtml1-transitional.dtd">
<html xmlns="http://www.w3.org/1999/xhtml">
<head>
<title>XML Based Menu</title>
<meta http-equiv="Content-Type"
    content="text/html; charset=iso-8859-1" />
<script type="text/javascript" src="sarissa/sarissa.js"></script>
<script type="text/javascript">
function initMenu(xmlFile) {
  var xml = Sarissa.getDomDocument();
  xml.async = false;
  xml.load(xmlFile);

  var nodes = xml.documentElement.childNodes;
  var output = '';
  for (var i = 0; i <= nodes.length - 1; i++) {
    if (nodes.item(i).nodeType != Node.ELEMENT_NODE) continue;
    output += '<a href="' + nodes.item(i).getAttribute('target') +
        '">' + nodes.item(i).getAttribute('label') + '</a><br />';
  }
  document.getElementById('menudiv').innerHTML = output;
}

window.onload = function() {
  initMenu('navmenu.xml');
};
</script>
</head>
```

```
<body>
<h1>My Menu</h1>
<div id="menudiv"></div>
</body>
</html>
```

Now that we have a function that prints our output to a `div` element, we can reuse this code and place our menu wherever we need it to appear on the page.

In the next section, we'll apply this knowledge to our CMS project by creating categories of articles, then defining a menu system for those categories.

What's the Point of Learning all This?

After reading all this, some of you may still be wondering, "Well, this is pretty silly—I can do all this with PHP on the server side and not have to worry about how different browsers handle things."

I have a few answers for that sort of sentiment:

1. You're exactly right.

2. Don't forget that learning the DOM is a useful tool not only for processing XML data in general, but for fiddling with the structures of HTML documents. This is a fundamental component of Dynamic HTML (DHTML) node collapsing, and the better you understand it, the better you can apply other DHTML techniques.

3. You need to remember that it's sometimes very useful to offload certain kinds of processing to the client. While this particular example showed a hard-coded navigation menu, it's not difficult to imagine a more customized example that uses data stored in cookies on the user's machine to create a personalized navigation menu. That kind of work can be left to the client without burdening the server unnecessarily.

Yes, XML can be seen as a linear sequence of characters and tags, but it can also be seen as a hierarchical tree structure. Having an understanding of the way XML documents are loaded into the DOM can only enhance your ability to make wise decisions about which type of server-side parsing you will use.

There's nothing inherently magical about XML beside the fact that it provides a standardized representation of data; in fact, with semantically appropriate tags, it can become information. What is somewhat magical is the fact that XML structures can be transformed into other entities, such as DOM object trees, which can themselves be processed, navigated, and changed.

Our CMS Project

Now that we've learned how to use JavaScript to load XML data, and to work with that data, let's use these newfound skills to add some capabilities to our CMS project.

IMPORTANT

Browser Compatibility Concerns

As I have already mentioned, client-side XML processing is currently not supported in all browsers. In particular, Safari and Opera browsers do not yet support even the simplest of XSLT transformations. If you plan to develop a CMS for public consumption, you should therefore steer clear of such techniques until wider browser support for these features is available. The server-side techniques I'll present in Chapter 7 are more powerful and free of browser incompatibilities.

For the sake of example, I'll implement a couple of minor features of our CMS using client-side XML processing, but for real-world applications you should keep browser compatibility issues in mind.

Right now, the site can display Web copy, articles, news items, and the like. At some point, though, you can imagine that the Website will be full of content items. There may be hundreds of articles, news items, and so on. So many, in fact, that the content items may become a little hard to sift through.

What we need to do is add categories to the site. A smart, centralized category listing, and an easy way to assign content items to categories, can make it easier for visitors to navigate an otherwise undifferentiated mass of content.

When I start talking about categorization, most of my friends and colleagues usually roll their eyes and yearn to leave the room. But, I love to talk about categorization, ontologies, and things like that. I find them utterly fascinating in all kinds of ways. However, I promise to restrain myself in this chapter—this isn't a book about categorization, after all.

The easiest way to go about all this is to jump right in and discuss things as we go along. I'll try to keep the more esoteric discussions to sidebars, so you can come back to them later if you're in a hurry right now.

Here is a category listing for a site devoted to Web development topics:

File: **categories.xml**

```
<?xml version="1.0" encoding="iso-8859-1"?>
<categories>
  <category label="xml" status="live" id="1"/>
  <category label="php" status="live" id="2"/>
  <category label="asp" status="live" id="3"/>
  <category label="javascript" status="live" id="4"/>
  <category label="perl" status="live" id="5"/>
</categories>
```

Each category is described by its label, its ID, and its visibility status. The status attribute here is very important, because it allows us to remove from view all articles from any given category as needed. Giving each category item its own unique ID will also allow us to reference that category easily in other XML files.

Assigning Content to Categories

Okay, now that we have a category listing, how do we tell our XML-powered Website which content items belong to which categories? With the aid of a categoryid element that we'll build into news items, articles, and other content types.

A sample news document might look like this:

File: **news101404061004.xml**

```
<?xml version="1.0"?>
<news id="news101404061004">
  <authorid>1</authorid>
  <headline>xml headline 2</headline>
  <categoryid>1</categoryid>
  <url>http://www.myerman.com/</url>
  <description>yeah man!</description>
  <keywords>xml</keywords>
  <status>live</status>
  <pubdate>news101404061004</pubdate>
</news>
```

Our next step is to use this information in a meaningful way.

Retrieving Content by Category

Finally, we come to the most complicated part of the process. What we need to do is allow the user to browse our content by category. When a user clicks on a category, we need to display links to all the content items that fall under that category.

To this end, we'll add a new page to our site. First of all, we want to include our all-important header and navigation elements. Initially, the page should show a list of links—one for each category on our site—generated dynamically with JavaScript, as we've seen in this chapter. Each of these links will reload the same page, but with a list of the content items in that category displayed, thanks to some PHP code.

Let's do it one piece at a time. First, we initialize our PHP file by including com-mon.inc.php and loading the Sarissa library:

File: **cats.php** (excerpt)

```php
<?php
include_once 'common.inc.php';
?>
<!DOCTYPE html PUBLIC "-//W3C//DTD XHTML 1.0 Transitional//EN"
    "http://www.w3.org/TR/xhtml1/DTD/xhtml1-transitional.dtd">
<html xmlns="http://www.w3.org/1999/xhtml">
<head>
<title>Browse by Category</title>
<meta http-equiv="content-type"
    content="text/html; charset=iso-8859-1" />
<link rel="stylesheet" href="xmlcms.css" type="text/css" />
<script type="text/javascript" src="sarissa/sarissa.js"></script>
```

The JavaScript that will build the list of categories follows the exact same pattern we saw for the navigation menu example earlier in this chapter: a function named initMenu will be called when the document first loads.

File: **cats.php** (excerpt)

```javascript
<script type="text/javascript">
function initMenu(xmlFile) {
  var xml = Sarissa.getDomDocument();
  xml.async = false;
  xml.load(xmlFile);

  var nodes = xml.documentElement.childNodes;
  var output = '';
  for (var i = 0; i <= nodes.length - 1; i++) {
    if (nodes.item(i).nodeType != Node.ELEMENT_NODE) continue;
    if (nodes.item(i).getAttribute('status') == 'live') {
      output += '<a href="cats.php?catid=' +
          nodes.item(i).getAttribute('id') + '">' +
```

```
            nodes.item(i).getAttribute('label') + '</a><br />';
    }
  }
  document.getElementById('menudiv').innerHTML = output;
}

window.onload = function() {
  initMenu('xml/categories.xml');
};
</script>
</head>
```

The only significant addition (shown in bold here) is an `if` statement that checks that the `status` attribute of each category is `live` before displaying it in the list.

Next, we continue with our familiar boilerplate code for our basic HTML layout, making sure to include our top navigation and search sidebar files:

File: **cats.php (excerpt)**

```
<body>
<?php
include 'navtop.inc.php';
?>
<div id="navSide">
  <?php
  include 'search.inc.php';
  include 'news.inc.php';
  ?>
</div>
```

The final part is the hardest: we have to fill in the content area of the page. First off, we need a `div` element to house the category menu that will be generated by the JavaScript code above:

File: **cats.php (excerpt)**

```
<div id="mainContent">
  <h1>Browse By Category</h1>
  <div id="menudiv"></div>
  <hr/>
```

That takes care of letting the user select a category, but once that's done we need to display the content items in the selected category. That's where the PHP code comes in. Looking for a `$_GET['catid']` value, the script rifles through the `xml` directory in search of news, article, or Web copy files, spotting those that have a matching `categoryid` element and a `status` of `live`.

File: **cats.php (excerpt)**

```php
<?php
if (isset($_GET['catid'])) {
  $handle = opendir($fileDir);
  while (($file = readdir($handle)) !== FALSE) {
    if (is_dir($fileDir . $file)) continue;
    if (!eregi("^(news|article|webcopy).*\.xml$", $file))
      continue;

    $xml = simplexml_load_file($fileDir . $file);
    if ((string)$xml->categoryid == $_GET['catid'] &&
        (string)$xml->status == "live") {
      $id = htmlentities($xml['id']);
      $label = htmlentities($xml->headline);
      echo "<a href=\"innerpage.php?id={$id}\">{$label}</a> ";
    }
  }
}
?>
</div>
</body>
</html>
```

Our last step is to open our search widget file and add the following line to the bottom of the file:

File: **search.inc.php (excerpt)**

```php
<p><a href="cats.php">Browse by Category</a></p>
```

Doing this will create a link to `cats.php` from every page on the site. Figure 6.7 shows what our `cats.php` page looks like when someone has clicked on a category listing.

Summary

Now that we've learned how to manipulate XML with JavaScript and DHTML, it's time to turn our attention to PHP's XML functions. In the next chapter, we'll delve deeper into PHP 5's SimpleXML functions, as well as some other DOM-related functions. We'll also round out our CMS tool by creating all the administrative forms we'll need to manage the site.

Figure 6.7. Browsing by category.

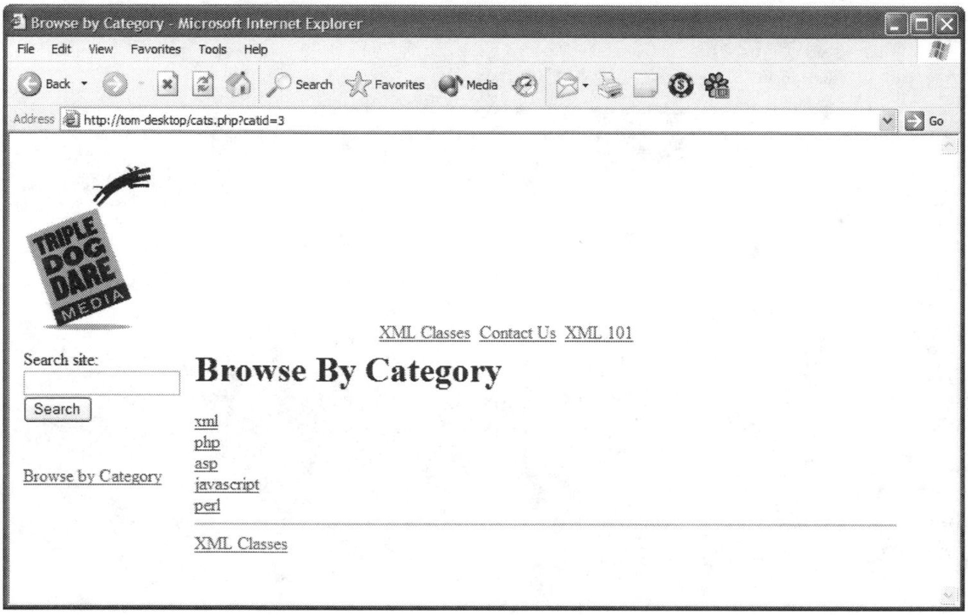

Manipulating XML with PHP

In previous chapters, we processed XML on the client-side, using DOM and XSLT. Now, we're going to learn how to process XML on the server side, using such tools as SAX, DOM, and SimpleXML.

Generally speaking, there are two ways to handle XML processing: the Document Object Model (DOM), which we have already seen, and the **Simple API for XML (SAX)**. With the DOM, you build a hierarchical tree structure to which you can refer repeatedly. With SAX, you treat XML documents as a series of events—one event per element or attribute—and respond to those events as the document is parsed.

Each approach has its pros and cons. DOM builds memory-intensive trees, but, once they're built, the DOM provides plenty of tools to navigate, process, and manipulate those tree structures. SAX is only really good at handling your XML documents in a linear fashion, which means less flexibility; however, it is fast and easy to learn.

PHP 5.0 provides a third approach to handling XML processing—an approach that we've already seen in action. SimpleXML builds a hierarchical object structure like the DOM. The difference is that this structure is optimized for extracting and processing information, whereas the DOM provides a more general-purpose, heavy API for manipulating the structure of the tree.

In this chapter, we'll cover SAX, DOM, and SimpleXML, in that order. By the end of these discussions, you should have a good understanding of how the different APIs can be used to handle XML documents.

Using SAX

Imagine that you build an XML document, then break it apart and lay it end to end on an assembly line. You can see processing instructions, start tags, content, end tags, and so on, all laid out before you in a long line.

You hit a button and your document starts to move down the assembly line, past a guy with a bullhorn. Every time a tag, comment, entity, processing instruction, or chunk of text (character data) goes by, the guy with the bullhorn shouts out, "I see a _____!" That's pretty much what happens with the SAX parser.

Unfortunately, to do anything interesting with SAX, you have to hand-roll your own functions to handle start tags, end tags, and character data, by taking immediate action in response to each. If you want to store any information from the document in a temporary data structure for later use, you have to figure that out for yourself—SAX won't do it for you. They don't call it the Simple API for XML for nothing!

So, why would you use SAX? It might be especially handy in the following situations:

❑ You're dealing with a large XML document that would take up too much memory if it were turned into a DOM tree.

❑ You need to get your parser up and running quickly.

❑ You're doing a limited amount of processing, or processing that is very straightforward and linear (i.e. translating particular XML elements into HTML elements).

❑ You don't need to modify the original XML document.

Given the right circumstances (a large XML document, for instance), SAX will run circles around DOM. However, it's important to understand that, in some cases, it really is more appropriate to use a tree structure—we'll discuss those cases a little later.

The default SAX parser for PHP is Expat,[1] a C library that's durable, tried and true, and is enabled by default in most PHP installations. You don't need to install any additional libraries—everything is built into PHP already. How do you use it? Let's step through a very quick tutorial.

The first step is to create a simple XML file for processing. Here's the file we'll use in this section:

File: **keyword-data.xml**

```xml
<?xml version="1.0" encoding="iso-8859-1"?>
<keywords>
  <keyword>XML</keyword>
  <keyword>PHP</keyword>
  <keyword>Perl</keyword>
  <keyword>JavaScript</keyword>
  <keyword>ASP</keyword>
</keywords>
```

Great—now, we're ready to code some PHP! Before we begin, though, it's a good idea to have an idea of the end result we want to achieve. In this case, we want to transform this list of keyword elements into an HTML bullet list, as illustrated in Figure 7.1.

Figure 7.1. A SAX-processed list of keywords.

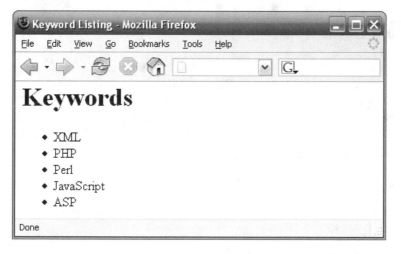

----

[1] http://expat.sourceforge.net/

Creating Handlers

Before we can do anything else with SAX in PHP, we have to create the functions that "handle" the start tags, end tags, and character data. These functions will be called by the SAX parser as it processes the XML—we don't call these functions ourselves.

Our first handler, which we'll call `start_element`, will be responsible for handling all the start tags in our XML document. We could name this handler anything we liked; as you'll see in a moment, we will tell PHP the names of the handlers we've created for it.

The handler function for start tags must accept three arguments: a reference to the SAX parser (which we'll create shortly), the name of the element whose start tag has been encountered, and an array of the element's attributes (and their values).

As you can see below, the handler in this case is nothing more than a `switch` statement that looks for an XML tag name, and responds by outputting the appropriate HTML code.

File: **saxdemo.php (excerpt)**

```php
function start_element($parser, $element_name, $element_attrs) {
  switch ($element_name) {
    case 'KEYWORDS':
    echo '<h1>Keywords</h1><ul>';
    break;
    case 'KEYWORD':
    echo '<li>';
    break;
  }
}
```

In SAX, all Tag Names are Uppercase

By default, the SAX parser in PHP performs a process called **case folding**, in which any lowercase characters in tag or attribute names are replaced with their uppercase equivalents before they are handed to your handler functions. This is why the element names `'KEYWORDS'` and `'KEYWORD'` in this example are all in uppercase. If it really bugs you, the PHP Manual contains some information[2] on how to disable case folding, but it's easier just to go with the flow and write your code to accommodate it.

---

[2] http://www.php.net/xml#xml.case-folding

We'll call our next handler function `end_element`. This handler is called to respond to end tags in the document, and uses the same `switch` statement structure we saw above to output the appropriate HTML code when each end tag is detected.

File: **saxdemo.php (excerpt)**

```
function end_element($parser, $element_name) {
  switch ($element_name) {
    case 'KEYWORDS':
      echo '</ul>';
      break;
    case 'KEYWORD':
      echo '</li>';
      break;
  }
}
```

Finally, we need a way to handle character data. Let's create a `character_data` function that prints out the value of every node it sees. Remember that in XML, "character data" is the name given to any text that's not markup; this handler would print out all the stuff that resides between an element's start and end tags.

File: **saxdemo.php (excerpt)**

```
function character_data($parser, $data) {
  echo htmlentities($data);
}
```

Now that we've defined our custom tag and content handling functions, it's time to instantiate our parser and get to work.

Creating the Parser and Processing the XML

The next steps are relatively easy—most of the heavy lifting is handled by our handler functions. All we have to do is create our parser and tell it which functions we've created to handle start tags, end tags, and character data:

File: **saxdemo.php (excerpt)**

```
$parser = xml_parser_create();
xml_set_element_handler($parser, 'start_element', 'end_element');
xml_set_character_data_handler($parser, 'character_data');
```

Once we've done that, we can use the standard PHP `fopen` function to open our XML document:

File: **saxdemo.php** (excerpt)

```
$fp = fopen('keyword-data.xml', 'r')
    or die ("Cannot open keyword-data.xml!");
```

With the XML document in hand, we can use a simple `while` loop to read in manageable chunks (4KB is a reasonable size), and run them through the parser with the `xml_parse` function. If there's an error at any point, we use PHP's `die` function to print out the error message supplied by `xml_error_string` based on the error number given by `xml_get_error_code`. `xml_get_current_line_number` is used to point to the specific line where the error occurred.

File: **saxdemo.php** (excerpt)

```
while ($data = fread($fp, 4096)) {
  xml_parse($parser, $data, feof($fp))
      or die(sprintf('XML ERROR: %s at line %d',
          xml_error_string(xml_get_error_code($parser)),
          xml_get_current_line_number($parser)));
}
```

Once we're done with our loop, we free the parser with `xml_parser_free`.

File: **saxdemo.php** (excerpt)

```
xml_parser_free($parser);
```

That was a lot to take in, so let's step though the tasks again:

1. Create handlers for start tags, end tags, and character data.

2. Initiate your parser.

3. Register your custom handlers with the parser.

4. Open the XML file.

5. Loop through the file, sending each chunk of data through the parser.

6. Use built-in error trapping to detect problems.

7. Free up the parser once you're done.

As you can see, the SAX approach is very simple and straightforward. However, it lacks some of the more powerful features of other approaches, like DOM.

Using DOM

Now that you know something about SAX, it's time to understand how PHP's DOM functionality works. The DOM is a robust, complex piece of engineering designed to handle a raft of contingencies. In fact, being able to handle anything you throw at it is the major strength of DOM. Its major weakness is that it's very complex and can be overwhelming—not to mention that it can really bog down your resources if you load a large document into memory.

We've already discussed the use of DOM on the client side. On the server side, we're talking about the same DOM—luckily for us, it's a standardized interface. The easiest way to talk about DOM on the server is to compare it with what we already know about SAX. You know from the previous section that you can use SAX to process XML documents in a linear fashion.

PHP's DOM functionality takes a different approach. It loads an XML document into memory and converts it into its own hierarchical object structure, providing two very important features that SAX does not. The first is that the XML structure can be manipulated in memory, allowing nodes to be added, removed, changed, and rearranged. The second is that DOM allows the document to be inspected again and again, in random-access fashion, instead of just linearly.

Let's reuse our simple XML file from the SAX section so we can make an apples-to-apples comparison:

File: **keyword-data.xml**

```xml
<?xml version="1.0" encoding="iso-8859-1"?>
<keywords>
  <keyword>XML</keyword>
  <keyword>PHP</keyword>
  <keyword>Perl</keyword>
  <keyword>JavaScript</keyword>
  <keyword>ASP</keyword>
</keywords>
```

Now that we have a file, let's create a DOM parser and load our XML.

Creating a DOM Parser

To create our parser, we create a DOMDocument object. Before we use it, we'll turn its whitespace handling feature off to prevent spaces, tabs, and line breaks between tabs from being treated as text nodes:

File: **domdemo.php** (excerpt)

```
$doc = new DOMDocument();
$doc->preserveWhiteSpace = false;
```

Next, we load our XML document and grab a reference to our document element:

File: **domdemo.php** (excerpt)

```
$doc->load("keyword-data.xml");
$root = $doc->documentElement;
```

Retrieving Elements

Once we've created the parser and loaded our XML file, we can retrieve information from the document. One of the easiest ways to work with the DOM is to retrieve elements using the `getElementsByTagName` method.

The `getElementsByTagName` method allows you to grab all elements contained within another element that have a particular name. We can use this method to grab all the individual `keyword` elements in the sample document and store them in an array:

File: **domdemo.php** (excerpt)

```
$keywords = $root->getElementsByTagName('keyword');
```

Since we called the method on the root element of the document, the `$keywords` array now contains every `keyword` element in the XML document. We can now iterate through the `$keywords` array to make sure each element is valid. We can then perform some processing on that element.

File: **domdemo.php** (excerpt)

```
echo '<ul>';
foreach ($keywords as $kw) {
  echo '<li>' . htmlentities($kw->nodeValue) . '</li>';
}
echo '</ul>';
```

The result would appear in the Web browser as shown in Figure 7.2.

Figure 7.2. Keyword processing example.

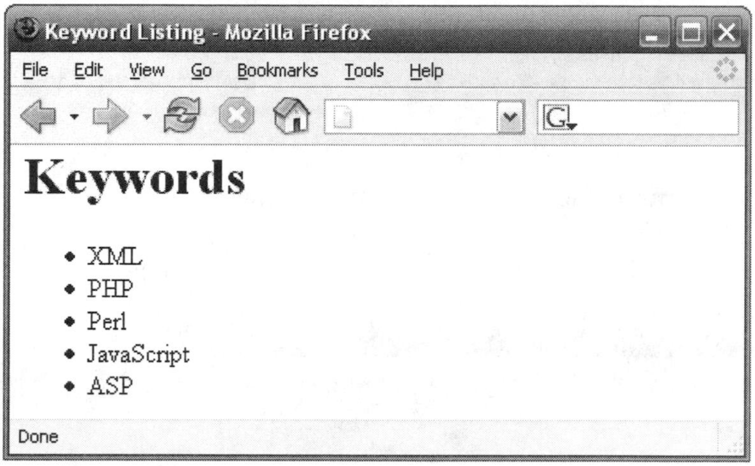

So far, the results are identical to those we achieved with SAX. The main difference is the approach taken: in SAX, we had to create custom handlers to handle different tags as they rolled off the assembly line one after the other; with DOM, we get to access the different levels of a hierarchical node structure in any order we like.

There's one additional point that can be made about working with XML and DOM. If you want to change what is output, or the format of your XML changes, it's usually easier to keep up with these alterations in DOM than in SAX.

For example, imagine each of our keyword elements had a status attribute, like this:

File: **keyword-data2.xml** (excerpt)

```
<?xml version="1.0" encoding="iso-8859-1"?>
<keywords>
  <keyword status="live">XML</keyword>
  <keyword status="in progress">PHP</keyword>
  <keyword status="live">Perl</keyword>
  <keyword status="live">Javascript</keyword>
  <keyword status="in progress">ASP</keyword>
</keywords>
```

Now, we want to print out each keyword's status along with the keyword itself. To do this, we need only make a simple change:

File: **domdemo2.php (excerpt)**

```
echo '<ul>';
foreach ($keywords as $kw) {
  echo '<li>' . htmlentities($kw->nodeValue) .
      ' (' . htmlentities($kw->getAttribute('status')) . ')</li>';
}
echo '</ul>';
```

This small alteration prints as shown in Figure 7.3.

Figure 7.3. Tweaking the keyword listing.

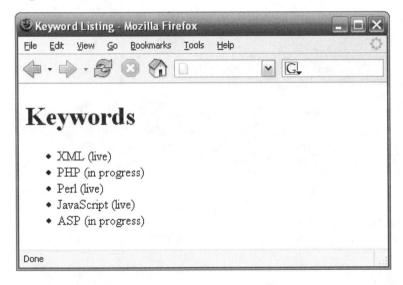

If we wanted to print out only the live keywords, all we'd have to do would be to add a simple if test:

File: **domdemo3.php (excerpt)**

```
echo '<ul>';
foreach ($keywords as $kw) {
  if ($kw->getAttribute('status') == 'live') {
    echo '<li>' . htmlentities($kw->nodeValue) . '</li>';
  }
}
echo '</ul>';
```

This displays as shown in Figure 7.4.

Figure 7.4. Displaying only live keywords.

Creating Nodes

As I mentioned earlier, the DOM allows you to add new nodes, and manipulate existing ones. Let's create a new `keyword` element and add it to our existing DOM structure.

We can add a new node using the `create_element` method of the `DOMDocument` object. All we have to do is pass in the name of our new node, and optionally its node value (the text it should contain):

File: **domdemo4.php** (excerpt)
```
$newKW = $doc->createElement('keyword', 'XSLT');
```

Once that's done, we have to attach the new keyword node to our DOM structure. We can do so using the `appendChild` method, but we must be careful to tell the DOM exactly where we're adding the node.

In our case, the job is very easy. All we have to do is add our new keyword element to our established `$root` variable (remember, this variable represents our document's root element—in this case, `keywords`).

File: **domdemo4.php** (excerpt)
```
$root->appendChild($newKW);
```

With a modified document in hand, you can now do several things with it. The most common is to output the XML code of the modified document, either to a file on the server, or to the Web browser.

Printing XML from DOM

Printing a DOM structure as XML code is fairly straightforward. All we have to do is use the `saveXML` method of the `DOMDocument`. By setting the `formatOutput` property of the object to `true` first, you can produce neatly indented XML code.

File: **domdemo4.php (excerpt)**

```
$doc->formatOutput = true;
echo '<p>Updated XML source code:</p>';
echo '<pre>' . htmlentities($doc->saveXML()) . '</pre>';
```

We've barely scratched the surface of DOM functionality with this quick discussion. We'll get into it a lot more in this and later chapters, though—especially as we'll need it to create XML documents on-the-fly.

Using SimpleXML

Before the introduction of SimpleXML in PHP 5, developers could only manipulate and process XML with SAX and DOM. Both of those approaches were solid, but both required the developer to have a thorough understanding of what he or she was getting into.

Then, along came SimpleXML. As the name implies, SimpleXML seeks to simplify the way a PHP developer interacts with, processes, and manipulates XML data. What makes it so wonderful? Basically, SimpleXML loads XML data into a hierarchy of objects and arrays of objects. It then allows you to access that array using familiar methods like `foreach` loops and array indexes.

To put it another way, the developers behind SimpleXML recognized the fact that a large part of XML usage concerns the extraction and processing of information, so they made those types of operations very easy.

As we saw in Chapter 4, SimpleXML assigns each tag in an XML file a property that matches its element name. Take a look at this very simple XML document:

```
<document>
  <msg>Hello</msg>
</document>
```

Here, we'd be able to access the value of the <msg> tag using PHP's object oriented arrow notation as follows:

```
echo $xml->msg;
```

Element Name Changes Affect PHP Code

IMPORTANT

There's a huge drawback to this approach! If your XML element names change for any reason, you'll have to go back and change your SimpleXML logic to match the new names. The best way to avoid problems like this is to make sure your XML documents are already stable and structured the way you need them. If you do make changes to the XML after you start coding PHP, be sure to go back and change your code to match.

Let's go over each of the major features of SimpleXML.

Loading XML Documents

SimpleXML has to work on something, so the first thing you need to do is identify the XML you want to process. SimpleXML can either load a file into memory or work on XML code in the form of a PHP string.

To open a file, use the `simplexml_load_file` function, like this:

File: **sxmldemo.php (excerpt)**
```
$keywords = simplexml_load_file('keyword-data2.xml');
```

You could also provide your XML as a variable, then load that variable into memory using the `simplexml_load_string` function:

File: **sxmldemo2.php (excerpt)**
```
$xml = <<<XML
<?xml version="1.0" encoding="iso-8859-1"?>
<keywords>
  <keyword status="live">XML</keyword>
  <keyword status="in progress">PHP</keyword>
  <keyword status="live">Perl</keyword>
  <keyword status="live">JavaScript</keyword>
  <keyword status="in progress">ASP</keyword>
</keywords>
XML;
$keywords = simplexml_load_string($xml);
```

Declaring PHP Strings with Heredocs

The PHP string containing the XML code in the above example is declared using **heredoc syntax**. If you're unfamiliar with this syntax, you can read about it in the PHP Manual.[3]

Regardless of the approach you take here, the result will be a hierarchy of objects and arrays called `$keywords`. We can now access different parts of that structure using standard PHP object and array syntax.

The XML Element Hierarchy

When an XML element contains multiple child elements with the same name (as does our `keywords` element in this example), those children are stored as an array in the object hierarchy. We can therefore use array indexes to access the information we need. For example, we can use this syntax to access the various keywords stored in our XML document:

```
echo $keywords->keyword[0]; // prints "XML"
echo $keywords->keyword[1]; // prints "PHP"
```

Notice that in each case, we use the `$keywords` object, which represents the root element of the document, followed by the arrow operator, and the name of the child node we're interested in (in this case, `keyword`). As this is an array, we use `keyword[0]` to access the first `keyword` element. To access the second, we use `keyword[1]`, and so on.

Sometimes, you'll want to obtain all the values in an XML element array created by SimpleXML. As you might suspect, you can use a simple PHP `foreach` loop to do this:

File: **sxmldemo.php/sxmldemo2.php** (excerpt)

```
echo '<ul>';
foreach ($keywords->keyword as $kw) {
  echo '<li>' . htmlentities($kw) . '</li>';
}
echo '</ul>';
```

When an element contains only one child element of a given type, however, no array is created. Instead, you can access the element directly. Let's say that our XML file wasn't quite as simple as it is. Let's suppose that it had another level

---

[3] http://www.php.net/language.types.string#language.types.string.syntax.heredoc

of elements—child nodes of each `keyword` element. Here's what that might look like:

```
<keywords>
  <keyword status="live">
    <name>XML</name>
    <url>http://www.example.com/xml/</url>
  </keyword>
  <keyword status="in progress">
    <name>PHP</name>
    <url>http://www.example.com/php/</url>
  </keyword>

  ...
</keywords>
```

If we wanted to print out the `name` and `url` element values for the first `keyword`, here's how we could do it:

```
echo $keywords->keyword[0]->name; // "XML"
echo $keywords->keyword[0]->url; // "http://www.example.com/xml/"
```

It doesn't get any easier than that! SimpleXML is so much easier than working with a DOM structure or declaring custom SAX handler functions.

As we have just seen, SimpleXML element objects may be used where strings are required and they will behave as strings, containing the text value that the corresponding XML element contains. It is important to be aware, however, that these objects are not in fact strings. This distinction comes into effect in cases where a string is not required, and therefore PHP will not perform the conversion for you. Here's an example:

```
if ($keywords->keyword[0] == 'XML') {
  echo 'The first keyword is XML.';
}
```

Looking at our sample XML document, we would expect this `if` statement to execute and display the message, but it won't because `$keywords->keyword[0]` is an object, and is therefore not equal to the string `'XML'`. In order to make this code behave as expected, you must perform the conversion yourself by **casting** the object to a string:

```
if ((string)$keywords->keyword[0] == 'XML') {
  echo 'The first keyword is XML.';
}
```

If you're not a PHP guru, it can be a little hard to figure out when you have to cast to a string and when PHP will do it for you. The examples in this book should help somewhat, but if in doubt, cast the value to a string yourself—that way you'll always be sure PHP is treating the value as you intended.

XML Attribute Values

You can access the value of an attribute by treating the element object as an array, and using the attribute's name as an array key.

For example, to print out the value of the first `keyword` element's `status` attribute, we could use the following:

```
echo $keywords->keyword[0]['status']; // prints "live"
```

As with element values, however, things become tricky when you try to compare attribute values to PHP strings, as they are actually objects at heart. For example, imagine you want to display only "live" keywords. You might assume that it would be as easy as this:

```
foreach ($keywords->keyword as $kw) {
  if ($kw['status'] == 'live') { // wrong!
    echo '<li>' . htmlentities($kw) . '</li>';
  }
}
```

The above code snippet looks reasonable. However, PHP can't compare apples to oranges—in this case, objects to a strings—so none of the keywords will be displayed.

To make this work, we have to cast our attribute object to a string:

File: **sxmldemo3.php (excerpt)**

```
foreach ($keywords->keyword as $kw) {
  if ((string)$kw['status'] == 'live') {
    echo '<li>' . htmlentities($kw) . '</li>';
  }
}
```

Let's call this "the hard way." An easier method of filtering the values you retrieve from an XML document exists, thanks to XPath.

XPath Queries

There is another way to filter XML elements based on an attribute's value; it involves using the `xpath` method we saw in Chapter 4. You'll recall that this method allows us to pass XPath queries into SimpleXML and receive the results in the form of an array.

The easiest way to grab all the `keyword` elements that have their `status` attribute set to `live` is to run the following XPath query from the `keyword` element in our document:

```
keyword[@status="live"]
```

This query will look at all `keyword` elements that are children of the current element, and extract those that have a `status` of `live`. Here's how to do it with SimpleXML:

File: **sxmldemo4.php (excerpt)**

```php
foreach ($keywords->xpath('keyword[@status="live"]') as $kw) {
  echo '<li>' . htmlentities($kw) . '</li>';
}
```

What does our XPath query buy us? For one thing, we no longer have to perform a string comparison inside PHP: XPath takes care of that for us. If you're familiar with database development in PHP, this kind of operation is similar to letting your SQL statement do the work of filtering database values before returning them to your script. Furthermore, our code is now a bit simpler to look at, and hopefully, easier to maintain.

Granted, you may look at the second construction and say to yourself, "That's so much more complicated then casting an object to a string for comparison purposes."

Well, some say tom*ay*to, some say tom*ah*to. And in Texas, some say tuhmayter.

Using SimpleXML to Update XML

If you're already beginning to like SimpleXML, I have some good news! SimpleXML allows you to update values in a straightforward fashion. Let's say we wanted to change the third keyword in our example from PHP to JSP. Here's how we'd do it:

```
$keywords->keyword[2] = 'JSP';
```

To change the value of an attribute, we would simply add the appropriate attribute name as an array key:

```
$keywords->keyword[2]['status'] = 'live';
```

To save or print out the updated XML code, we'd use the `asXML` method:

```
echo $keywords->asXML();
```

Fixing SimpleXML Shortcomings with DOM

As elegant and simple as SimpleXML is, it does have a few shortcomings. For one thing, it's not possible (at the time of writing) to add new nodes to an XML document, just change the values of existing ones. Nor is it possible to delete nodes. Style sheets cannot easily be attached to your XML for transformational purposes. And finally, as you've seen, the PHP code is highly dependent on the names of the XML tags—if they change, updating the code can be a real headache.

However, SimpleXML has a very handy feature that allows it to interoperate with other PHP XML functionality. Namely, this functionality allows you to import DOM documents and convert them into SimpleXML data structures.

What's the benefit of that? The functionality allows you to do some of the heavy lifting using native DOM functionality in PHP; you can then convert it to SimpleXML and do the rest of your work there.

To see this in action, let's start by loading up an XML document with DOM and making a change to it that we couldn't do with SimpleXML:

File: **sxmldemo5.php (excerpt)**

```
$doc = new DOMDocument();
$doc->preserveWhiteSpace = false;
$doc->load("keyword-data2.xml");
$root = $doc->documentElement;

$newKW = $doc->createElement('keyword', 'JSP');
$newKW->setAttribute('status', 'live');
$root->appendChild($newKW);
```

With a new element added to the DOM structure, we can use the `simplexml_import_dom` function to import it into a SimpleXML data structure.

We can then use the SimpleXML API to do whatever's required—for example, to search for and display nodes with a certain attribute value.

File: **sxmldemo5.php (excerpt)**

```php
$keywords = simplexml_import_dom($doc);
echo '<ul>';
foreach ($keywords->xpath('keyword[@status="live"]') as $kw) {
  echo '<li>' . htmlentities($kw) . '</li>';
}
echo '</ul>';
```

This will display the list of keywords with a status of live, including "JSP", which was added using DOM.

When to Use the Different Methods

You might be wondering when it's appropriate to use SAX, DOM, and/or SimpleXML. Here are a few rules of thumb:

❑ If you have a very simple XML document that needs only linear processing, and you don't need to modify the document, SAX is a good candidate.

❑ If you need to process a more complex XML document, but only to extract information, SimpleXML is a good choice.

❑ If you need to create XML documents from scratch, or make heavy modifications to existing documents, use DOM.

Our CMS Project

It's now time to create the administrative side of our CMS. Our administrative tools will allow authorized users to log in to the CMS and administer the different parts of the Website. In this chapter, I'll walk you through building the following functionality:

❑ login/verification page

❑ administrative index (from which CMS users gain access to other pages)

❑ article create page

❑ article edit page

❏ article delete page

Once we're done with these pages, we're going to continue our discussion of the administrative tool in Appendix B, mostly because a lot of it is fairly repetitive and can be sidelined. That discussion includes:

❏ news create/edit/delete pages

❏ binary file create/edit/delete pages

❏ category create/edit/delete pages

❏ admin create/edit/delete pages

All pages in the administration area reside in the `admin` directory of the site.

IMPORTANT

Disable Magic Quotes

All of the PHP scripts in this book assume you have the **magic quotes** feature of PHP disabled. This can be done by setting the `magic_quotes_gpc` option in your server's `php.ini` file to `Off`.

If this feature is left on, you'll find a lot of unwanted backslashes (\) appearing in your content as you manipulate it using the administration scripts we'll develop in this section and in Appendix B.

The Login Page

The login page is very simple. It involves a basic HTML `form` that allows administrators to enter a username and password. Any complexity comes from structuring the HTML so that it can be styled effectively using CSS.

File: `login.php`

```php
<?php
session_start();
?>
<!DOCTYPE html PUBLIC "-//W3C//DTD XHTML 1.0 Transitional//EN"
    "http://www.w3.org/TR/xhtml1/DTD/xhtml1-transitional.dtd">
<html xmlns="http://www.w3.org/1999/xhtml">
<head>
<title>Please Log In</title>
<meta http-equiv="Content-Type"
    content="text/html; charset=iso-8859-1">
<link rel="stylesheet" type="text/css" href="../xmlcms.css" />
```

```
<link rel="stylesheet" type="text/css" href="login.css" />
</head>
<body>
<form class="login" action="verify.php" method="post">
<h1>Please log in</h1>
<div class="fields">
  <label for="username">User name</label>
  <input type="text" id="username" name="username" class="text" />
  <label for="password">Password</label>
  <input type="password" id="password" name="password"
      class="password" />
</div>
<div class="actions">
  <input type="submit" value="Submit" />
  <input type="reset" value="Reset" />
</div>
<p class="error"><?php echo $_SESSION['error']; ?></p>
</form>
</body>
</html>
```

In addition to the basic site style sheet (`xmlcms.css`), this page also uses a style sheet especially for laying out the login form. Again, this isn't a book on CSS, so we won't spend time on the details of this file, but here is the code for completeness:

File: **login.css**

```
form.login {
  width: 290px;
  margin: 1em auto;
  padding: 4px;
  background: #ccc;
}
form.login h1 {
  text-align: center;
  font-size: medium;
  background: #fff;
  margin: 1px;
}
form.login .fields {
  text-align: right;
}
form.login label {
  float: left;
  width: 130px;
  text-align: right;
```

```
}
form.login .actions {
  text-align: center;
}
form.login input.text, form.login input.password {
  width: 150px;
  margin-bottom: 1px;
}
form.login .error {
  color: red;
  margin: 0;
  padding: 0;
}
```

Getting back to the login page itself, notice that the form's `action` is set to a page called `verify.php`. The PHP logic on this page needs to check the entered values against a list of administrators that's kept in `admin.xml`.

Protect Your XML Files

IMPORTANT

For the purposes of the examples in this book and its code archive, we have placed the XML files that contain the content, categories, authors, and administrative users in a subdirectory of the main site. But, although we have gone to some length to protect sensitive information in those files (encrypting the passwords of our administrators, for example), it's still a good idea to protect those files from direct access over the Web by casual visitors to your site.

To protect these files, you can either configure your Web server to prevent browsers from accessing the directory, or you can move the directory out of your site's Web-accessible directory structure. In the latter case, you'll need to adjust the `common.inc.php` file to point to the directory's new location, so that all of the scripts on the site can still find the XML files.

Encrypted Passwords

As we've seen, the password values stored in `admin.xml` are encrypted for added security. To use the sample `admin.xml` file included in the code archive for this book, you need to know that the initial password of all three administrators stored in that file (`joe`, `bill`, and `tom`) is `password`.

If there's a match, the PHP code will set a session variable and redirect the user to the administration index page. If not, PHP sends the user back to the `login.php` page, with a special session variable (`$_SESSION['error']`) containing an error message for display.

Here is the code. Notice that we're using SimpleXML in this case, because it's the fastest way to load the information from `admin.xml`.

File: **verify.php**

```php
<?php
include_once '../common.inc.php';

$admins = simplexml_load_file($fileDir . 'admin.xml');
foreach ($admins->admin as $admin) {
  if ($_POST['username'] == (string)$admin->username and
      crypt($_POST['password'], (string)$admin->password) ==
      (string)$admin->password) {
    $_SESSION['login'] = true;
    header('location: index.php');
    exit;
  }
}
$_SESSION['error'] = 'Wrong user name or password. Try again.';
header('location: login.php');
?>
```

Notice that, since we'll be encrypting our passwords in `admin.xml`, we have to take the password provided by the user, encrypt it the same way, and then compare that user input to the password that's stored in the XML file. If you're unfamiliar with PHP's `crypt` function, you can read all about it in the PHP Manual.[4]

As anyone could enter a URL for one of the administration pages, we must add an extra piece of security to protect those pages' content. At the top of each page, we need to check to see if the value of the session variable `$_SESSION['login']` is set to `true`. If it isn't, we'll send the user back to the `login.php` page. As we'll be reusing this functionality, it's a good idea to place this check inside an include file:

File: **security.inc.php**

```php
<?php
include_once '../common.inc.php';

if (@$_SESSION['login'] !== true) {
  header('location: login.php');
  $_SESSION['error'] = 'You must log in before you can access
      administration pages.';
  exit;
```

---

[4] http://www.php.net/crypt

```
}
?>
```

 Tip

Disable Security for Initial Setup

When you are first setting up your site, you may not yet *have* any administrators set up. But then how are you supposed add administrators if you can't log in? To add your first administrator accounts, you'll want to disable security by simply commenting out the contents of `security.inc.php`, so that the file doesn't do anything. You'll then be able to browse the admin pages freely, and add an administrator or two. You can then re-enable security and log in using one of the accounts you created.

The last thing we need is a logout page, which we can link to so that users can log out of the site before they leave their computer:

File: **logout.php**

```php
<?php
include_once '../common.inc.php';

$_SESSION['login'] = false;
header('location: index.php');
?>
```

The Admin Index Page

The first page of our administration tool provides access to all site functionality and content, including administrative users, articles, news items and other content types.

The code for this page is very concise. All we want to do is provide links to each of the major parts of the administration tool.

File: **index.php**

```php
<?php
include 'security.inc.php';
?>
<!DOCTYPE html PUBLIC "-//W3C//DTD XHTML 1.0 Transitional//EN"
    "http://www.w3.org/TR/xhtml1/DTD/xhtml1-transitional.dtd">
<html xmlns="http://www.w3.org/1999/xhtml">
<head>
<meta http-equiv="Content-Type"
    content="text/html; charset=iso-8859-1" />
<title>Welcome to the Admin Index Page</title>
```

```
<link rel="stylesheet" type="text/css" href="../xmlcms.css" />
</head>
<body>
<h1>Welcome to the Admin Index Page</h1>
<p>
  <a href="articletool.php">Manage Articles</a><br />
  <a href="newstool.php">Manage News Items</a><br />
  <a href="admintool.php">Manage Administrators</a>
</p>
<p><a href="logout.php">Log out</a></p>
</body>
</html>
```

Each of the areas represented by those links will have the same functionality. Each area will allow CMS users to create, edit, and delete items. Let's go through each of these tasks in turn for the first area—articles.

Working with Articles

Our article administration area will allow CMS users to create new articles, edit existing ones, and delete them as required. Since articles are the most important part of our site, we'll start with them, then move on to news items and site administrators in Appendix B.

For the main page of our article administration area, we'll need a list of all the articles on the site. You should be relatively familiar with the PHP code required to do this by now:

File: **articletool.php**

```php
<?php
include 'security.inc.php';
include_once '../common.inc.php';
?>
<!DOCTYPE html PUBLIC "-//W3C//DTD XHTML 1.0 Transitional//EN"
    "http://www.w3.org/TR/xhtml1/DTD/xhtml1-transitional.dtd">
<html xmlns="http://www.w3.org/1999/xhtml">
<head>
<meta http-equiv="Content-Type"
    content="text/html; charset=iso-8859-1" />
<title>Article Index</title>
<link rel="stylesheet" type="text/css" href="../xmlcms.css" />
</head>
<body>
<h1>Article Index</h1>
```

```
<p><a href="articletool_create.php">Create New Article</a></p>
<p><a href="index.php">Cancel</a></p>
<ul>
<?php
$handle = opendir($fileDir);
while (($file = readdir($handle)) !== FALSE) {
  if (is_dir($fileDir . $file)) continue;
  if (!eregi("^article.*\.xml$", $file)) continue;

  $articleFile = simplexml_load_file($fileDir . $file);
  echo '<li>' . htmlentities($articleFile->headline);
  echo ' <a href="articletool_edit.php?id=' . $articleFile['id'] .
    '">edit</a>';
  echo ' <a href="doArticleDelete.php?id=' . $articleFile['id'] .
    '">delete</a></li>';
}
?>
</ul>
</body>
</html>
```

Creating New Articles

The article creation page is very important—it allows site administrators to create new XML articles on the site using a simple Web form interface. Each of the form fields maps to an element in the XML document structure we first planned in Chapter 1 and revisited in Chapter 3.

As a refresher, here's what one of our articles should look like when it's created:

```
<?xml version="1.0" encoding="iso-8859-1"?>
<article id="article12499300388912">
  <authorid>1</authorid>
  <categoryid>1</categoryid>
  <headline>Using XML with PHP</headline>
  <description>PHP offers many ways to work with XML</description>
  <pubdate>2004-06-26</pubdate>
  <status>live</status>
  <keywords>XML PHP SAX DOM SimpleXML</keywords>
  <body><![CDATA[
    <h1>Using XML with PHP</h1>
    <p>PHP is very powerful. It offers many ways to work with
      XML.</p>
  ]]></body>
</article>
```

In particular, be aware of the need to generate a unique ID, and to fill in all the various pieces of metadata.

Let's create a form that contains fields for all of this information. We start out with the familiar check to make sure that the user is logged in:

File: **articletool_create.php** (excerpt)

```php
<?php
include 'security.inc.php';
include_once '../common.inc.php';
?>
```

We follow that with the start of our HTML, including a link to a new style sheet named `forms.css`, which will contain the rules to lay out large administration forms like this one:

File: **articletool_create.php** (excerpt)

```html
<!DOCTYPE html PUBLIC "-//W3C//DTD XHTML 1.0 Transitional//EN"
    "http://www.w3.org/TR/xhtml1/DTD/xhtml1-transitional.dtd">
<html xmlns="http://www.w3.org/1999/xhtml">
<head>
<meta http-equiv="Content-Type"
    content="text/html; charset=iso-8859-1" />
<title>Create a New Article</title>
<link rel="stylesheet" type="text/css" href="../xmlcms.css" />
<link rel="stylesheet" type="text/css" href="forms.css" />
</head>
<body>
```

Finally, we create our form. Most of it is made up of plain form fields, but for selecting an author and category we need dynamic listings, which we extract from the appropriate files using SimpleXML.

File: **articletool_create.php** (excerpt)

```html
<h1>Create a New Article</h1>
<p><a href="articletool.php">Cancel</a></p>
<form action="doArticleCreate.php" method="post">
<div class="fields">
  <p>
    <label for="headline">Headline</label>
    <input type="text" id="headline" name="headline"
        class="text" />
  </p>
  <p>
    <label for="author">Author</label>
```

```
    <select id="authorid" name="authorid">
      <?php
      $authors = simplexml_load_file($fileDir . 'authors.xml');
      foreach ($authors->author as $author) {
        echo '<option value="' . htmlentities($author['id']) .
          '">' . htmlentities($author->name) . '</option>';
      }
      ?>
    </select>
  </p>
  <p>
    <label for="category">Category</label>
    <select id="categoryid" name="categoryid">
      <?php
      $cats = simplexml_load_file($fileDir . 'categories.xml');
      foreach ($cats->category as $cat) {
        echo '<option value="' . htmlentities($cat['id']) . '">' .
          htmlentities($cat['label']) . '</option>';
      }
      ?>
    </select>
  </p>
  <p>
    <label for="status">Status</label>
    <select id="status" name="status">
      <option value="in progress">In Progress</option>
      <option value="live">Live</option>
    </select>
  </p>
  <p>
    <label for="keywords">Keywords</label>
    <input type="text" id="keywords" name="keywords" class="text"
    />
  </p>
  <p>
    <label for="description">Description</label>
    <textarea id="description" name="description"></textarea>
  </p>
  <p>
    <label for="body">Article Body (HTML)</label>
    <textarea id="body" name="body"></textarea>
  </p>
</div>
<div class="actions">
  <input type="submit" value="Add Article" />
  <input type="reset" value="Reset" />
```

```
</div>
</form>
</body>
</html>
```

Here's the CSS code that performs the layout of this imposing form:

File: **forms.css**

```
form .actions {
  text-align: center;
}
form p {
  clear: left;
  margin: 1px 0;
}
form label {
  float: left;
  width: 15%;
  padding-right: 10px;
  text-align: right;
}
input.text, input.password, select {
  width: 300px;
}
textarea {
  width: 70%;
  height: 4em;
}
textarea#body {
  height: 30em;
}
```

The form's action is set to the doArticleCreate.php page, which uses DOM functions to create an XML article from the information in the form. Because this is a little complex, I'll go over the code in pieces.

The first part of the file initializes our new XML document, setting the version and creating the root element, article.

File: **doArticleCreate.php** (excerpt)

```
<?php
include 'security.inc.php';
include_once '../common.inc.php';

$doc = new DOMDocument();
```

```
$root = $doc->createElement('article');
$root = $doc->appendChild($root);
```

Next, we add an `id` attribute to the `article` node. The ID will be the word `article` followed by a timestamp. On the off-chance that more than one article is created in the same second, we check for an existing file with the same ID in its name, and increment the timestamp by one until a non-clashing ID is found.

File: **doArticleCreate.php (excerpt)**

```
$timestamp = date('YmdHis');
do {
  $id = 'article' . $timestamp++;
} while (file_exists($fileDir . $id . '.xml'));
$root->setAttribute('id', $id);
```

Now that we've created the root, it's time to create each of that element's children, in the correct order. The first is `authorid`. Notice that the `authorid` element is a child of `article`, and that the ID itself is a child of `authorid`.

File: **doArticleCreate.php (excerpt)**

```
$author = $doc->createElement('authorid');
$root->appendChild($author);
$atext = $doc->createTextNode($_POST['authorid']);
$author->appendChild($atext);
```

We use the same technique to generate the `categoryid`, `headline`, `description`, `status`, and `keywords` elements. The value of `pubdate` is generated on-the-fly by the script, but otherwise it's the same.

File: **doArticleCreate.php (excerpt)**

```
$cat = $doc->createElement('categoryid');
$root->appendChild($cat);
$ctext = $doc->createTextNode($_POST['categoryid']);
$cat->appendChild($ctext);

$head = $doc->createElement('headline');
$root->appendChild($head);
$htext = $doc->createTextNode($_POST['headline']);
$head->appendChild($htext);

$desc = $doc->createElement('description');
$root->appendChild($desc);
$dtext = $doc->createTextNode($_POST['description']);
$desc->appendChild($dtext);
```

```
$pub = $doc->createElement('pubdate');
$root->appendChild($pub);
$pubtext = $doc->createTextNode(date('Y-m-d'));
$pub->appendChild($pubtext);

$stat = $doc->createElement('status');
$root->appendChild($stat);
$stext = $doc->createTextNode($_POST['status']);
$stat->appendChild($stext);

$key = $doc->createElement('keywords');
$root->appendChild($key);
$ktext = $doc->createTextNode($_POST['keywords']);
$key->appendChild($ktext);
```

Next, we process the body text. Remember that we are planning to store our article body information as HTML, which means it will contain a bunch of tags. If we use DOM, as we have so far, to output this value as text, it'll work just fine, but the resulting XML file will be difficult to read, with character entities like < and > scattered throughout.

As mentioned in Chapter 1, to keep the code readable we will instead store the body text as a CDATA section within our XML file, so that special characters within do not have to be converted to character entities. Instead of using createTextNode, we'll use createCDATASection. We'll place all the HTML text from the form inside that command.

File: **doArticleCreate.php** (excerpt)

```
$body = $doc->createElement('body');
$root->appendChild($body);
$cdata = $doc->createCDATASection($_POST['body']);
$body->appendChild($cdata);
```

Next, we write this entire XML tree to a file, using the ID generated earlier as a filename:

File: **doArticleCreate.php** (excerpt)

```
$filename = $fileDir . $id . '.xml';
$doc->save($filename);
```

Finally, now that we're finished with all of this, we need to send the user back to articletool.php, where they should see the newly-created file listed in the master article list.

File: **doArticleCreate.php** (excerpt)

```
header('location: articletool.php');
```

Editing an XML Article

Generally speaking, editing an XML article is much the same as creating an article, except that you have to load an existing article's values into the form, and write the submitted changes out to the file.

Let's start with the code for the form page. The first part should be pretty familiar to you—it verifies that the user has logged in.

File: **articletool_edit.php** (excerpt)

```
<?php
include 'security.inc.php';
include_once '../common.inc.php';
```

Next, we open the file for the document the user wishes to edit. Because we won't be modifying the file just yet, we can use SimpleXML to open the file and pull out the information we need.

File: **articletool_edit.php** (excerpt)

```
if (!isset($_GET['id']) || $_GET['id'] == '' ||
    !file_exists($fileDir . $_GET['id'] . '.xml')) {
  header('location: articletool.php');
  exit;
}
$file = simplexml_load_file($fileDir . $_GET['id'] . '.xml');
?>
```

Now, we simply have the markup for a form very similar to the one in articletool_create.php, except that this time we pull the existing value for each field out of the $file variable.

File: **articletool_edit.php** (excerpt)

```
<!DOCTYPE html PUBLIC "-//W3C//DTD XHTML 1.0 Transitional//EN"
    "http://www.w3.org/TR/xhtml1/DTD/xhtml1-transitional.dtd">
<html xmlns="http://www.w3.org/1999/xhtml">
<head>
<meta http-equiv="Content-Type"
    content="text/html; charset=iso-8859-1" />
<title>Edit Article</title>
<link rel="stylesheet" type="text/css" href="../xmlcms.css" />
<link rel="stylesheet" type="text/css" href="forms.css" />
```

```
</head>
<body>
<h1>Edit Article</h1>
<p><a href="articletool.php">Cancel</a></p>
<form action="doArticleUpdate.php" method="post">
<input type="hidden" name="id"
    value="<?php echo htmlentities($_GET['id']); ?>" />
<div class="fields">
  <p>
    <label for="headline">Headline</label>
    <input type="text" id="headline" name="headline" class="text"
        value="<?php echo htmlentities($file->headline); ?>" />
  </p>
  <p>
    <label for="author">Author</label>
    <select id="authorid" name="authorid">
      <?php
      $authors = simplexml_load_file($fileDir . 'authors.xml');
      foreach ($authors->author as $author) {
        if ((string)$author['id'] == (string)$file->authorid) {
          echo '<option value="' . htmlentities($author['id']) .
              '" selected="selected">' .
              htmlentities($author->name) . '</option>';
        } else {
          echo '<option value="' . htmlentities($author['id']) .
              '">' . htmlentities($author->name) . '</option>';
        }
      }
      ?>
    </select>
  </p>
  <p>
    <label for="category">Category</label>
    <select id="categoryid" name="categoryid">
      <?php
      $cats = simplexml_load_file($fileDir . 'categories.xml');
      foreach ($cats->category as $cat) {
        if ((string)$cat['id'] == (string)$file->categoryid) {
          echo '<option value="' . htmlentities($cat['id']) .
              '" selected="selected">' .
              htmlentities($cat['label']) . '</option>';
        } else {
          echo '<option value="' . htmlentities($cat['id']) .
              '">' . htmlentities($cat['label']) . '</option>';
        }
      }
```

```
      ?>
    </select>
  </p>
  <p>
    <label for="status">Status</label>
    <select id="status" name="status">
      <option value="in progress"
          <?php if ((string)$file->status == 'in progress')
          echo 'selected="selected"'?>>In Progress</option>
      <option value="live"
          <?php if ((string)$file->status == 'live')
          echo 'selected="selected"'?>>Live</option>
    </select>
  </p>
  <p>
    <label for="keywords">Keywords</label>
    <input type="text" id="keywords" name="keywords" class="text"
value="<?php echo htmlentities($file->keywords); ?>" />
  </p>
  <p>
    <label for="description">Description</label>
    <textarea id="description" name="description">
<?php echo htmlentities($file->description); ?></textarea>
  </p>
  <p>
    <label for="body">Article Body (HTML)</label>
    <textarea id="body" name="body">
<?php echo htmlentities($file->body); ?></textarea>
  </p>
</div>
<div class="actions">
  <input type="submit" value="Update Article" />
  <input type="reset" value="Reset" />
</div>
</form>
</body>
</html>
```

The doArticleUpdate.php file that processes this form is very similar to the doArticleCreate.php script:

File: **doArticleUpdate.php**

```php
<?php
include 'security.inc.php';
include_once '../common.inc.php';
```

```php
$doc = new DOMDocument();
$root = $doc->createElement('article');
$root = $doc->appendChild($root);

$id = $_POST['id'];
$root->setAttribute('id', $id);

…

$filename = $fileDir . $id . '.xml';
unlink($filename);
$doc->save($filename);

header('location: articletool.php');
?>
```

Deleting an XML Article

Deleting an XML file is very simple. When an ID is passed to the doArticleDelete.php page, it deletes the corresponding file and send the user back to the articletool.php page:

File: **doArticleDelete.php**

```php
<?php
include 'security.inc.php';
include_once '../common.inc.php';

$filename = $fileDir . $_GET['id'] . '.xml';
unlink($filename);

header('location: articletool.php');
?>
```

At this point, we've built a login page, an administrative index, and pages for the addition, editing, and deletion of articles. We'll discuss the rest of our administrative pages in Appendix B. Don't be surprised if we reuse the code from these initial administrative pages to quickly knock up the rest of the administration tool!

Summary

We've learned a lot about using SAX, DOM, and SimpleXML functionality in PHP in this chapter. With this, and your knowledge of client-side processing, you should be well-armed to handle most XML processing tasks. In the second part of this chapter, we created the administrative forms we'll need to manage our Website articles.

In the next chapter, we'll discuss RSS and RDF, two standards that are commonly used for making headlines and other feeds of information available to third parties in XML format.

RSS and RDF

We've covered a good deal of information in this book, including XML, XSLT, XPath, and PHP functions for processing XML. In this chapter, we're going to take what we've learned and apply it to RSS and RDF, two exciting technologies that are used to share and disseminate XML data.

What are RSS and RDF?

Depending on where you look and who you ask, RSS stands for **Really Simple Syndication**, **Rich Site Summary**, or **RDF Site Summary**. Regardless of what the acronym stands for, RSS is an XML format for distributing or syndicating content. For example, Weblogs, or "blogs," are syndicated using this kind of XML format.

RDF stands for **Resource Description Framework**, which forms the backbone of some but not all RSS standards. It's a metadata standard for describing Web resources—not only the Web pages themselves, but also their authors, the dates and times at which they were last updated, their keywords and titles, and so on. That's all I'm going to say about this for the moment—we'll pick up a discussion of RSS versions after we've run through a basic example.

What's the Big Deal?

Imagine that you're a cartoonist or columnist working in relative obscurity on a small city's daily newspaper. You create good stuff, but you're not known very well outside your local region. The easiest way to make more money and reach a wider audience is to do what other respected writers and cartoonists have done for decades—syndicate your material! If you strike the right syndication deal, your articles or art may start appearing in dozens or hundreds of media outlets, thereby increasing your pay and your exposure.

Syndication is also a good thing from the reader's point of view. In this modern age, you no longer have to send away for the hometown paper in order to keep up with your favorite columnists or cartoonists. It's very likely that your favorite columnist or cartoonist is featured in your local newspaper.

It's the same idea online. You may or may not get rich by syndicating your content, but you can certainly increase your exposure. Syndication also represents a convenient service for your audience members, who don't have to remember to search for your content or visit your site and dig through all your other information to see if you've published anything new—users simply subscribe and keep getting updates. If you have RSS up and running, whenever you add an article or other interesting content item to your site, you can create an RSS entry that points to this content. This new entry will show up in RSS aggregators and listings on Website belonging to your subscribers.

What Kind of Information Should be Featured in an RSS Feed?

When you create an RSS feed, keep these rules of thumb in mind:

1. The content must be list-oriented. List-oriented content includes news headlines, article summaries, rankings, job listings, bookmarks, search result listings, event calendars, press release summaries, and other information.

2. The content should cover topics in which your audience has an interest. Another way to look at this is to ask yourself, is the content useful or instructional? Does it keep subscribers up-to-date with an industry or its trends? Is the material newsworthy?

3. To warrant use of the RSS feed format, the content should change frequently.

Before We Get Started

I'm going to show you some straightforward ways to get up and running with RSS. Be aware, though, that some parts of RSS/RDF (especially RDF syntax) can be obscure and confusing. You might not know which elements of the RDF syntax are required, for example, because the RDF specification can be pretty hard to plow through. The goal of this chapter is merely to provide you with a clear idea of how the world of RSS works.

To begin, let's take a look at RSS in action. Figure 8.1 shows a program called SharpReader[1] reading an RSS feed from sitepoint.com. To read an RSS feed, all you have to do is provide SharpReader with the URL of that feed.

Once you know where a feed is located, you can click the Subscribe button on SharpReader to keep receiving updates. If sitepoint.com updates its RSS feed, then subscribers, too, receive updates. In fact, if you have SharpReader running, little windows will pop up, displaying headlines from your subscribed feeds, on the side of your screen.

Figure 8.1. Using SharpReader to view the SitePoint RSS feed.

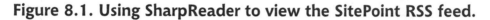

---

[1] http://www.sharpreader.com/

Creating Your First Basic RSS Feed

Let's create an RSS file (or feed) from scratch. No matter how big, small, simple, or complicated the feed may be, at the heart of every RSS file lies a list of content items. Your RSS file can contain one item, 1,000 items, or anything in between (or beyond), but without at least one item, you really don't have an RSS file.

What does such an item comprise? Three very important parts:

❑ A title

❑ A link

❑ A description

Let's say that you maintain a Website that covers the world of Web development. In particular, your articles explore a particular niche: ecommerce Web development. Furthermore, let's imagine that you've just published a new article about the use of PHP to integrate PayPal into a Website. Now you want to point to this article and let your subscribers know it's available to them.

It's likely that you gave your article HTML `<title>` and `<meta name="description"`>` tags. You don't have to use this title and description when you create your RSS item, though it certainly doesn't hurt. However, you *do* have to accurately point to the proper URL to allow subscribers to link to the information.

Here's how your information might look before we start to wrap XML tags around each piece:

```
Making PHP work with PayPal
http://www.tripledogdaremedia.com/articles/paypal-php.html
Everything you need to know to create PHP scripts that are PayPal
friendly.
```

To denote a title, we'll use `<title>` tags:

```
<title>Making PHP work with PayPal</title>
```

For the URL, use `<link>` tags:

```
<link>http://www.tripledogdaremedia.com/articles/paypal-php.html
</link>
```

For the description, use <description> tags:

```
<description>Everything you need to know to create PHP scripts
   that are PayPal friendly.</description>
```

To make this particular group of tags and content into an RSS item, we need to place it within an item element:

File: **headline.xml (excerpt)**

```
<item>
  <title>Making PHP work with PayPal</title>
  <link>http://www.tripledogdaremedia.com/articles/paypal-php.html
  </link>
  <description>Everything you need to know to create PHP scripts
     that are PayPal friendly.</description>
</item>
```

Congratulations, you've completed your first RSS item! But we're not done yet. We need to place our item into a channel element. Channels describe the source of the information—usually, your Website.

RSS channels have the same elements as RSS items: title, link, and description. For example, here's a channel containing the RSS item we created above:

File: **headline.xml (excerpt)**

```
<channel>
  <title>Ecommerce Development</title>
  <link>http://www.tripledogdaremedia.com/articles/</link>
  <description>If it's about ecommerce and Web development, we'll
     write about it!</description>
  <item>
    <title>Making PHP work with PayPal</title>
    <link>
    http://www.tripledogdaremedia.com/articles/paypal-php.html
    </link>
    <description>Everything you need to know to create PHP
       scripts that are PayPal friendly.</description>
  </item>
</channel>
```

All you have to do now is wrap the entire file with an <rss> tag, add the XML declaration, and you have a well-formed RSS feed:

File: **headline.xml**

```
<?xml version="1.0"?>
<rss version="0.91">
  <channel>
    <title>Ecommerce Development</title>
    <link>http://www.tripledogdaremedia.com/articles/</link>
    <description>If it's about ecommerce and Web development,
      we'll write about it!</description>
    <item>
      <title>Making PHP work with PayPal</title>
      <link>
      http://www.tripledogdaremedia.com/articles/paypal-php.html
      </link>
      <description>Everything you need to know to create PHP
        scripts that are PayPal friendly.</description>
    </item>
  </channel>
</rss>
```

Notice that we're using version 0.91 of RSS; this means we're not yet using RDF. We'll talk about the differences between the various RSS versions, and how they relate to RDF, a little later in this chapter.

You can easily add more items to a channel using the syntax rules we saw above. Simply create your items with the proper `title`, `description`, and `link` elements, and place them inside the appropriate `channel` element in your RSS feed.

The last thing you need to do is to save the file. It's a good idea to give your RSS file a descriptive name with `.xml` or `.rss` as the file extension: `ecommercefeed.xml` or `ecommercefeed.rss`, for example.

Telling the World about your Feed

Now that you have an RSS feed, you need to tell folks about it so they can subscribe. There are two ways to get the word out: add a link from your site to your RSS feed, and subscribe to RSS aggregators.

Providing a Link on your Site

It's quite possible that other Website owners might want to syndicate your content on their sites. This arrangement can be good for both of you—the site owner doesn't have to create content, as you've provided it, and you get exposure to their audience. If you provide a link to your RSS feed from your site, other site owners can easily point their PHP-, ASP.NET-, Perl-, Python-, and JSP-based RSS tools toward your feed, and add to their own sites pointers to your information.

A link to our sample RSS feed might look like this:

```
<a href="headline.xml">RSS feed</a>
```

To further promote your RSS feed, you can also include a `<link>` tag in your page header (`<head>`), so that RSS-enabled browsers and search engines can see your feed:

```
<link rel="alternate" type="application/rss+xml" title="RSS Feed"
    href="headline.xml" />
```

That's really all there is to it!

Subscribing to RSS Aggregators

RSS aggregators, or news aggregators, are services that allow you to add your RSS feed to an existing catalog of RSS feeds. Other users can search for and subscribe to your feed, either on the Web or through a standalone, downloadable RSS feed reader (*also* called an aggregator). Here are two of the more popular RSS news aggregators:

❑ News Is Free[2] is a long-standing Web-based news aggregator. Using the free service, you can create customized "pages" for different topics, then have headlines from various resources automatically filled into those pages.

❑ Radio UserLand[3], a popular blog-building tool, is also another long-standing news aggregator. You can subscribe to a feed simply by entering its URL.

Make Sure your RSS is Valid

These services will likely require that you validate your RSS file before you submit it. You can find numerous RSS validators by Googling for "rss validator," but one is available from the W3C:

http://www.w3.org/RDF/Validator/

Now that we've covered the basics of RSS, let's dig into the details a little more.

---

[2] http://www.newsisfree.com
[3] http://www.radiouserland.com

Going Beyond the Basics

Notice in our example that we were using a particular version of RSS.

File: **headline.xml (excerpt)**

```
<rss version="0.91">
```

This RSS is known as Really Simple Syndication, and was jointly developed by Netscape and Userland Corporation.[4] The idea behind this version of RSS is to provide a very simple tool for content syndication.

As you already know from the example, with RSS version 0.91, you can have one or more `channel` elements, each with at least one `item` element. Each `item` element must contain a `title` and a `link` and can also contain a `description` element. The same goes for the `channels` themselves.

Other channel metadata tags that you can include are:

`<image>`   to specify a thumbnail image for the channel

`<webMaster>`   to provide email addresses for those responsible for the feed
`<managingEditor>`

`<lastBuildDate>`   to indicate when the feed was last updated

For the details on these and other RSS 0.91 elements, you can refer to the RSS 0.91 specification.[5] More recent versions of the specification exist. Both RSS 0.92[6] (December 2000) and RSS 2.0[7] (October 2002) add more tags, and lift restrictions on certain tags (e.g. in 0.91 the `<link>` tag had to point to an HTTP or FTP resource; in 2.0 any valid URI will do). But since 0.91 is forwards-compatible with these standards (a valid RSS 0.91 document is also a valid RSS 2.0 document), RSS 0.91 continues to be the best starting place for beginners who don't need the more advanced features of the later standards.

---

[4] http://www.userland.com/
[5] http://backend.userland.com/rss091
[6] http://backend.userland.com/rss092
[7] http://blogs.law.harvard.edu/tech/rss

RDF and RSS 1.0

RSS 1.0 is something of a lone wolf. Although it was designed to do the same thing as other versions of RSS, it has very little to do with the other standards. In many ways, it is actually more advanced than RSS 2.0, and it is therefore the preferred choice of many forward-looking Web developers.

First of all, the "RSS" in RSS 1.0[8] stands for RDF Site Summary. This particular flavor of RSS, released just prior to RSS 0.92 in December 2000, uses RDF, the Resource Description Framework, to define what the files look like. In a hand-wavy sort of way, RDF is a standard for describing *anything* and what it has to do with *anything else*. Vague enough for you?

Without actually getting into the details of RDF,[9] which is quite a powerful and complex collection of specifications, let me assure you that there is a lot more to it than an XML document format for describing lists of things; but in the context of RSS 1.0, that's exactly how it's used. The advantage of using RDF is that RSS 1.0 documents can take part in larger software systems designed around RDF. One such system that is still in the planning stages is the Semantic Web,[10] a re-imagination of the World Wide Web that will allow computer programs to seek out and pull together disparate services and bits of information from across the Web to accomplish tasks for you, without your having to track down all those things yourself.

But hey, that's all coming tomorrow (or possibly the day after tomorrow). Right now, the complexity of RDF just makes syndicating content with RSS 1.0 a little more difficult than with the other RSS standards. Let's see just *how* difficult... Here's the RSS 1.0 version of the simple RSS 0.91 document we saw earlier:

File: **headline.rdf**

```
<?xml version="1.0"?>
<rdf:RDF
    xmlns:rdf="http://www.w3.org/1999/02/22-rdf-syntax-ns#"
    xmlns="http://purl.org/rss/1.0/">
  <channel
      rdf:about="http://www.tripledogdaremedia.com/articles/">
    <title>Ecommerce Development</title>
    <link>http://www.tripledogdaremedia.com/articles/</link>
    <description>If it's about ecommerce and Web development,
```

---

[8] http://web.resource.org/rss/1.0/
[9] http://www.w3.org/RDF/
[10] http://www.w3.org/2001/sw/

```
        we'll write about it!</description>

    <items>
      <rdf:Seq>
        <rdf:li rdf:resource=
"http://www.tripledogdaremedia.com/articles/paypal-php.html"/>
      </rdf:Seq>
    </items>
  </channel>

  <item rdf:about=
"http://www.tripledogdaremedia.com/articles/paypal-php.html">
    <title>Making PHP work with PayPal</title>
    <link>
    http://www.tripledogdaremedia.com/articles/paypal-php.html
    </link>
    <description>Everything you need to know to create PHP scripts
      that are PayPal friendly.</description>
  </item>
</rdf:RDF>
```

The first thing you'll notice about this document is the pair of XML namespace declarations in the root element of the document:

File: **headline.rdf** (excerpt)

```
<rdf:RDF
    xmlns:rdf="http://www.w3.org/1999/02/22-rdf-syntax-ns#"
    xmlns="http://purl.org/rss/1.0/">
```

As these declarations indicate, RSS 1.0 is actually a mixture of at least two groups of XML tags and attributes: the RDF standard tags/attributes, which are given the rdf: namespace prefix, and the RSS-specific tags/attributes, which will use the default namespace. As required by the RDF standard, the root element of the document is RDF.

Things become a little more familiar with the channel element:

File: **headline.rdf** (excerpt)

```
<channel
    rdf:about="http://www.tripledogdaremedia.com/articles/">
  <title>Ecommerce Development</title>
  <link>http://www.tripledogdaremedia.com/articles/</link>
  <description>If it's about ecommerce and Web development,
    we'll write about it!</description>
```

So far, the only change from RSS 0.91's `channel` element is the addition of an RDF `about` attribute to the tag. At a glance, you might think that it makes no sense to put the URL of the site to which this channel refers in this attribute, since it's already given by the `link` element inside the `channel`. This attribute actually serves as a unique identifier for the `channel`, as required by RDF. It is simply a convention of RDF that a URI is used for this purpose, in the same way that URIs are used to identify XML namespaces.

But if you got upset about the `about` attribute, you aren't going to like the rest of the `channel` element at all...

File: **headline.rdf** (excerpt)

```
  <items>
    <rdf:Seq>
      <rdf:li rdf:resource=
"http://www.tripledogdaremedia.com/articles/paypal-php.html"/>
    </rdf:Seq>
  </items>
 </channel>
```

Instead of embedding a list of `item` elements right inside the `channel`, RSS 1.0 follows the RDF requirement that all the *things* that the document describes (be they channels, items, or even images) appear as children of the root `RDF` element. Instead, the `channel` contains a single `items` element, which contains an RDF table of contents (TOC).

RDF supports at least two types of TOC: bags and sequences. A bag is the RDF equivalent of an HTML unordered list (`<ul>`), whereas a sequence is like an ordered list (`<ol>`). Since the order of items in RSS feeds is important, RSS 1.0 uses an RDF sequence (`<rdf:Seq>`). A sequence contains one or more RDF list items (`<rdf:li>`), each with an RDF `resource` attribute that points to the unique URI for an item in the feed.

With the `channel` taken care of, we can now define our `items`:

File: **headline.rdf** (excerpt)

```
  <item rdf:about=
"http://www.tripledogdaremedia.com/articles/paypal-php.html">
    <title>Making PHP work with PayPal</title>
    <link>
    http://www.tripledogdaremedia.com/articles/paypal-php.html
    </link>
    <description>Everything you need to know to create PHP scripts
```

```
        that are PayPal friendly.</description>
    </item>
```

Again, this looks a lot like the RSS 0.91 version, except for the RDF `about` attribute, which provides a URI that uniquely identifies the item. This is the URI that the `items` element in the `channel` points to in order to include it in the channel.

Adding Information with Dublin Core

Now, when you saw the namespace declarations that were required at the top of an RSS 1.0 file, I bet you thought, "Oh man, I have to type all that stuff *every time* I create an RSS feed? Nuts to that." Well, who can blame you? As it turns out, however, giving the RSS 1.0 the benefit of XML namespaces allows us to extend the format with tags from other XML namespaces.

The people behind RSS have even provided three additional sets of XML tags, each with its own namespace (these are called **modules**), as part of the RSS 1.0 specification. The most popular of these is the Dublin Core[11] set of metadata elements, which lets you specify additional properties for `channels` and `items` in your RSS feeds.

To use Dublin Core, you need to declare its namespace in your RSS feed, along with the others:

File: **headlinedc.rdf (excerpt)**

```
<rdf:RDF
    xmlns:rdf="http://www.w3.org/1999/02/22-rdf-syntax-ns#"
    xmlns:dc="http://purl.org/dc/elements/1.1/"
    xmlns="http://purl.org/rss/1.0/">
```

You can then add Dublin Core elements to your RSS feed. Here's our example `item` element, with a bit of Dublin Core flair:

File: **headlinedc.rdf (excerpt)**

```
  <item rdf:about=
"http://www.tripledogdaremedia.com/articles/paypal-php.html">
    <title>Making PHP work with PayPal</title>
    <link>
    http://www.tripledogdaremedia.com/articles/paypal-php.html
    </link>
    <description>Everything you need to know to create PHP scripts
```

---

[11] http://web.resource.org/rss/1.0/modules/dc/

```
      that are PayPal friendly.</description>
    <dc:subject>Server-Side Scripting</dc:subject>
    <dc:creator>Thomas Myer</dc:creator>
    <dc:date>2005-06-25</dc:date>
  </item>
```

Dublin Core, as its esoteric name might suggest, actually has a rich and full life outside of the RSS 1.0 specification. For full details on Dublin Core and the elements it provides, visit the Dublin Core Metadata Initiative.[12]

When to use RSS 1.0

When you look at the different versions of RSS, you might ask yourself when you would use which version. That's a good question.

For most cases, as in most of the examples in this chapter, you would use the 0.91 version of RSS, or possibly version 2.0 if you like its advanced features. These formats provide the simplest, quickest, and easiest solution for your feeds. These versions of RSS are not hard to understand, and building systems that process them isn't hard to do.

RSS 1.0 provides more robust syntax that allows you to incorporate specialized tags for additional information. For example, you can use Dublin Core's set of tags to track information about authors, publication dates, last-edit dates, and so on. You can even devise your own sets of tags and mix them in for your own devious purposes, all within the generalized resource description framework provided by RDF.

A Brief Note on Atom

The AtomEnabled project[13] is a recently-devised initiative to develop standard APIs and data formats for publishing content on the Web. It includes its own XML-based syndication format[14] that presents an alternative to RSS feeds. Sam Ruby of IBM is most often credited with many of the core ideas behind Atom, which include common metadata terms to support the description of author name, publication date, resource identifier and location, and content.

There isn't enough space in this book to cover Atom, but you may wish to look into the format and possibly support it along with the RSS version(s)

---

[12] http://dublincore.org/

[13] http://www.atomenabled.org/

[14] http://www.atomenabled.org/developers/syndication/atom-format-spec.php

of your feeds. Because it is XML, it can be processed with SimpleXML and XSLT, just like RSS.

Parsing RSS Feeds

Now that we know something about RSS files, let's walk through how you would add a script to your site to parse an RSS feed and display the information properly.

To keep things simple, we'll continue to use our RSS 0.91 example from earlier in the chapter. The only change we'll make is to add two more items to the channel.

File: **headlines.xml**

```xml
<?xml version="1.0"?>
<rss version="0.91">
  <channel>
    <title>Ecommerce Development</title>
    <description>If it's about ecommerce and Web development,
      we'll write about it!</description>
    <link>http://www.tripledogdaremedia.com/articles/</link>
    <item>
      <title>Making PHP work with PayPal</title>
      <description>Everything you need to know to create PHP
        scripts that are PayPal friendly.</description>
      <link>
      http://www.tripledogdaremedia.com/articles/paypal-php.html
      </link>
    </item>
    <item>
      <title>Building a PHP Shopping Cart</title>
      <description>A quick how-to on building a PHP-based shopping
        cart.</description>
      <link>
http://www.tripledogdaremedia.com/articles/shoppingcart-php.html
      </link>
    </item>
    <item>
      <title>SEO and PHP</title>
      <description>Boosting your ecommerce site's visibility with
        SEO, the PHP way.</description>
      <link>
      http://www.tripledogdaremedia.com/articles/seo-php.html
      </link>
    </item>
```

```
    </channel>
</rss>
```

Parsing our Feed with SimpleXML

We're going to parse this feed with SimpleXML. The first thing we need to do is load that file into our parser and then do our work. For this example, we'll use a local file for the RSS feed:

File: **parserss.php** (excerpt)

```php
<?php
$rssfeed = simplexml_load_file('headlines.xml');
```

Of course, in the real world, we would more likely be loading the RSS feed from another site. Thankfully, you can pass SimpleXML a URL just as easily:

```php
$rssfeed = simplexml_load_file(
    'http://www.tripledogdaremedia.com/sample.rss');
```

Once we have it loaded into SimpleXML, all we have to do is start looping through each channel in the file with a simple foreach loop. Along the way, we'll print out the channel's title, description, and link:

File: **parserss.php** (excerpt)

```php
foreach ($rssfeed->channel as $channel) {
    echo '<h1>' . htmlentities($channel->title) . '</h1>';
    echo '<p>' . htmlentities($channel->description) . '</p>';
    echo '<p><a href="' . htmlentities($channel->link) . '">' .
        htmlentities($channel->link) . '</a></p>';
```

Now that we've printed out that information, we can start an inner loop and print out each item. For this exercise, I've decided to use a bullet list, but you could just as easily format it as a data table:

File: **parserss.php** (excerpt)

```php
    echo '<ul>';
    foreach ($channel->item as $item) {
        echo '<li><a href="' . htmlentities($item->link) . '">';
        echo htmlentities($item->title) . '</a><br />';
        echo htmlentities($item->description) . '</li>';
    }
    echo '</ul>';
}
?>
```

As you can see, this script is very small (fewer than 20 lines) and very easy to maintain, thanks to SimpleXML's simplified syntax. The result is illustrated in Figure 8.2.

Figure 8.2. Parsing RSS with SimpleXML.

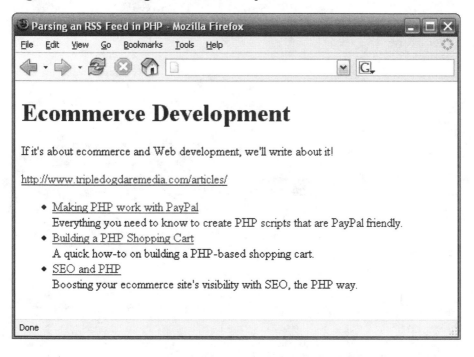

If you wanted to, it would be very easy to include this SimpleXML code snippet into a larger design—for example, a sidebar of article links featured on your site's homepage.

RSS 1.0, DOM or SAX?

Kevin Yank has an excellent article entitled PHP and XML: Parsing RSS 1.0,[15] which covers the use of both SAX and DOM for parsing RSS 1.0 documents.

---

[15] http://www.sitepoint.com/article/php-xml-parsing-rss-1-0/1

Our CMS Project

Any self-respecting article-based site nowadays needs an RSS feed. But rather than simply offering a feed for the latest articles on our site, let's allow each user to select the categories he or she is interested in and generate a feed of the newest articles in those categories on-the-fly.

Creating an RSS Feed

To achieve our goal, we need two new PHP scripts: one that presents a form for the user to select the categories of interest, and another that processes that form submission to produce a customized RSS feed.

Creating the Form

Here is our form. You will notice that we are using SimpleXML, as we have before, to produce a list of categories from which to choose.

File: **feedselect.php**

```php
<?php
include_once 'common.inc.php';
?>
<!DOCTYPE html PUBLIC "-//W3C//DTD XHTML 1.0 Transitional//EN"
    "http://www.w3.org/TR/xhtml1/DTD/xhtml1-transitional.dtd">
<html xmlns="http://www.w3.org/1999/xhtml">
<head>
<meta http-equiv="Content-Type"
    content="text/html; charset=iso-8859-1" />
<title>Feed Designer</title>
</head>
<body>
<h1>Feed Designer</h1>
<p>Create your own customized RSS feed to be notified of the
  latest articles published in your areas of interest.</p>
<p>Which categories would you like to monitor?</p>
<form action="feed.php" method="get">
<?php
$cats = simplexml_load_file($fileDir . 'categories.xml');
foreach ($cats->category as $cat) {
  if ((string)$cat['status'] == 'live') {
    echo '<p><label>';
    echo '<input type="checkbox" name="cat[]" value="' .
        htmlentities($cat['id']) . '" checked="checked" />';
```

```
        echo htmlentities($cat['label']) . '</label></p>';
    }
}
?>
<input type="submit" value="Generate Feed" />
</form>
</body>
</html>
```

Note that the form is set to submit using the `get` method, which will allow the user to bookmark the resulting page, and use it in an RSS reader to continually monitor the custom feed.

Simple enough, right? Now let's get down to the business of generating the RSS feed.

Processing the Form Post Results

The form is set to post to `feed.php`. This PHP script is considerably more complicated than our form. It must first build up our RSS feed with the proper channel information, and then parse the articles on our site, adding the ten most recent that are live and in the selected categories to the feed.

We'll go through it a piece at a time. First, we use PHP's DOM functions to start a new XML document, declaring RSS version 0.91 in our root `rss` element:

File: **feed.php (excerpt)**

```php
<?php
include_once 'common.inc.php';

$doc = new DOMDocument();
$root = $doc->createElement('rss');
$doc->appendChild($root);
$root->setAttribute('version', '0.91');
```

We then add our `channel` element with its `title`, `description`, and `link` elements, all of which have fixed values.

File: **feed.php (excerpt)**

```php
$channel = $doc->createElement('channel');
$root->appendChild($channel);

$title = $doc->createElement('title');
$channel->appendChild($title);
```

```
$text = $doc->createTextNode('Example.com Articles');
$title->appendChild($text);

$desc = $doc->createElement('description');
$channel->appendChild($desc);
$text = $doc->createTextNode('Articles from example.com');
$desc->appendChild($text);

$link = $doc->createElement('link');
$channel->appendChild($link);
$text = $doc->createTextNode('http://www.example.com/');
$link->appendChild($text);
```

Now for the hard part: picking out the latest live articles on the site that fall within the selected categories. Actually, it's not too different from the sort of processing we've done before:

File: **feed.php (excerpt)**

```
$handle = opendir($fileDir);
$articles = array();
while (($file = readdir($handle)) !== FALSE) {
  if (is_dir($fileDir . $file)) continue;
  if (!eregi("^article.*\.xml$", $file)) continue;
  $articles[] = $file;
}
rsort($articles);

$cats = @$_GET['cat'];
if (!is_array($cats)) $cats = array();
$itemsToGo = 10;
foreach ($articles as $file) {
  $article = simplexml_load_file($fileDir . $file);
  if ((count($cats) == 0 or
      in_array((string)$article->categoryid, $cats)) and
      (string)$article->status == 'live') {
```

First we use our standard means of looping through the article XML files on our site, but instead of processing them immediately, we'll store them in an array variable named $articles. Once we have our full list of article files, we sort them in reverse order, from latest to oldest (remember, articles have timestamps in their filenames), using PHP's rsort function.

The categories selected by the user arrive in the $_GET['cat'] variable as an array. If no such variable was submitted (i.e. if the user didn't select any categories, or if the feed.php script was loaded directly), then an empty array is created to take its place. We then set a variable called $itemsToGo to track the number of articles we wish to display (ten in this case).

For each article found in the XML files of our site, we check if its categoryid may be found in the list of acceptable categories (if the list is empty, we accept all articles), and if its status is set to live. If those conditions are met, we can go ahead and create an item element for the article in the feed:

File: **feed.php (excerpt)**

```php
$item = $doc->createElement('item');
$channel->appendChild($item);

$iTitle = $doc->createElement('title');
$item->appendChild($iTitle);
$text = $doc->createTextNode($article->headline);
$iTitle->appendChild($text);

$iDesc = $doc->createElement('description');
$item->appendChild($iDesc);
$text = $doc->createTextNode($article->description);
$iDesc->appendChild($text);

$iLink = $doc->createElement('link');
$item->appendChild($iLink);
$text = $doc->createTextNode(
    'http://www.example.com/innerpage.php?id=' .
    $article['id']);
$iLink->appendChild($text);

    if (--$itemsToGo < 1) break;
  }
}
```

Note the if statement at the end, which bails out of the loop once ten articles have been selected for display.

Finally, we write out our XML document to the browser, first sending a header to indicate the appropriate content type for an RSS feed:

```php
header('content-type: application/xml');
echo $doc->saveXML();
?>
```

As a finishing touch, add a link to the feedselect.php page to the front page of the site:

File: **search.inc.php**

```
<form id="searchWidget" method="post" action="doSearch.php">
 Search Site:
 <input name="term" type="text" id="term" />
 <input name="search" type="submit" id="search" value="Search" />
</form>
<p><a href="cats.php">Browse by Category</a></p>
<p><a href="sitemap.php">Site Map</a></p>
<p><a href="feedselect.php">RSS</a></p>
```

Summary

In this chapter, we worked our way around the different RSS standards, and learned how RDF fits into the picture. In a practical example, we saw how to consume an RSS feed from another site and display the headlines as part of our own site. We then used this new-found knowledge to also add a bit of functionality to our CMS project: a customizable headline feed.

9

XML and Web Services

It's time to talk about Web Services—specialized mini-programs that applications written in any language can access over the Internet, thanks to XML. For the most part, we'll look at XML-RPC—an older, but simpler XML standard for Web Services—but we'll also make time for a glance at the latest protocol, SOAP. After that, we'll dive in and add a simple Web Service to our CMS, where we'll use XML-RPC to provide information about articles in the system. This will provide yet another means for our content to be distributed across the Web.

What is a Web Service?

A Web Service is, as its name implies, any service made available over the Web. But what does that mean?

In other words, Web Services take the human-centric Web to the next level. The Web today is mostly about humans using browsers to search for and download information. Web Services provide an application-centric vision of the Web, in which applications provide services and information to each other. Web Services use XML-based messages to allow applications to interact with each other in an automated fashion.

Most Web Services are designed in such a way that individual programming languages don't really matter—I might build my Web Service with PHP, and someone else might build a program to interact with it using ASP.NET, but who cares? The fact is, we're passing standard XML messages back and forth, and so that becomes the glue that holds everything together regardless of what programming language originated the messages.

What makes for a good Web Service? Well, for one thing, they should be **self-describing**, with easy-to-understand public interfaces. Another thing that makes for a good Web Service is its **discoverability**. If you publish a Web Service, it should be easy to find by those who need to use it. There's a whole cloud of peripheral technologies surrounding Web Services that address their description and discovery. We won't cover those technologies in this book; instead, we'll focus on actually building practical Web Services.

The three most common XML data formats used for building Web Services are:

XML Remote Procedure Call (XML-RPC)
This chapter will demonstrate this method.

Simple Object Access Protocol (SOAP)
We will be taking only a brief glance at SOAP.

Custom XML documents
We won't be covering this aspect of Web Services in this chapter.

What's the Big Deal?

To many folks, Web Services don't seem all that different from CGI scripts or even the kind of PHP, ASP.NET, and JSP scripts that extract information from databases. In fact, companies long ago realized they needed software that would interact with other software—credit card processors being one major example.

So here's the big deal. Until the age of Web Services (sounds impressive, no?) most of these efforts were largely ad hoc. They used proprietary methods and approaches, myriad programming languages, and nonstandard ways of requesting services and information.

A bank, let's say, might have a system in place that runs on Java but expects specially formatted queries to service requests. It might have an arcane set of commands that must be sent through in just the right way to work... and the result of a query might come back as fixed-length data records that have to be parsed just so. Another bank might have a C++ system to do the very same thing, but it might use colon-delimited data files and command sequences similar to UNIX commands, because most of its clients interact via a UNIX shell. To work with either of these banks, you would have to write customized software that understood the needs and quirks of each system.

Web Services strive to do away with this confusion. With a good Web Service in place, you can standardize the way you get requests for information, standardize the way you respond to those requests, and publish the interface so that others can easily request services. In this case, it doesn't matter if you're using Java and the other guy wants to use Perl or PHP.

The other big deal focuses on removing the human user from a number of interactions. Let's face it: if you could reroute some of the more mundane requests you receive every day, wouldn't you do it?

What are Web Services Good At?

Any time you want to share information that is otherwise hard to find, or is frequently accessed, you have a candidate for a Web Service. Let me give you a couple of examples.

Let's say that you run a bookstore in a small town. In fact, you run a specialty bookstore selling detective and crime novels only. You decide to boost your Website's offerings by listing select detective novels available on Amazon.com.

Granted, you could enter these items manually into your own inventory listing, or you could write a PHP script to go scrape Amazon.com pages for information. Both these approaches leave a lot to be desired.

Instead, you could sign up to use Amazon.com's Web Service, which allows you to query an inventory listing based on multiple criteria, and get back a list of those items. You can then write code to format the list and post it automatically onto your Website. Stock quotes, weather reports, travel alerts, and auctions are all good candidates for this sort of approach.

Here's another example: one involving Web Services as the great integrator. You work for a Fortune 100 company that has gigabytes of data stored away in ancient, reliable mainframes. Someone from the Marketing department calls your boss, wanting access to this data. But you don't have time to teach this person how to work the mainframe, and, even if you did, it's not a good idea to give the user direct access.

So you build a Web Service that allows data queries to the mainframe, and transmits any result sets back to the user in XML format. The business user doesn't have to understand where the data is, what it looks like, or even how to get it. All he or she has to do is send in an XML-formatted request; your Web Service then replies with its own XML response.

All across the corporate world, Web Services are being used to solve these kinds of "last mile" issues with integration, not to mention their value as a quick way to keep aging systems viable.

Where to find Web Services

You can find some of the more popular Web Services at these locations:

Amazon.com   http://www.amazon.com/gp/aws/landing.html

Google Web APIs   http://www.google.com/apis/

XMethods Service Listing   http://www.xmethods.net/

XML-RPC

XML-RPC is a very simple protocol that uses XML messages to perform remote procedure calls. A remote procedure call is a fancy way to describe a program on one computer calling a function stored on another computer.

XML-RPC requests are sent via HTTP POST, and responses are embedded in the HTTP response. XML-RPC is platform-independent and very easy to learn. You can find out more about the XML-RPC standard at http://www.xmlrpc.com/.

Here's a very simple hypothetical example involving a weather service. All a user has to do is provide a standard method name and pass in a US ZIP code to get back a temperature reading:

```
<?xml version="1.0" encoding="ISO-8859-1"?>
<methodCall>
  <methodName>getCurrentTempByZip</methodName>
  <params>
    <param><value>78701</value></param>
  </params>
</methodCall>
```

Let's suppose further that this is the response that comes back:

```
<?xml version="1.0" encoding="ISO-8859-1"?>
<methodResponse>
  <params>
    <param>
      <value><int>98</int></value>
    </param>
  </params>
</methodResponse>
```

You can easily see that a basic service like this could involve just a very simple form with a ZIP code field and a submit button. The response could easily be transformed into HTML using XSLT, SimpleXML, or DOM.

Because XML-RPC is so simple, a lot of Web Services newbies start with it (though many stay right there and never go on to SOAP). We'll get into more detail about the different pieces of requests and responses in a little while.

First, let's break down the three most important parts of XML-RPC: data structure, request, and response.

The XML-RPC Data Model

XML-RPC supports eight different data types: six simple types and two compound ones. The simple types are shown in Table 9.1.

These basic types are always wrapped in a `value` element, as we saw in our very simple XML-RPC response example:

```
<value><int>98</int></value>
```

Table 9.1. Simple XML-RPC Data Types

Data Type	Example
int or i4 32-bit integers between −2,147,483,648 and 2,147,483,647	`<int>98</int>` `<i4>98</i4>`
double 64-bit floating point numbers	`<double>98.6</double>`
boolean true (1) or false (0)	`<boolean>1</boolean>`
string ASCII text	`<string>Hello there</string>`

dateTime.iso8601
 	
Dates in ISO8601 format (*YYYYMM-DDTHH:MM:SS*)
	`<dateTime.iso8601>`
	`   20050701T16:31:22`
	`</dateTime.iso8601>`

base64
 	
Binary information encoded in Base64
	`<base64>`
	`   SGVsbG8sIFdvcmxkIQ==`
	`</base64>`

So much for simple types; what about complex types? Well, there are two complex types—arrays and structs—which are made up of combined simple types. For example, an array may contain numerous double or string values.

An array is indicated by an `array` element, which is just a list of `values` contained in a single `data` element. The following example could be a list of temperatures taken at a clinic:

```
<value>
  <array>
    <data>
      <value><double>98.7</double></value>
      <value><double>99.3</double></value>
      <value><double>99.5</double></value>
      <value><double>97.9</double></value>
    </data>
```

```
    </array>
    </value>
```

There's no reason why your arrays can't contain mixed content, as in the following example, which could constitute a record of an account balance at a certain time and date:

```
    <value>
      <array>
        <data>
          <value><double>100.30</double></value>
          <value><string>Thomas Myer</string></value>
          <value><int>34783773993</int></value>
          <value><dateTime.iso8601>20050701T16:31:22
</dateTime.iso8601></value>
        </data>
      </array>
    </value>
```

An XML-RPC struct is similar to an array, except it uses name-value pairs. These name-value pairs are contained within member elements. Let's revisit our previous example and make clearer the kind of data we're describing:

```
    <value>
      <struct>
        <member>
          <name>AccountOwner</name>
          <value><string>Thomas Myer</string></value>
        </member>
        <member>
          <name>AccountBalance</name>
          <value><double>100.30</double></value>
        </member>
        <member>
          <name>AccountNumber</name>
          <value><int>34783773993</int></value>
        </member>
        <member>
          <name>TimeStamp</name>
          <dateTime.iso8601>20050701T16:31:22</dateTime.iso8601>
        </member>
      </struct>
    </value>
```

Notice that it's not necessary to identify each of the name elements as a string—XML-RPC assumes that.

XML-RPC Requests

An XML-RPC request is very simple: each request is a combination of HTTP headers and XML content. The XML content is a single XML file whose root element is `methodCall`. This root element contains two other elements, `methodName` and `params`. The `methodName` element identifies the function to call, while the `params` element contains a list of `param` elements that represent arguments or data passed to the function.

Here's a sample request that calls a `getAccountBalance` method. We pass in two parameters: an account ID and a password for that account:

```
<?xml version="1.0" encoding="ISO-8859-1"?>
<methodCall>
  <methodName>getAccountBalance</methodName>
  <params>
    <param>
      <value>
        <struct>
          <member>
            <name>accountid</name>
            <value><string>19393002011</string></value>
          </member>
          <member>
            <name>password</name>
            <value><string>fakepassword</string></value>
          </member>
        </struct>
      </value>
    </param>
  </params>
</methodCall>
```

The HTTP header part of the request equation would look something like this:

```
POST /targetscript HTTP/1.1
User-Agent: identifier
Host: script.host.name
Content-Type: text/xml
Content-Length: request length in bytes
```

The sections shown in italics above will change from request to request, and from client to client. For instance, if the script that listens for requests is located at http://services.example.com/bankAccountRPC, then our headers might look like this:

```
POST /bankAccountRPC HTTP/1.1
User-Agent: xmlRPC-Client-1.0
Host: services.example.com
Content-Type: text/xml
Content-Length: 482
```

When we assemble the header and the XML content inside a standard HTTP POST, we get an ordinary HTTP request with a standardized payload:

```
POST /bankAccountRPC HTTP/1.1
User-Agent: xmlRPC-Client-1.0
Host: services.example.com
Content-Type: text/xml
Content-Length: 482

<?xml version="1.0" encoding="ISO-8859-1"?>
<methodCall>
  <methodName>getAccountBalance</methodName>
  <params>
    <param>
      <value>
        <struct>
          <member>
            <name>accountid</name>
            <value><string>19393002011</string></value>
          </member>
          <member>
            <name>password</name>
            <value><string>fakepassword</string></value>
          </member>
        </struct>
      </value>
    </param>
  </params>
</methodCall>
```

Later in this chapter, we'll generate a request like this on-the-fly, so it's important to be fully aware of the format required.

XML-RPC Responses

There are two kinds of XML-RPC responses: the successful and the unsuccessful. The unsuccessful responses are called **faults**. Faults vary from one implementation to another, but usually a fault returns a struct that tells you where and why your code went wrong. For example, there might be a problem on line 20 of your request, because no method exists to handle the request you sent in (a common error if you happen to spell badly).

Here's how a fault might appear:

```
<?xml version="1.0" encoding="ISO-8859-1"?>
<methodResponse>
  <fault>
    <value>
      <struct>
        <member>
          <name>faultCode</name>
          <value>
            <int>20</int>
          </value>
        </member>
        <member>
          <name>faultString</name>
          <value>
            <string>No method exists by that name.</string>
          </value>
        </member>
      </struct>
    </value>
  </fault>
</methodResponse>
```

Successful XML-RPC responses also contain a `methodResponse` root element, but this time it contains a `params` element. In the current version of XML-RPC, a response can contain only one `param` child element of `params`, but that `param` can contain an `array` or `struct` to pass back multiple values if need be.

Here's an example response to our example request from the previous section. Notice that we use a `struct` to return multiple pieces of information from the original request:

```
<?xml version="1.0" encoding="ISO-8859-1"?>
<methodResponse>
```

```
<params>
  <param>
    <value>
      <struct>
        <member>
          <name>AccountOwner</name>
          <value><string>Thomas Myer</string></value>
        </member>
        <member>
          <name>AccountBalance</name>
          <value><double>100.30</double></value>
        </member>
        <member>
          <name>AccountNumber</name>
          <value><int>34783773993</int></value>
        </member>
        <member>
          <name>TimeStamp</name>
          <dateTime.iso8601>20040701T16:31:22</dateTime.iso8601>
        </member>
      </struct>
    </value>
  </param>
</params>
</methodResponse>
```

What do we Use to Process XML-RPC?

XML-RPC is platform-independent, so you can use ASP.NET, Perl, Python, JSP, and of course, PHP to handle requests and send back responses. We will be building an XML-RPC Web Service in the CMS section, and that's where we'll get into the nitty gritty PHP code.

First, though, let's take a brief walk through SOAP.

SOAP

Like XML-RPC, Simple Object Access Protocol (SOAP) uses a request-response paradigm to get things done. It also uses HTTP as a transport mechanism. SOAP is also platform-independent and is therefore ideal for allowing different systems to communicate.

But I'm afraid that's where the similarities end. SOAP is a much more robust environment for handling heavy-duty requests. It is also much more complicated to use, though it is more extensible than XML-RPC. SOAP allows for user-defined data types, the ability to specify the message recipient, and some other features.

Since XML-RPC does everything we'll need in this book and more, we'll only pause for a high-level overview of SOAP. To get a feel for it, let's revisit our simple weather service, this time using SOAP:

```
<?xml version="1.0" encoding="ISO-8859-1"?>
<env:Envelope
    xmlns:env="http://www.w3.org/2001/09/soap-envelope/">
  <env:Body>
    <w:getTempByZip
        xmlns:w="http://www.example.com/weather">
      <w:zip>78701</w:zip>
    </e:getTempByZip>
  </env:Body>
</env:Envelope>
```

A couple of things need to be addressed right away:

❏ SOAP is structurally and syntactically more complex than XML-RPC. It uses XML namespaces and can even use XML schemas (a complex successor to DTDs).

❏ A SOAP request consists of at least two structural elements: an `Envelope` and a `Body`. The `Envelope` contains the `Body`, and the `Body` contains your request.

❏ Apart from that, the request still just identifies a method and provides a list of parameters that gets passed to the Web Service.

As with XML-RPC, a SOAP request begets a response. Let's take a look at what a really simple response to our request looks like:

```
<?xml version="1.0" encoding="ISO-8859-1"?>
<env:Envelope
    xmlns:env="http://www.w3.org/2001/09/soap-envelope/">
  <env:Body>
    <w:getTemperatureResponse
        xmlns:w="http://www.example.com/weather">
      <w:temp>98</w:temp>
    </w:getTemperatureResponse>
  </env:Body>
</env:Envelope>
```

In our example response, we get back a single integer to indicate the temperature at the given ZIP code. Again, the syntax is more complicated than XML-RPC, but the structure is easy to understand: send in a request, get back a response.

What we Haven't Covered

There's a lot that we haven't covered here about SOAP; in fact, the examples we've just seen barely scratch the surface. Not only is SOAP itself replete with syntactically obscure ways of identifying data types, handling errors, tracking multi-request transactions and more, but related standards for locating and describing SOAP Web Services also exist, each with their own complexities.

Practically speaking, SOAP and it's associated standards were designed for automated tools to generate and process, with higher-level APIs masking the details from developers like you and me.

That said, if you want to learn more about SOAP, take a look at some of the following resources:

❑ SOAP specifications at W3C:

http://www.w3.org/TR/soap/

❑ *Web Services Demystified*, an article by Kevin Yank:

http://www.sitepoint.com/article/web-services-demystified

❑ *SOAP Tutorial* at W3Schools.com:

http://www.w3schools.com/soap/default.asp

Our CMS Project

In this section, we're going to create an XML-RPC server and client for use with our CMS. Our first XML-RPC script will be very simple indeed—it will only return a count of live articles on the system. Our other scripts will be more sophisticated, allowing us to search for and retrieve links to articles in the system.

Before we get started, I have to warn you that the PHP XML-RPC functions aren't necessarily a joy to use, but they provide a solid base from which to create your own XML-RPC-based Web Services.

Building an XML-RPC Server

PHP comes with an optional extension for writing and consuming XML-RPC services. This extension isn't enabled by default; you'll need to compile it using `--with-xmlrpc` on Unix-style installations, or add the `php_xmlrpc.dll` file to your `php.ini` file on Windows.[1]

PHP's XML-RPC extension has several functions that deal with servers, the most important being:

`xmlrpc_server_create`   Tells PHP to create a new server.

`xmlrpc_server_register_method`   Registers a PHP function with the XML-RPC client, making it available to requesting clients as a method.

`xmlrpc_server_call_method`   Passes a client request to the server and sends the server's response back to the client.

`xmlrpc_server_destroy`   Frees up memory used by an XML-RPC server.

Let's get started!

Your First XML-RPC Method

The first thing we need to do is define and register the functions we want to expose as XML-RPC methods. This will allow XML-RPC clients to make requests and get back meaningful responses.

For our XML-RPC server, we want to provide functionality around the articles on our Website. The first method we want to create provides a raw count of live articles available on the site. Let's start by building the PHP function that will support this method.

Every function that will be registered as an XML-RPC method must take three arguments, in this order:

---

[1] If reconfiguring PHP isn't an option for you, an alternative is to use the XML-RPC package in PEAR [http://pear.php.net/package/XML_RPC].

1. The name of the XML-RPC method requested (not necessarily the same name as the function that handles the request).

2. An array containing the arguments passed with the request.

3. Any data sent in the `appData` parameter of the `xmlrpc_server_call_method` (more about this in a moment).

Here's our first function, called `getCountArticles`:

File: **rpcserver.php** (excerpt)

```php
function getCountArticles($methodName, $params, $appData) {
  global $fileDir;
  $count = 0;
  $handle = opendir($fileDir);
  while (($file = readdir($handle) !== FALSE) {
    if (is_dir($fileDir . $file)) continue;
    if (!eregi('^article.*\.xml$', $file)) continue;

    $xmlItem = simplexml_load_file($fileDir . $file);
    if ((string)$xmlItem->status == 'live') {
      $count++;
    }
  }
  return $count;
}
```

Once we have this basic function created, we have to register it as a method with XML-RPC to make it available for client requests. To register a method, you must first create an XML-RPC server using `xmlrpc_server_create`, and then call the `xmlrpc_server_register_method` function with three arguments:

❑ The handle of the server created with `xmlrpc_server_create`.

❑ The name to register the method under (i.e., what needs to be in the `<methodName>` of a request for this method).

❑ The name of the PHP function that will handle requests for this method.

The following code shows how to register our function as an XML-RPC method. Notice that, for simplicity's sake, we've made the XML-RPC method's name the same as the PHP function's name.

File: **rpcserver.php** (excerpt)

```
$xmlRpcServer = xmlrpc_server_create();
xmlrpc_server_register_method($xmlRpcServer, 'getCountArticles',
    'getCountArticles');
```

Creating a Search Method

Now that we have our first, very rudimentary XML-RPC method, let's create a second, more complex one that will allow us to search for articles in the system. This function will be very similar to the search engine we implemented in Chapter 5. The only real difference is that it will get its search term from the $params array.

File: **rpcserver.php** (excerpt)

```
function searchArticles($methodName, $params, $appData) {
  global $fileDir;
  $term = $params[0];
  $handle = opendir($fileDir);
  $items = array();
  while (($file = readdir($handle)) !== FALSE) {
    if (is_dir($fileDir . $file)) continue;
    if (!eregi("^article.*\.xml$", $file)) continue;

    $xmlItem = simplexml_load_file($fileDir . $file);
    if ((stripos($xmlItem->keywords, $term) !== FALSE or
        stripos($xmlItem->headline, $term) !== FALSE or
        stripos($xmlItem->description, $term) !== FALSE) and
        (string)$xmlItem->status == 'live') {
      $item = array();
      $item['id'] = (string)$xmlItem['id'];
      $item['headline'] = (string)$xmlItem->headline;
      $items[] = $item;
    }
  }
  return $items;
}
```

As before, the script uses SimpleXML to grab the information we want and return a series of headlines and unique document IDs to the client.

Of course, we also have to register our new function:

File: **rpcserver.php** (excerpt)

```
xmlrpc_server_register_method($xmlRpcServer, 'searchArticles',
    'searchArticles');
```

Processing a Request

Now that you've created a method and registered it with an XML-RPC server, you have to process an incoming request. To do this, you have first to capture the incoming HTTP POST data, which contains the request:

File: **rpcserver.php** (excerpt)

```
$requestXml = @$HTTP_RAW_POST_DATA;
```

Now hand the request to the xmlrpc_server_call_method function, which identifies the method that was called, extracts any arguments, then dispatches it to the function you registered:

File: **rpcserver.php** (excerpt)

```
$response =
    xmlrpc_server_call_method($xmlRpcServer, $requestXml, '');
```

Finally, let's send the XML response back to the client:

File: **rpcserver.php** (excerpt)

```
header('content-type: text/xml');
echo $response;
```

Once you've printed a response for the client, you can free up your resources using the xmlrpc_server_destroy function:

File: **rpcserver.php** (excerpt)

```
xmlrpc_server_destroy($xmlRpcServer);
```

The Finished XML-RPC Server Script

Here's the finished script:

File: **rpcserver.php**

```
<?php
include_once 'common.inc.php';

$xmlRpcServer = xmlrpc_server_create();
xmlrpc_server_register_method($xmlRpcServer, 'getCountArticles',
```

```
    'getCountArticles');
xmlrpc_server_register_method($xmlRpcServer, 'searchArticles',
    'searchArticles');

$requestXml = $HTTP_RAW_POST_DATA;
$response = xmlrpc_server_call_method($xmlRpcServer, $requestXml,
    '');
header('content-type: text/xml');
echo $response;
xmlrpc_server_destroy($xmlRpcServer);

function getCountArticles($methodName, $params, $appData) {
  global $fileDir;
  $count = 0;
  $handle = opendir($fileDir);
  while (($file = readdir($handle) !== FALSE)) {
    if (is_dir($fileDir . $file)) continue;
    if (!eregi('^article.*\.xml$', $file)) continue;

    $xmlItem = simplexml_load_file($fileDir . $file);
    if ((string)$xmlItem->status == 'live') {
      $count++;
    }
  }
  return $count;
}

function searchArticles($methodName, $params, $appData) {
  global $fileDir;
  $term = $params[0];
  $handle = opendir($fileDir);
  $items = array();
  while (($file = readdir($handle)) !== FALSE) {
    if (is_dir($fileDir . $file)) continue;
    if (!eregi("^article.*\.xml$", $file)) continue;

    $xmlItem = simplexml_load_file($fileDir . $file);
    if ((stripos($xmlItem->keywords, $term) !== FALSE or
        stripos($xmlItem->headline, $term) !== FALSE or
        stripos($xmlItem->description, $term) !== FALSE) and
        (string)$xmlItem->status == 'live') {
      $item = array();
      $item['id'] = (string)$xmlItem['id'];
      $item['headline'] = (string)$xmlItem->headline;
      $items[] = $item;
    }
```

```
    }
    return $items;
}
?>
```

Building an XML-RPC Client that Counts Articles

Now that we have a server, it's time to create a client. However, I've got some bad news: the XML-RPC extension for PHP doesn't make HTTP requests by itself. However, it *does* come with some very handy include files that allow you to create clients very easily.

First, you'll have to download the XML-RPC EPI PHP extension PHP source package from http://xmlrpc-epi.sourceforge.net/. Click the Downloads link on that site and grab the latest version of the xmlrpc-epi-php package (0.51 as of this writing). Extract the file and copy the contents of the /sample/utils directory (including utils.php) into a directory in your PHP include_path. In the next couple of examples, I'll assume you've placed in your include_path a directory named xmlrpc_utils containing these files. I've included these files in the code archive for your convenience.

Once we have the necessary library files installed, we can make short work of the client. The function that does all the work when we call our methods is xu_rpc_http_concise. This function is defined in the xmlrpc_utils/utils.php file that's now located in our PHP include_path.

Let's get on with the example. The first thing we have to do in our client script is include the XML-RPC utility library:

File: **rpcclient-count.php (excerpt)**

```php
<?php
error_reporting(E_ALL ^ E_NOTICE);
include_once 'xmlrpc_utils/utils.php';
```

Note that I've disabled reporting of notice-level errors at the top of this script, as the utils.php file produces several of these.

Next, set three variables, $server, $port, and $uri, to point to your server, the port on which the server is listening, and the location of the XML-RPC server script you set up, respectively. You'll be using these variables soon.

File: **rpcclient-count.php** (excerpt)
```
$host = 'www.example.com'; // or 'localhost' for local machine
$port = 80;
$uri = '/rpcserver.php'; // or URI of the XML-RPC server
```

Now it's time to use the `xu_rpc_http_concise` function provided by the `utils.php` library to send a request and get a response. This method takes one argument, a PHP associative array that contains the following elements in order:

❑ The name of the method to call

❑ The host

❑ The URI of the XML-RPC server

❑ The port number

The result of the request is returned as an ordinary value that you can then manipulate or print.

File: **rpcclient-count.php** (excerpt)
```
$result = xu_rpc_http_concise(
    array(
        'method' => 'getCountArticles',
        'host' => $host,
        'uri' => $uri,
        'port' => $port
    )
);

header('content-type: text/plain');
echo 'The number of articles on server ' . $host . ' is ' .
    $result . '.';
?>
```

When this is run, it should print something like:

```
The number of articles on server www.example.com is 12.
```

Debugging XML-RPC Requests

If you have any trouble getting an XML-RPC request to work, you can ask `xu_rpc_http_concise` to display debugging information. To do this, simply add a `'debug'` parameter to the array you pass to the function:

```
$result = xu_rpc_http_concise(
    array(
        'method' => 'getCountArticles',
        'host' => $host,
        'uri' => $uri,
        'port' => $port,
        'debug' => TRUE
    }
};
```

The Entire XML-RPC Client

File: **rpcclient-count.php**

```php
<?php
include_once 'xmlrpc_utils/utils.php';

$host = 'www.example.com'; // 'localhost' for the local machine
$port = 80;
$uri = '/rpcserver.php'; // or URI of the XML-RPC server

$result = xu_rpc_http_concise(
    array(
        'method' => 'getCountArticles',
        'host' => $host,
        'uri' => $uri,
        'port' => $port
    )
);

header('content-type: text/plain');
echo 'The number of articles on server ' . $host . ' is ' .
    $result . '.';
?>
```

Building an XML-RPC Client that Searches Articles

Okay, we've written a script to invoke the simpler of our two XML-RPC methods, accessing the number of live articles on the site. Now, let's build a client that will run a search. As before, we'll need to include our XML-RPC utility library, and set variables for host, port, and URI.

We also need to add a variable that will contain our search term, which we'll likely get from a request variable:

File: **rpcclient-search.php (excerpt)**

```php
include 'xmlrpc_utils/utils.php';

$host = 'www.example.com'; // 'localhost' for the local machine
$port = 80;
$uri = '/rpcserver.php'; // or URI of the XML-RPC server

$term = $_REQUEST['searchterm'];
```

Next, we send over our request with xu_rpc_http_concise. Notice that our search term becomes the value associated with the args key.

File: **rpcclient-search.php (excerpt)**

```php
$result = xu_rpc_http_concise(
    array(
        'method' => 'searchArticles',
        'args' => $term,
        'host' => $host,
        'uri' => $uri,
        'port' => $port
    )
);
```

This time, the response will be an array, so we'll need to do some processing to display the result of the search:

File: **rpcclient-search.php (excerpt)**

```php
foreach ($result as $article) {
  echo '<p>' . $article['headline'] . '<br />';
  echo '<a href="http://' . $host . '/innerpage.php?id=' .
    htmlentities($article['id']) . '">Read content</a></p>';
}
```

The Entire XML-RPC Client

Run this code by passing a searchterm variable in the URL (e.g. http://www.example.com/rpcclient-search.php?searchterm=xml), and you should receive a list of results with links to the full articles in return.

File: **rpcclient-search.php**

```php
<?php
include_once 'xmlrpc_utils/utils.php';

$host = 'www.example.com'; //  'localhost' for the local machine
```

```php
$port = 80;
$uri = '/rpcserver.php'; // or URI of the XML-RPC server

$term = $_REQUEST['searchterm'];

$result = xu_rpc_http_concise(
    array(
        'method' => 'searchArticles',
        'args' => $term,
        'host' => $host,
        'uri' => $uri,
        'port' => $port
    )
);
?>
<!DOCTYPE html PUBLIC "-//W3C//DTD XHTML 1.0 Transitional//EN"
    "http://www.w3.org/TR/xhtml1/DTD/xhtml1-transitional.dtd">
<html xmlns="http://www.w3.org/1999/xhtml">
<head>
<title>Search Results</title>
<meta http-equiv="content-type"
    content="text/html; charset=iso-8859-1" />
</head>
<body>
<?php
foreach ($result as $article) {
  echo '<p>' . $article['headline'] . '<br />';
  echo '<a href="http://' . $host . '/innerpage.php?id=' .
    htmlentities($article['id']) . '">Read content</a></p>';
}
?>
</body>
</html>
```

Summary

In this chapter, we took a whirlwind look at the modern phenomena that are Web Services. Given the amount of hype this technology gets, I'll forgive you if you were underwhelmed by the reality. From the developer's perspective, XML-RPC is truly a simple technology.

To be fair, we looked at Web Services only within the context of PHP scripting. When Web Services get really exciting is when a program or script in one language can exploit functionality provided by a program or script written in another language. If you want to get a feel for this, spend some time browsing around for an XML-RPC service or two that would be useful on your site, and see how easy it is to call this service in your own PHP code.

10

XML and Databases

Welcome to the last chapter of the book! We have only one more thing to cover: the relationship between XML and databases, which will be the focus of this chapter. Once we've discussed the theory, we'll get our hands dirty adding to our CMS a PHP script and database tables that will give us the ability to back up versions of our XML content.

XML and Databases

If you've been around Web application development for any period of time, you probably know that most PHP, ASP, ColdFusion, and JSP development out there right now involves a database. In PHP's case, the database of choice for most developers is MySQL. You may already be very familiar with the tasks of building tables, defining fields, extracting data, and adding, updating, and deleting records.

Throughout this book, we've mostly talked XML. You could say that XML is a document-centric technology—the shape or format that XML takes is usually some kind of document or file. But to focus on XML's document-centricity ignores the fact that XML is essentially a self-describing semantic unit that contains discrete capsules of data. It also belies the fact that an increasing amount of XML traffic occurs in non-document contexts—think about all those SOAP requests and responses flying back and forth over HTTP, for example.

Indeed, at times, an XML document looks very much like a database. It's this duality—document and database—that makes working with XML so intriguing.

But how does XML work with actual databases, and vice versa? Why would we use them together? When would we use one and not the other? Is it appropriate to use both at the same time? Can you store XML in database tables? Is it possible to convert between SQL and XML data formats? What's the best type of database to work with: relational, post-relational, or a native XML database?

Let's take a stroll down the path created by these questions, and see if we can't shed a little light on the subject.

Why use XML and Databases Together?

This question seems like the most obvious place to start. If you're using a database, why use XML? And if you're using XML, why use a database? Well, the answers to these questions can take you down many different paths.

For example, you might use your database to store a series of revisions to XML content. When you create a piece of XML content, you could store this XML-tagged content in the database with a revision ID. If you made any updates to that content, each of those updates could also be stored with its own specific revision ID. If you then wanted to retrieve a particular version of your XML content, you'd have a relatively easy way to do it: you'd retrieve the initial piece of content along with its revisions, and construct the revised content from those pieces.

Another example might involve using XML primarily in a data-centric way (in other words, as data parcels for your Web Services). Storing this XML in a database provides a record of the transactions that occur over time.

Relational Database? Native XML Database? Somewhere in Between?

The next thing we need to tackle is the type of database we'll use when working with XML. As of this writing, the market offers four different approaches:

Relational
Under this approach, we either place entire documents directly into database fields, or normalize each XML document's elements into appropriate tables and fields. **Normalizing** refers to the process by which we break XML documents (that are hierarchical in nature) into discrete data values, making them

suitable for the database (which is table-column-row-oriented) to store. In the language of database vendors, this process is known as "decomponentizing XML structures to an atomic level."

With very simple XML documents, this process is straightforward. However, with lots of attributes, elements, namespaces, and external entities, we'd need to be very careful in order to make this approach work. And don't forget that, depending on your needs, you're also likely to need a means of converting the values stored in the database back into a self-contained XML document—potentially more work to occupy the wee hours in the face of impending deadlines.

Native XML

A variety of vendors provide both commercial and open source native XML databases. These products allow you to store XML documents (also called snippets or node collections) directly into the database without having to shoehorn those XML structures into conventional database tables. Information queries, extractions, and merges are handled with tools like XPath, XQuery, and XSLT, either inside or outside the database application. As such, anyone who has experience with these XML technologies can, in many cases, use that knowledge to work with native XML databases.

At the time of this writing, few native XML databases support the full XML feature set, and insufficient key tests have been run to establish interoperability and portability between environments. In fact, there's safety in choosing a relational (or post-relational) approach, simply because the user community is larger, and has already done a good job of figuring out best practices.

Following are some links to articles about native XML databases:

❑ *Introduction to Native XML Databases*
  http://www.xml.com/pub/a/2001/10/31/nativexmldb.html

❑ *Native XML Databases: Bad Idea for Data?*
  http://www.ibm.com/developerworks/xml/library/x-xdnat.html

❑ *Native XML Database Vendors*
  http://www.service-architecture.com/products/xml_databases.html

Post-relational

So-called post-relational databases are relational databases with built-in support for XML and object-oriented data structures. This gives us the ability to store hierarchical or recursive information in a single field, run complex full-text searches, and/or use XPath/XQuery[1] to retrieve data.

Flat-file

A flat-file database is a very simple type of database in which each line represents a record. Each field in a record can be of fixed length or of varying length with some kind of delimiter (such as a comma). Because a flat-file database has no relational capabilities, this approach can generate a lot of redundant information.

One way to store XML in a flat-file database would be to create a lookup file that contained pointers to XML document files, with a title for each file.

Which of these approaches is best? Again, the answer is, "it depends." One of the biggest factors in choosing one approach over another will be your level of experience with software development in general, and database development in particular. For example, a lot more support is available for relational databases, so if you think you'll benefit from a large community of peers to help you through the sticky spots, that might be the best way to go.

Another big factor to consider is the type of data you intend to store. If the structure of your XML information is uniform and predictable, then it will fit nicely into the regimented fields required by a relational database. If your XML information is diverse or only semi-structured, the native XML database format's ability to store that data in whatever form it may take will be a huge benefit.

Finally, consider what you intend to do with the XML information once it's in the database. If you're just running queries and extracting different elements (or collections of elements), the native XML format will do nicely—in fact, you'll be able to use native XML tools like XPath and XQuery. On the other hand, if you need to perform calculations (like sum, average, and count) or run relational lookups on your XML information, you'll want the features of a relational database. For instance, if you want to look up a customer's unique ID, then figure out how many outstanding invoices that customer has, it's not likely that the native XML database will have any built-in tools to help you. In such circumstances, you'll need to build those tools yourself.

---

[1]XQuery is a query language that is analogous to SQL and allows you to formulate searches on XML nodes and content.

In our CMS project, we'll use the database to store backups and versions of our XML documents. As such, we'll take the relational database approach.

Converting Relational Data to XML

Before we entrust our precious content to a database, let's make sure we can get that XML data back *out* again. Let's try doing exactly that with a MySQL database, first using the phpMyAdmin tool, then using the mysqldump command, and finally, with the help of a hand-rolled converter written in PHP.

After we've gained some experience converting database data to XML, we'll move on to look at our CMS project.

Using phpMyAdmin to Export XML

You're probably already familiar with phpMyAdmin, the all-purpose MySQL interface that's built in PHP to allow you to administer your MySQL Web databases. But did you know that you could use phpMyAdmin to export your MySQL data in XML format? You can—and it can be a definite time-saver!

Figure 10.1. The phpMyAdmin main screen.

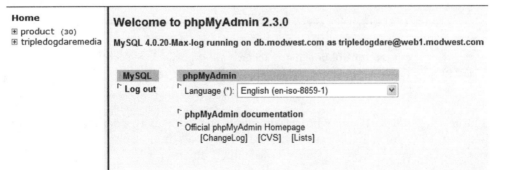

Let's use the phpMyAdmin tool, shown in Figure 10.1, to export a table full of data to XML format. First, click the plus sign that appears next to the name of the database that contains the table you want. Click that table name, then click the Export tab located at the top of the display.

In the Export screen, choose the Export to XML Format and Save as File options, then click Go. Figure 10.2 shows the Export screen in action.

Figure 10.2. The phpMyAdmin export screen.

| wse | SQL | Select | Insert | Export | Operations | Options | En |

View dump (schema) of table

- ○ Structure only
- ○ Structure and data
- ○ Data only

- ○ CSV for Ms Excel data

- ○ CSV data :
  - Fields terminated by `;`
  - Fields enclosed by `"`
  - Fields escaped by `\`
  - Lines terminated by `\r\n`

- ◉ Export to XML format

Structure
- ☐ Add 'drop table'
- ☐ Enclose table and field names with backquotes

Data
- ☐ Complete inserts
- ☐ Extended inserts
- Dump `23` row(s) starting at record # `0` .

☑ Save as file (☐ "zipped" ☐ "gzipped")

[Go]

You can control how many records are exported by selecting a number from the Dump field on the right-hand side of the screen.

The result is an XML file whose filename is the same as the database table you just exported (for example, `members.xml`). Here's a sample snippet of an exported file from a hypothetical database table named `survey`:

```
<?xml version="1.0" encoding="iso-8859-1"?>

<!--
-
- phpMyAdmin XML-Dump
- version 2.3.0
- http://phpwizard.net/phpMyAdmin/
- http://www.phpmyadmin.net/ (download page)
-
```

```
- Host: db.yourhosting.com
- Generation Time: Jul 10, 2004 at 07:30 PM
- Server version: 4.00.20
- PHP Version: 4.3.1
- Database : 'mydatabase'
-
-->

<mydatabase>
  <!-- table  survey -->
    <survey>
        <surveyID>5</surveyID>
        <name>Carol Smith</name>
        <email>carol@tripledogdaremedia.com</email>
        <phone>555-2685</phone>
        <industry>hightech</industry>
        <orgname>Sample Commerce</orgname>
        <orgsize>501-1000</orgsize>
        <currentwebsite>y</currentwebsite>
        <howlong>more than 2 yrs</howlong>
        <howoften>once a week</howoften>
        <typewebsite>dynamic</typewebsite>
        <typeos>windows</typeos>
        <stamp>2004-06-18 07:06:33</stamp>
    </survey>
</mydatabase>
```

Notice that phpMyAdmin's XML output utility uses the database name as the root element for the XML file it creates.

Using `mysqldump` to Export XML

You can do essentially the same thing that phpMyAdmin does with a very simple `mysqldump` command. This command line utility, which ships with MySQL, allows you to export database content as XML data.

Here's the format of the `mysqldump` command:

```
mysqldump -u user -ppassword --xml dbname table > outputfile
```

Here, *user* is your MySQL username, *password* is your MySQL password (note that there is no space between the `-p` and the *password* value), *dbname* is the MySQL database name, *table* is the name of the table you want to dump out, and *outputfile* identifies the path and filename of your output file.

For instance, if, in your Website's database, you had a database named `website` containing a table named `survey` that you wanted to dump out to an XML file, you'd run the following command from the command line:

```
mysqldump -u myuser -pmypass --xml website survey > survey.xml
```

Running this command with MySQL version 4.1 produces an XML file that has the following format:

```
<?xml version="1.0"?>
<mysqldump>
  <database name="dbName">
    <table_structure name="tableName">
      <field Field="field1" Type="int(10) unsigned" … />
      <key Table="fieldkeyword" Non_unique="0" Key_name="PRIMARY"
           … />
      <options Name="tableName" Engine="MyISAM" Version="9" … />
    </table_structure>
    <table_data name="tableName">
      <row>
        <field name="field1">data</field>
      </row>

      <!-- more row tags follow -->

    </table_data>
  </database>
</mysqldump>
```

The XML output is contained within a `<mysqldump>` tag. In this case, it has one child tag, `<database>`, whose `name` attribute indicates the database whose contents are being dumped. Inside the `<database>` tag are two more tags: `<table_structure>` and `<table_data>`. The `<table_structure>` tag contains information about the structure of the table that's being dumped, such as the fields it contains, their formats, the related key information, and the `mysqldump` options used to create that dump. The `<table_data>` tag contains the name of the table being dumped, and holds a series of `<row>` tags, which represent the actual rows of data. Each `<row>` tag contains one or more `<field>` tags that hold the data for the fields in that row.

As you can see, it wouldn't be that hard to put together a simple shell script that contained the username, password, database name, table name, and output file name of a database, then to run it periodically using `cron`. That shell script would look something like this:

```
#!/bin/sh
user=$1
pw=$2
dbname=$3
dbtable=$4
path=$5
/usr/bin/mysqldump -u $user -p$pw --xml $dbname $dbtable > $path
```

We use chmod +x on the Linux command line to make it executable. Then, we create another shell script to call the original shell script multiple times (once for each table from which we need XML data):

```
#!/bin/sh
./dump2XML.sh myuser mypw mydb table1 /htdocs/www/xml/table1.xml
./dump2XML.sh myuser mypw mydb table2 /htdocs/www/xml/table2.xml
./dump2XML.sh myuser mypw mydb table3 /htdocs/www/xml/table3.xml
```

Once this shell script is made executable, we set up a crontab to run it every day (or at a frequency of our choice) and bingo! We have a simple back-end process for dumping out MySQL data as XML.

The crontab that would run our script every day at 1:00am might look like this:

```
0 1 * * * /path/to/MasterShellScript.sh
```

Hand-Rolling an XML Converter

Converting a complex database structure to XML can be a daunting task, particularly if the SQL data structure is highly normalized. As a gentle introduction, we're going to take on the much simpler task of converting a single table to XML with a custom script. This PHP 5 script will connect to a MySQL database of our choosing, and then translate the contents of the table into an XML document:

File: **sqldump.php** (excerpt)

```php
<?php
// Replace these arguments with your own values
connectDatabase('localhost', 'user', 'password', 'database');

// parameters: table name, where constraints (optional),
// row limit (optional)
printTableContent('table', 'status="active"', 2);

function connectDatabase($server, $user, $pw, $db) {
  $GLOBALS['link'] = mysqli_connect($server, $user, $pw, $db);
```

```
  if (mysqli_connect_errno()) {
    echo 'Connect failed: ' . mysqli_connect_error();
    exit();
  }
}
```

As you can see, the real magic happens in the `printTableContent` function, which takes the name of the table to be dumped, as well as an optional WHERE condition and LIMIT clause. It starts out by using these arguments to build an SQL SELECT query:

File: **sqldump.php** (excerpt)

```
function printTableContent($table, $where = FALSE, $limit = FALSE)
{
  $sql = 'SELECT * FROM ' .
      mysqli_escape_string($GLOBALS['link'], $table);
  if ($where !== FALSE) {
    $sql .= ' WHERE ' .
        mysqli_escape_string($GLOBALS['link'], $where);
  }
  if ($limit !== FALSE) {
    $sql .= ' LIMIT ' .
        mysqli_escape_string($GLOBALS['link'], $limit);
  }
```

It then, of course, executes the query:

File: **sqldump.php** (excerpt)

```
$result = mysqli_query($GLOBALS['link'], $sql);
if (mysqli_errno($GLOBALS['link'])) {
  echo mysqli_error($GLOBALS['link']);
  exit();
}
```

Since the tags we use in the XML will be based on the names of the fields (columns) in the table, we must capture those in an array:

File: **sqldump.php** (excerpt)

```
$fields = array();
$fieldCount = mysqli_num_fields($result);
for ($i = 0; $i < $fieldCount; $i++) {
  $meta = mysqli_fetch_field($result);
  $fields[] = $meta->name;
}
```

Now it's just a matter of looping through the rows of our result set, and for each row looping through the fields, all the while using the DOM API to build an XML document containing the values:

File: **sqldump.php (excerpt)**

```php
$dom = new DOMDocument();
$tableEl = $dom->appendChild($dom->createElement($table));
while ($row = mysqli_fetch_array($result)) {
  $rowEl = $tableEl->appendChild($dom->createElement('record'));
  foreach ($fields as $field) {
    $fieldEl = $rowEl->appendChild($dom->createElement($field));
    $fieldEl->appendChild($dom->createTextNode($row[$field]));
  }
}
```

With the document in hand, all we need to do is print it out:

File: **sqldump.php (excerpt)**

```php
header('content-type: application/xml');
echo $dom->saveXML();
}
?>
```

If we ran this script on the `survey` table we saw in an earlier example, the output would appear as follows:

```xml
<?xml version="1.0"?>
<survey>
  <record>
    <surveyID>5</surveyID>
    <name>Carol Smith</name>
    <email>carol@tripledogdaremedia.com</email>
    <phone>555-2685</phone>
    <industry>hightech</industry>
    <orgname>Sample Commerce</orgname>
    <orgsize>501-1000</orgsize>
    <currentwebsite>y</currentwebsite>
    <howlong>more than 2 yrs</howlong>
    <howoften>once a week</howoften>
    <typewebsite>dynamic</typewebsite>
    <typeos>windows</typeos>
    <stamp>2004-06-18 07:06:33</stamp>
  </record>

  <record>
```

```
    <surveyID>4</surveyID>
    <name>Jen Davidson</name>
    <email>jdavidson@tripledogdaremedia.com</email>
    <phone>555-9366</phone>
    <industry>medical</industry>
    <orgsize>1-5</orgsize>
    <currentwebsite>y</currentwebsite>
    <howlong>more than 2 yrs</howlong>
    <howoften>too hard/don't know how</howoften>
    <typeos>windows</typeos>
    <stamp>2002-06-18 06:06:58</stamp>
  </record>
</survey>
```

This solution's very simple and won't be able to handle complex data relationships, but as a quick and dirty extraction and conversion tool for single table data, it does all right. Add complexity as needed and season to taste.

Our CMS Project

We've come a long way with our CMS project, but we still have one last touch to add: we're going to perform a nightly backup of all the XML files in the `xml` directory. To pull this off, we'll have to open up each XML document in the directory, grab all of that file's content, then update the database with each piece of content.

Building the MySQL Table

To make administration a little easier, we're going to back up our data to two tables. The first table, `xmlfile`, will contain pointers to our files. The second table, `xmlcontent`, will contain daily snapshots of the contents of each file. Here are the SQL commands we'll use to create those tables:

File: **xmlbackup.sql**

```
CREATE TABLE xmlfile (
  xmlfileid INT NOT NULL AUTO_INCREMENT PRIMARY KEY,
  xmlfilename varchar(255) NOT NULL,
  createtime DATETIME NOT NULL
);

CREATE TABLE xmlcontent (
  xmlcontentid INT NOT NULL AUTO_INCREMENT PRIMARY KEY,
  xmlfileid INT NOT NULL,
```

```
  xmlcontent TEXT,
  updatetime INT NOT NULL,
  status ENUM('current', 'not current') DEFAULT 'not current' NOT
    NULL
);
```

Note that the `xmlfile` table keeps track of date/time that the file is first backed up. The `xmlcontent` table keeps track of the date/time of each update and whether or not it is the current (latest) snapshot of the file.

Building the PHP

Now that we've established our tables in MySQL, we can develop a common-sense solution using PHP. First, we connect to the database:

File: **xmlbackup.php (excerpt)**

```php
<?php
include_once 'common.inc.php';

/* replace these values with ones for your database */
$link = mysqli_connect('localhost', 'user', 'password',
    'database');
if (mysqli_connect_errno()) {
  echo 'Connect failed: ' . mysqli_connect_error();
  exit();
}
```

Now, our script will basically work like this: for each file in the XML file directory, the script will check if the `xmlfile` table contains a record for that file. If it doesn't, it will add a new record for the file. In either case, it will then add a record of the file's current contents to the `xmlcontent` table.

First up, here's the by-now-familiar file loop:

File: **xmlbackup.php (excerpt)**

```php
$handle = opendir($fileDir);
while (($file = readdir($handle)) !== FALSE) {
 if (is_dir($fileDir . $file)) continue;
 if (!eregi('\.xml$', $file)) continue;
```

Next, we grab the content of each file:

File: **xmlbackup.php (excerpt)**

```php
  $content = file_get_contents($fileDir . $file);
```

With the file in hand, we can now check if it's registered in the `xmlfile` table, and get its ID if it is:

File: **xmlbackup.php (excerpt)**

```php
$sql = 'SELECT xmlfileid FROM xmlfile WHERE xmlfilename="' .
    mysqli_escape_string($link, $file) . '"';
$result = mysqli_query($link, $sql);
if (mysqli_errno($link)) {
  echo mysqli_error($link);
  exit();
}
if ($row = mysqli_fetch_array($result)) {
  $xmlfileid = $row['xmlfileid'];
```

If it's not registered in the table, we must insert a new record for the file, and obtain its ID:

File: **xmlbackup.php (excerpt)**

```php
} else {
  $sql = 'INSERT INTO xmlfile (xmlfilename, createtime) ' .
      'VALUES ("' . mysqli_escape_string($link, $file) . '", ' .
      time() . ')';
  $result = mysqli_query($link, $sql);
  if (mysqli_errno($link)) {
    echo mysqli_error($link);
    exit();
  }
  $xmlfileid = mysqli_insert_id($link);
}
```

Whether the file is newly-registered, or if we retrieved its existing record from the `xmlfile` table, we now have its ID. We can now insert a new record for it into the `xmlcontent` table. But first, we make sure to set any other records that exist for the file with a `status` of `not current`:

File: **xmlbackup.php (excerpt)**

```php
$sql = 'UPDATE xmlcontent SET status="not current" ' .
    'WHERE xmlfileid=' . $xmlfileid;
$result = mysqli_query($link, $sql);
if (mysqli_errno($link)) {
  echo mysqli_error($link);
  exit();
}
$sql = 'INSERT INTO xmlcontent ' .
    '(xmlfileid, xmlcontent, updatetime, status) ' .
```

```
    'VALUES (' . $xmlfileid . ', "' .
    mysqli_escape_string($link, $content) . '", ' . time() .
', "current")';
  $result = mysqli_query($link, $sql);
  if (mysqli_errno($link)) {
    echo mysqli_error($link);
    exit();
  }
```

The last step is to close our database link and directory handle:

File: **xmlbackup.php (excerpt)**

```
}
mysqli_close($link);
closedir($handle);
?>
```

Setting up a Cron Schedule to Run Periodically

Now that we have the PHP script working with our MySQL database, we need to set up a cron schedule to run the script at different times—for instance, shortly after midnight, and in the early afternoon.

We could set up our cron task to run twice a day (at 12:30am and 2:30pm) with the following crontab entry (assuming that the name of our backup script is xml-backup.php):

```
30 0,14 * * * /usr/bin/php /path/to/xmlbackup.php
```

For full details of setting up cron tasks, run man crontab at the command prompt of your Linux (or similar) server.

On Windows servers, you can instead set this up using the Task Scheduler and the command-line interface version of PHP.

The key here is to balance the need to make frequent version updates against our performance requirements. The result? A quick script that makes a database backup of all of our files. We can now use the MySQL backup to restore files if needed, or even to perform database queries of our XML content.

Clean Up Your Database

This script will of course store a complete copy of every XML file on your site to the database each time it is run. If you don't want your database to grow out of control, you should update the script to purge out-of-date backups as per your requirements. Since this is all about PHP scripting and has nothing to do with XML, I'll leave that to you as an exercise.

Summary

In this chapter, we learned about XML and databases. We considered the various options when it comes to storing XML data in a database, and concluded that there are great benefits to be had from some of the newer technologies in this area, but that support can be a problem if you don't know what you're doing. We also looked at how to retrieve relational data out of a database and build an XML file out of it on-the-fly. Finally, we created a simple backup script for our XML that stores the previous and current versions of the XML data files at the heart of our site.

What's left to cover? Well, you'll want to look at Appendix A to review a list of PHP's XML functions. This list will give you a better idea of the extensive support that's available for XML in PHP 5. And don't forget that Appendix B finishes up our CMS project by covering the various PHP scripts that make up the administrative interface for the site.

Appendix A: PHP XML Functions

In this appendix, we'll outline the major PHP XML functions available for SAX, DOM, and SimpleXML.

SAX Functions

The PHP SAX implementation supports James Clark's expat parser. The SAX toolkit lets you parse XML documents only—it doesn't support XML document validation. It supports the US-ASCII, ISO-8859-1 and UTF-8 character encodings.

Error Code Constants

The SAX implementation uses the following integer constants as error codes:

- ❑ XML_ERROR_NONE

- ❑ XML_ERROR_NO_MEMORY

- ❑ XML_ERROR_SYNTAX

- ❑ XML_ERROR_NO_ELEMENTS

- ❑ XML_ERROR_INVALID_TOKEN

- ❑ XML_ERROR_UNCLOSED_TOKEN

- ❑ XML_ERROR_PARTIAL_CHAR

- ❑ XML_ERROR_TAG_MISMATCH

- ❑ XML_ERROR_DUPLICATE_ATTRIBUTE

- ❑ XML_ERROR_JUNK_AFTER_DOC_ELEMENT

- ❑ XML_ERROR_PARAM_ENTITY_REF

- ❑ XML_ERROR_UNDEFINED_ENTITY

- ❑ XML_ERROR_RECURSIVE_ENTITY_REF

❑ XML_ERROR_ASYNC_ENTITY

❑ XML_ERROR_BAD_CHAR_REF

❑ XML_ERROR_BINARY_ENTITY_REF

❑ XML_ERROR_ATTRIBUTE_EXTERNAL_ENTITY_REF

❑ XML_ERROR_MISPLACED_XML_PI

❑ XML_ERROR_UNKNOWN_ENCODING

❑ XML_ERROR_INCORRECT_ENCODING

❑ XML_ERROR_UNCLOSED_CDATA_SECTION

❑ XML_ERROR_EXTERNAL_ENTITY_HANDLING

❑ XML_OPTION_CASE_FOLDING

❑ XML_OPTION_TARGET_ENCODING

❑ XML_OPTION_SKIP_TAGSTART

❑ XML_OPTION_SKIP_WHITE

Function Listing

The following SAX functions, presented in alphabetical order, are supported.

utf8_decode

```
string utf8_decode(string data)
```

This function converts a string containing UTF-8 encoded characters into a string containing single-byte ISO-8859-1 characters.

utf8_encode

```
string utf8_encode(string data)
```

This function converts the given string data into UTF-8, and returns the encoded string, leaving the supplied string intact. UTF-8 is a standard mechanism used by Unicode to encode wide character values into a byte stream. UTF-8 is transparent to plain ASCII characters, and can be used with normal string manipulation functions when the string contains only these characters.

xml_error_string

```
string xml_error_string(int code)
```

This function returns a textual description of a given error code, or FALSE if no description is found for the given error code. You can retrieve an error code by calling xml_get_error_code (see below).

xml_get_current_byte_index

```
int xml_get_current_byte_index(resource parser)
```

This function returns the number of bytes of the XML document the parser has processed, or FALSE if the parser is invalid.

xml_get_current_column_number

```
int xml_get_current_column_number(resource parser)
```

This function returns the column on the current line (as given by xml_get_current_line_number) at which the parser is located, or FALSE if the parser is invalid. So, if it's at the start of a line, it returns 0. If it's ten characters in, it returns 10.

xml_get_current_line_number

```
int xml_get_current_line_number(resource parser)
```

This function returns the line number at which the parser is currently located in its data buffer, or FALSE if the parser is invalid.

xml_get_error_code

```
int xml_get_error_code(resource parser)
```

This function returns one of the error codes listed in the section called "Error Code Constants" of this appendix (XML_ERROR_NONE if no error has occurred).

xml_parse

```
bool xml_parse(resource parser, string data[, bool is_final])
```

Use this function to parse a string of XML. When the XML document is parsed, the handlers for the configured events are called in accordance with the parsed document, after which the function returns TRUE for success or FALSE to indicate an error.

The first parameter, *parser*, is a reference to the parser that's to be used.

The second parameter, *data*, contains the XML data to parse.

The last parameter, *is_final*, indicates whether this is the last chunk of text that will be passed to the parser. You can use this parameter to perform progressive parsing, handing the parser a series of small chunks of XML data. Some errors can only be detected at the end of a document, and this argument lets you tell the parser that this has been reached.

xml_parse_into_struct

```
int xml_parse_into_struct(resource parser, string data,
    array &values[, array &index])
```

This function provides a means of using the lightweight SAX parser without the bother of event handling. You pass it one or two arrays, which it fills based on the XML document provided in the *data* argument.

The first array, *values*, will be filled with elements corresponding to the tags in the document, in the order they occur. Each entry in the array will be an array containing information about:

❑ An opening tag for an element with child elements

```
array
(
    'tag' => 'tagname',
    'type' => 'open',
    'level' => n
)
```

where *tagname* is the name of the tag, and *n* is the depth of the element in the document (1 for the root element).

❏ A closing tag for an element with child elements

```
array
(
    'tag' => 'tagname',
    'type' => 'close',
    'level' => n
)
```

❏ An element with no child elements (i.e., empty or containing only a text value)

```
array
(
    'tag' => 'tagname',
    'type' => 'complete',
    'level' => n,
    'value' => 'content'
)
```

where *content* is the text value contained in the element, if any.

If you supply an array for the *index* argument, it will be filled with one entry for each tag name in the document. That entry will contain an array of integer indices, pointing to the entries in the *values* array that correspond to that tag name. In other words, if you pass $index as the *index* argument, then $values[$index['*tagname*'][0]] will contain the first "opening", "closing", or "complete" entry for a *tagname* element in the document. Using this array, you can quickly pick out pairs of start/end tag entries in the *values* array and then parse the contents of those tags using the *values* entries between them.

xml_parse_into_struct returns 1 if successful or 0 if it fails.

xml_parser_create

```
resource xml_parser_create([string encoding])
```

This function creates a new XML parser and returns a resource handle, which references the parser, for use by the other XML functions.

The optional encoding specifies the character encoding of the XML input to be parsed. Supported encodings include ISO-8859-1 (default), UTF-8 and US-ASCII.

xml_parser_create_ns

```
resource xml_parser_create_ns([string encoding[,
    string separator]])
```

This function creates a new XML parser with XML namespace support, and returns a resource handle referencing the parser. This resource handle can then be used by other XML functions.

When a namespace-aware parser is used, tag parameters passed to the various handler functions will consist of the namespace prefix and tag name separated either by the string specified in separator, or :, the default (for example, ex:message).

The optional encoding specifies the character encoding of the XML input to be parsed. The supported encodings are ISO-8859-1 (default), UTF-8 and US-ASCII.

xml_parser_free

```
bool xml_parser_free(resource parser)
```

This function frees the memory used by the parser. It returns TRUE if successful, or FALSE if the supplied parser is invalid.

xml_parser_get_option

```
mixed xml_parser_get_option(resource parser, int option)
```

This function retrieves the value of an option from a parser, or returns FALSE if the parser or option is invalid.

The following options are available:

XML_OPTION_CASE_FOLDING
This option controls whether case-folding is enabled for an XML parser, and is enabled by default.

XML_OPTION_TARGET_ENCODING
This option sets the target encoding that is to be used in an XML parser. By default, it is set to reflect the source encoding used by xml_parser_create.

xml_parser_set_option

```
bool xml_parser_set_option(resource parser, int option,
    mixed value)
```

This function sets the value of an option for a parser. The available options are as listed for xml_parser_get_option. This function returns FALSE if the parser is invalid, or the option could not be set. Otherwise, the option is set and TRUE is returned.

xml_set_character_data_handler

```
bool xml_set_character_data_handler(resource parser,
    callback handler)
```

This function sets the character data handler function for the XML parser. The handler argument is a string containing the name of a function that must exist when xml_parse is called to parse the document.

The function named by handler must accept two arguments: parser and data.

❑ The first argument, parser, is a reference to the XML parser calling the handler.

❑ The second argument, data, contains the character data as a string.

If you wish to set up a method as a handler function, pass to handler a two-item array containing a reference to the object as the first item, and the name of the method as the second item.

If the handler function is set to an empty string, or to FALSE, the handler in question is disabled. TRUE is returned if the handler is set up; FALSE is returned if the parser is not valid.

xml_set_default_handler

```
bool xml_set_default_handler(resource parser, callback handler)
```

This function sets the default handler function for the XML parser. The handler comprises a string containing the name of a function that must exist when xml_parse is called to parse the document.

The function named by handler must accept two arguments: parser and data.

❑ The first argument, *parser*, is a reference to the XML parser that calls the handler.

❑ The second argument, *data*, contains the character data. This can be the XML declaration, document type declaration, entities or other data for which no other handler exists.

If you wish to set up a method as a handler function, pass to *handler* a two-item array containing a reference to the object as the first item, and the name of the method as the second item.

If the handler function is set to an empty string, or to FALSE, the handler in question is disabled. TRUE is returned if the handler is set up; FALSE is returned if the parser is invalid.

xml_set_element_handler

```
bool xml_set_element_handler(resource parser,
    callback start_element_handler, callback end_element_handler)
```

This function sets the element handler functions for the XML parser. *start_element_handler* and *end_element_handler* are strings containing the names of functions that must exist when xml_parse is called to parse the document.

The function named by *start_element_handler* must accept three arguments: *parser*, *name*, and *attributes*.

❑ The first argument, *parser*, is a reference to the XML parser calling the handler.

❑ The second argument, *name*, contains the name of the element for which this handler is called. If case-folding is in effect for this parser, the element name will appear in uppercase letters.

❑ The third argument, *attribs*, is an associative array containing the element's attributes (if any exist). The keys of this array are the attribute names; the values are the attribute values. Attribute names are case-folded on the same criteria as element names. Attribute values are not case-folded.

The function named by *end_element_handler* can accept two parameters: *parser* and *name*.

❑ The first argument, *parser*, is a reference to the XML parser that calls the handler.

❑ The second argument, *name*, contains the name of the element for which this handler is called. If case-folding is in effect for this parser, the element name will appear in uppercase letters.

For both handlers, if you wish to set up a method as a handler function, pass to *start_element_handler* or *end_element_handler* a two-item array containing a reference to the object as the first item, and the name of the method as the second item.

If a handler function is set to an empty string, or FALSE, the handler in question is disabled. TRUE is returned if the handlers are set up; FALSE is returned if the parser is invalid.

xml_set_end_namespace_decl_handler

```
bool xml_set_end_namespace_decl_handler(resource parser,
    callback handler)
```

In theory, this function should let you set up a handler function that will be called after the closing tag of an element that contained a namespace declaration. As of this writing, however, this particular callback is not supported by the XML library used by PHP, so this function should not be used.

xml_set_external_entity_ref_handler

```
bool xml_set_external_entity_ref_handler(resource parser,
    callback handler)
```

This function sets up a handler function that is called when the XML parser encounters an external entity reference; that is an entity reference (*&entname;*) whose value is declared in the DTD as the content of an external file. The *handler* argument is a string containing the name of a function that must exist when xml_parse is called to parse the document.

The function named by *handler* must accept five arguments: *parser*, *open_entity_names*, *base*, *system_id* and *public_id*.

❑ The first argument, *parser*, is a reference to the XML parser calling the handler.

❏ The second argument, *open_entity_names*, contains a space-separated list of the external entities that have been opened to get to the current entity reference. For example, if the current entity reference &entityC; appears inside the value of &entityB;, which in turn appears inside &entityA;, then this argument will be the string entityA entityB entityC.

❏ The third argument, *base*, should in theory contain an absolute URL to be used as the base URL for resolving the relative URL in *system_id*. Because of the way the XML parser in PHP is implemented, this will always be an empty string.

❏ The fourth argument, *system_id*, contains the system identifier of the external entity—a URL pointing to the location where the entity's content file may be downloaded.

❏ The fifth argument, *public_id*, contains the public identifier string for a standardized external entity within your application. If no such identifier is declared for the entity in the DTD, this argument will be an empty string.

If you wish to set up a method as a handler function, pass to *handler* a two-item array containing a reference to the object as the first item, and the name of the method as the second item.

If the handler function is set to an empty string, or to FALSE, the handler in question is disabled. TRUE is returned if the handler is set up; FALSE is returned if the parser is not valid.

xml_set_notation_decl_handler

```
bool xml_set_notation_decl_handler(resource parser,
    callback handler)
```

This function sets up a handler function that is called when the XML parser encounters a notation declaration in the DTD of the document. Notation declarations let you assign names and identifiers for types of non-XML data that may be included in the XML document by means of an external entity reference. Such entities are called **unparsed entities**.

The *handler* argument is a string containing the name of a function that must exist when xml_parse is called to parse the document. The function named by *handler* must accept five arguments: *parser*, *notation_name*, *base*, *system_id* and *public_id*.

❏ The first argument, *parser*, is a reference to the XML parser calling the handler.

❏ The second argument, *notation_name*, contains the name assigned to the notation by the notation declaration.

❏ The third argument, *base*, should in theory contain an absolute URL to be used as the base URL for resolving the relative URL in *system_id*. Because of the way the XML parser in PHP is implemented, this will always be an empty string.

❏ The fourth argument, *system_id*, contains the system identifier of the notation—a URL often used to point to an application that can process the data type identified by this notation.

❏ The fifth argument, *public_id*, contains the public identifier string for a standardized notation within your application. If no such identifier is declared for the notation in the DTD, this argument will be an empty string.

If you wish to set up a method as a handler function, pass to *handler* a two-item array containing a reference to the object as the first item, and the name of the method as the second item.

If the handler function is set to an empty string, or to FALSE, the handler in question is disabled. TRUE is returned if the handler is set up; FALSE is returned if the parser is not valid.

xml_set_object

```
void xml_set_object(resource parser, object object)
```

An alternative means of setting up methods as handler functions, this function lets you specify an *object* of which all of the handler functions assigned to the *parser* are assumed to be methods. This is especially convenient when using an XML parser within a PHP class, where you can assign the current object as the provider of all handler functions:

```
xml_set_object($this->parser, $this);
```

xml_set_processing_instruction_handler

```
bool xml_set_processing_instruction_handler(resource parser,
    callback handler)
```

This function sets up a handler function that is called when the XML parser encounters a processing instruction (<?*target data*>). The *handler* argument is a string containing the name of a function that must exist when xml_parse is called to parse the document.

The function named by *handler* must accept three arguments: *parser*, *target* and *data*.

❑ The first argument, *parser*, is a reference to the XML parser calling the handler.

❑ The second argument, *target*, contains the target portion of the processing instruction (e.g. for <?php … >, it would contain php).

❑ The third argument, *data*, contains the data that appears within the processing instruction.

If you wish to set up a method as a handler function, pass to *handler* a two-item array containing a reference to the object as the first item, and the name of the method as the second item.

If the handler function is set to an empty string, or to FALSE, the handler in question is disabled. TRUE is returned if the handler is set up; FALSE is returned if the parser is not valid.

DOM Functions

The DOM is an extensive API, and DOM functions in PHP do a very good job of taking into consideration most of the supported functionality. As a result, the supported DOM function list is very large. As this is an object oriented API, it is largely made up of object classes, each with a series of properties and methods:

Object Listing

The DOM API is implemented in PHP by objects of the following classes:

DOMAttr

Represents an attribute in an XML document. Extends DOMNode, inheriting all of that class's properties and methods.

To create a new DOMAttr object directly, use the class's object constructor:

```
$attr = new DOMAttr(string name[, string value]);
```

where *name* is the attribute's name and *value* is the attribute's value.

Don't Use the Constructor!

If you directly create a new DOMAttr object, it will be read-only until you add it to the document (e.g. with appendChild). To create a writable DOMAttr, use the DOMDocument object's createAttribute method instead.

Methods

```
bool $attr->isId()
```

Returns TRUE if the attribute is defined as a unique ID in the DTD for the document, or FALSE if not. Since this requires knowledge of the DTD to check, you must validate the document (e.g. using the DOMDocument's validate method) before this method will return TRUE.

Properties

name
> The name of the attribute. Read-only.

ownerElement
> The DOMElement the attribute belongs to. Read-only.

value
> The value of the attribute.

DOMCharacterData

Represents a section of character data in an XML document. Extends DOMNode, inheriting all of that class's properties and methods.

You're probably looking for DOMText

The DOMText class is a subclass of DOMCharacterData, and represents actual text nodes in the document. For most practical purposes, you'll be dealing with that class, not this one.

Methods

```
$cdata->appendData(string data)
```

Appends the string *data* to the end of the existing data.

```
$cdata->deleteData(int offset, int count)
```

Deletes *count* characters of the current text data beginning at *offset*.

```
$cdata->insertData(int offset, string data)
```

Inserts the string *data* into the existing data at *offset*.

```
$cdata->replaceData(int offset, int count, string data)
```

Deletes *count* characters of the current text data beginning at *offset*, then replaces it with the string *data*.

```
string $cdata->substringData(int offset, int count)
```

Returns the substring beginning at *offset* and running for up to *count* characters.

Properties

data
> The complete string of text data.

length
> The length in characters of text data. Read-only.

DOMComment

Represents a comment in an XML document. Extends DOMCharacterData, inheriting all of that class's properties and methods.

To create a new DOMComment object directly, use the class's object constructor:

```
$comment = new DOMComment([string value]);
```

where *value* is the text content of the comment.

Don't Use the Constructor!

If you directly create a new DOMComment object, it will be read-only until you add it to the document (e.g. with appendChild). To create a writable DOMComment, use the DOMDocument object's createComment method instead.

DOMDocument

Represents an XML document. Extends DOMNode, inheriting all of that class's properties and methods.

To create a new DOMDocument object directly, use the class's object constructor:

```
$dom = new DOMDocument([string version[, string encoding]]);
```

where *version* is the XML version number for the document (e.g. 1.0), and *encoding* is the character encoding for the document (US-ASCII, ISO-8859-1 or UTF-8).

Methods

```
DOMAttr $dom->createAttribute(string name)
```

Creates a new DOMAttr object associated with this document for an attribute *name*.

```
DOMAttr $dom->createAttributeNS(string namespaceURI,
    string qualifiedName)
```

Creates a new DOMAttr object associated with this document within the namespace specified by the URI *namespaceURI* and with the prefix specified in the *qualifiedName* (i.e., *prefix:name*).

```
DOMCDATASection $dom->createCDATASection(string data)
```

Creates a new DOMCDATASection object associated with this document with the text content *data*.

```
DOMComment $dom->createComment(string data)
```

Creates a new DOMComment object associated with this document with the text content *data*.

```
DOMDocumentFragment $dom->createDocumentFragment()
```

Creates a new `DOMDocumentFragment` object associated with this document.

```
DOMElement $dom->createElement(string name[, string value])
```

Creates a new `DOMElement` object associated with this document with the specified tag *name* and optionally containing a text node with the text *value*.

```
DOMElement $dom->createElementNS(string namespaceURI,
    string qualifiedName[, string value])
```

Creates a new `DOMElement` object associated with this document within the namespace specified by the URI *namespaceURI* and with the prefix specified in the *qualifiedName* (i.e. *prefix:name*), and optionally containing a text node with the text *value*.

```
DOMEntityReference $dom->createEntityReference(string name)
```

Creates a new `DOMEntityReference` object associated with this document with the specified *name* (not including & and ;).

```
DOMProcessingInstruction $dom->createProcessingInstruction(
    string target[, string data])
```

Creates a new `DOMProcessingInstruction` object associated with this document with the specified *target* and optionally containing the specified *data* string.

```
DOMText $dom->createTextNode(string content)
```

Creates a new `DOMText` object associated with this document with the specified *content* string.

```
DOMElement $dom->getElementById(string elementId)
```

Fetches the `DOMElement` object for the document element with the ID *elementId*, if it exists. Because the DOM has no way of knowing which attribute to use as the ID until the document's DTD is parsed, you must first validate the document with the `DOMDocument`'s `validate` method.

```
DOMNodeList $dom->getElementsByTagName(string name)
```

Fetches a `DOMNodeList` object containing all of the `DOMElement` objects with the specified tag *name* in the document. A *name* of * will fetch all elements in the document.

```
DOMNodeList $dom->getElementsByTagNameNS(string namespaceURI,
    string localName)
```

Fetches a `DOMNodeList` object containing all of the `DOMElement` objects with the specified tag *localName* (without the prefix) in the document, and within the namespace with the specified URI. A *localName* or *namespaceURI* of * will fetch all elements within the specified *namespaceURI*, or all elements with the specified *localName*, respectively.

`DOMNode $dom->importNode(DOMNode importedNode[, bool deep])`

Copies the supplied *importedNode* (potentially from another document) into a new `DOMNode` object associated with this document. If *deep* is given and is `TRUE`, all child nodes are recursively copied as well.

`bool $dom->load(string filename)`

Loads the specified XML *filename* into this `DOMDocument` object. Can also be called statically to create a new `DOMDocument` object from a file using default options (i.e., `$dom = DOMDocument::load(filename);`).

`bool $dom->loadHTML(string source)`

Parses the provided HTML *source* code, which may or may not be well-formed (i.e., the parser deals with it as best it can), into this `DOMDocument` object. Can also be called statically to create a new `DOMDocument` object from HTML code using default options (i.e., `$dom = DOMDocument::loadHTML(source);`).

`bool $dom->loadHTMLFile(string filename)`

Loads the specified HTML *filename*, which may or may not be well-formed (i.e., the parser deals with it as best it can), into this `DOMDocument` object. Can also be called statically to create a new `DOMDocument` object from an HTML file using default options (i.e., `$dom = DOMDocument::loadHTMLFile(filename);`).

`bool $dom->loadXML(string source)`

Parses the provided XML *source* code into this `DOMDocument` object. Can also be called statically to create a new `DOMDocument` object from XML code using default options (i.e., `$dom = DOMDocument::loadXML(source);`).

`$dom->normalize()`

Normalizes this document according to standard XML normalization rules in preparation for comparison with potentially equivalent documents. Whitespace is collapsed, adjacent text nodes are combined, etc.

`bool $dom->relaxNGValidate(string filename)`

Validates the document according to the relaxNG[1] schema in the file specified by *filename*. Returns TRUE if valid, FALSE if not.

```
bool $dom->relaxNGValidateSource(string source)
```

Validates the document according to the relaxNG[2] schema *source* code provided. Returns TRUE if valid, FALSE if not.

```
mixed $dom->save(string filename)
```

Stores this document as an XML file with the given *filename*. Returns the size of the file in bytes, or FALSE if an error occurs.

```
string $dom->saveHTML()
```

Returns the HTML source code for this document.

```
mixed $dom->saveHTMLFile(string filename)
```

Stores this document as an HTML file with the given *filename*. Returns the size of the file in bytes, or FALSE if an error occurs.

```
string $dom->saveXML([DOMNode node])
```

Returns the XML source code for this document, or for the portion of this document rooted at *node*, if specified.

```
bool $dom->schemaValidate(string filename)
```

Validates the document according to the XML Schema file specified by *filename*. Returns TRUE if valid, FALSE if not.

```
bool $dom->schemaValidateSource(string source)
```

Validates the document according to the XML Schema *source* code provided. Returns TRUE if valid, FALSE if not.

```
bool $dom->validate()
```

Validates the document according to its DTD. Returns TRUE if valid, FALSE if not, or if no DTD is specified by the document.

```
int $dom->xinclude([int options])
```

---

[1] http://www.relaxng.org/
[2] http://www.relaxng.org/

Processes the document for XInclude[3] includes, substituting `<xi:include>` tags for the content they point to.

Properties

actualEncoding

The encoding actually being used by this document. Read-only.

config

The `DOMConfiguration` object that encapsulates the configuration of this document. Read-only.

doctype

The `DOMDocumentType` object that encapsulates the Document Type Declaration of this document. Read-only.

documentElement

The root `DOMElement` of this document. Read-only.

documentURI

The location of the document, or `NULL`.

encoding

The encoding assigned to this document (e.g., `US-ASCII`, `ISO-8859-1` or `UTF-8`).

formatOutput

If `TRUE`, the document code will be indented on output.

implementation

The `DOMImplementation` that is responsible for handling this document. Read-only.

preserveWhiteSpace

Defaults to `TRUE`, which preserves redundant whitespace. If set to `FALSE`, consecutive whitespace characters in the document are collapsed to a single space.

---

[3] http://www.w3.org/TR/xinclude/

recover

Set this to TRUE before loading a document you suspect will be not well-formed. The parser will do its best to recover from missing tags and other such problems.

resolveExternals

Set this to TRUE before loading a document to include the contents of external entities declared in the DTD of this document.

standalone

If TRUE, this document will identify itself as being self-contained. No external entities or DTDs will be required to fully parse it.

strictErrorChecking

Defaults to TRUE, and causes the parser to throw a DOMException whenever a parsing error occurs.

substituteEntities

If TRUE, the contents of entities declared in the DTD will be substituted into this document as it is parsed.

validateOnParse

If TRUE, causes the document to be validated automatically as it is parsed, avoiding the need to call the validate afterwards.

version

The XML version in use by this document (e.g. 1.0).

xmlEncoding

This gives the encoding specified by the XML declaration of the parsed document. Documents created in memory, or which do not specify an encoding, will give a value of NULL for this property. Read-only.

xmlStandalone

This indicates whether the parsed document was declared as standalone in its XML declaration. If not specified, this defaults to FALSE.

xmlVersion

This gives the encoding specified in the XML declaration of the parsed document. If not declared, this defaults to 1.0.

DOMDocumentType

Represents the document type declaration of an XML document. Extends `DOMNode`, inheriting all of that class's properties and methods.

Properties

entities

A `DOMNamedNodeMap` object containing the internal and external entities declared in the DTD. Read only.

internalSubset

A string containing the entire internal subset of the DTD, that is, the portion of the DTD that is contained within the document itself.

name

The name of the DTD—the name of the root element of a valid document. Read only.

notations

A `DOMNamedNodeMap` object containing the notations declared in the DTD. Read only.

publicId

The public identifier string for a well-known or application-standard document type. Read-only.

systemId

The system identifier for this document type, that is, the URL to the DTD for this document. Read-only.

DOMElement

Represents an element in an XML document. Extends `DOMNode`, inheriting all of that class's properties and methods.

To create a new `DOMElement` object directly, use the class's object constructor:

```
$el = new DOMElement(string name[, string value[,
    string namespaceURI]]);
```

where *name* is the element's name (with a namespace prefix if *namespaceURI* is specified), *value* is the element's optional text content (which will be created as a `DOMText` object), and *namespaceURI* is the optional namespace identifier for this element.

Don't Use the Constructor!

If you directly create a new `DOMElement` object, it will be read-only until you add it to the document (e.g. with `appendChild`). To create a writable `DOMElement`, use the `DOMDocument` object's `createElement` or `createElementNS` method instead.

Methods

`string $el->getAttribute(string name)`

Returns the value of this element's attribute with the specified *name*, or an empty string if the attribute does not exist.

`DOMAttr $el->getAttributeNode(string name)`

Returns the `DOMAttr` object for this element's attribute with the specified *name*, or `NULL` if the attribute does not exist.

`DOMAttr $el->getAttributeNodeNS(string namespaceURI,`
`    string localName)`

Returns the `DOMAttr` object for this element's attribute with the specified *local-Name* and *namespaceURI*, or `NULL` if the attribute does not exist.

`string $el->getAttributeNS(string namespaceURI, string localName)`

Returns the value of this element's attribute with the specified *localName* and *namespaceURI*, or an empty string if the attribute does not exist.

`DOMNodeList $el->getElementsByTagName(string name)`

Returns a `DOMNodeList` of all descendant elements (that is, all elements contained in this element) with the specified *name*, in the order they occur in the document.

`DOMNodeList $el->getElementsByTagNameNS(string namespaceURI,`
`    string localName)`

Returns a `DOMNodeList` of all descendant elements (that is, all elements contained in this element) with the specified *localName* and *namespaceURL*, in the order they occur in the document.

`bool $el->hasAttribute(string name)`

Returns TRUE if the attribute *name* has a value for this element.

```
bool $el->hasAttributeNS(string namespaceURI, string localName)
```

Returns TRUE if the attribute with *namespaceURI* and *localName* has a value for this element.

```
bool $el->removeAttribute(string name)
```

Removes the attribute with *name* from this element, if it exists. Returns TRUE if successful, FALSE if the attribute did not exist.

```
bool $el->removeAttributeNode(DOMAttr node)
```

Removes the attribute represented by the DOMAttr object *node* from this element. Returns TRUE if successful, FALSE on failure.

```
bool $el->removeAttributeNS(string namespaceURI, string localName)
```

Removes the attribute with the given *namespaceURI* and *localName* from this element. Returns TRUE if successful, FALSE on failure.

```
bool $el->setAttribute(string name, string value)
```

Sets the *value* of the attribute with the given *name* on this element. If it already exists, it is replaced. If it doesn't exist, it is added.

```
DOMAttr $el->setAttributeNode(DOMAttr attr)
```

Sets the attribute given by the DOMAttr object *attr* on this element. If it already exists, it is replaced and the original DOMAttr is returned. If it doesn't exist, it is added and NULL is returned.

```
DOMAttr $el->setAttributeNodeNS(DOMAttr attr)
```

Sets the attribute given by the DOMAttr object *attr* on this element. If it already exists, it is replaced and the original DOMAttr is returned. If it doesn't exist, it is added and NULL is returned.

```
$el->setAttributeNS(string namespaceURI, string qualifiedName,
    string value)
```

Sets the *value* of the attribute with the given *namespaceURI* and *qualifiedName* (i.e., *prefix:name*) on this element. If it already exists, it is replaced. If it doesn't exist, it is added.

Properties

tagName
The element name. Read-only.

DOMEntity

Represents an entity declared in an XML document's DTD. Extends DOMNode, inheriting all of that class's properties and methods.

Properties

actualEncoding
The encoding used to parse this external parsed entity, or NULL if this is an internal or unparsed entity, or if the encoding is not known.

encoding
The encoding specified in the declaration for this external parsed entity, or NULL if this is an internal or unparsed entity, or if the encoding is not known. Read-only.

notationName
The name of the notation assigned to this unparsed entity, or NULL if this is a parsed entity. Read-only.

publicId
The public identifier associated with a well-known or application-standard entity, or NULL if not defined. Read-only.

systemId
The system identifier associated with this entity (that is, the URL to the resource containing the entity's content), or NULL if not defined. Read-only.

version
The version number given in the declaration for this external parsed entity, or NULL if this is an internal or unparsed entity, or if the version is not known. Read-only.

DOMEntityReference

Represents a reference to an entity in an XML document. Extends DOMNode, inheriting all of that class's properties and methods.

To create a new DOMEntityReference object directly, use the class's object constructor:

```
$el = new DOMEntityReference(string name);
```

where *name* is the entity name.

Don't Use the Constructor!

It is standard practice to create DOMEntityReference objects using the DOMDocument object's createEntityReference method.

DOMException

Represents an error encountered when attempting to perform an illegal operation on an XML document.

Properties

code
The error code identifying the type of error. See Table A.1 for the possible values. Read-only.

DOMImplementation

Provides methods for performing general DOM operations not related to any particular DOM object.

To create a new DOMImplementation object directly, use the class's object constructor:

```
$domimpl = new DOMImplementation();
```

Don't Use the Constructor!

Most of the time, you will already have a DOMDocument object from which you can obtain the associated DOMImplementation object by getting the value of its implementation property. This ensures that PHP can use the most appropriate implementation of the DOM for the DOMDocument.

Methods

```
DOMDocument $domimpl->createDocument([string namespaceURI[,
    string qualifiedName[, DOMDocumentType doctype]]])
```

Creates a new DOMDocument, optionally with a root element with the specified *namespaceURI* and *qualifiedName* (i.e., *prefix:name*), and optionally with the specified document type declaration (*doctype*).

Table A.1. DOMException Error Code Constants

Constant	Value	Description
DOM_INDEX_SIZE_ERR	1	The index given is negative, or greater than the maximum allowed value.
DOM_STRING_SIZE_ERR	2	The given text string will not fit in a DOMString object.
DOM_HIERARCHY_REQUEST_ERR	3	A node was inserted in an illegal place in the document.
DOM_WRONG_DOCUMENT_ERR	4	A node associated with one document is used with another document.
DOM_INVALID_CHARACTER_ERR	5	The given name or value contains an invalid or illegal character.
DOM_NO_DATA_ALLOWED_ERR	6	Content was added to a node that does not allow content.
DOM_NO_MODIFICATION_ALLOWED_ERR	7	A read-only object was modified.
DOM_NOT_FOUND_ERR	8	A node that does not exist was referenced.
DOM_NOT_SUPPORTED_ERR	9	The DOM support in PHP does not provide the requested functionality.
DOM_INUSE_ATTRIBUTE_ERR	10	An attribute that is already in use elsewhere was added again.
DOM_INVALID_STATE_ERR	11	An object that is no longer usable was used.
DOM_SYNTAX_ERR	12	The given string is invalid, as it does not conform to the required format.
DOM_INVALID_MODIFICATION_ERR	13	The type of an object was modified illegally.
DOM_NAMESPACE_ERR	14	The specified operation violates namespace rules.
DOM_INVALID_ACCESS_ERR	15	The requested operation is not supported.
DOM_VALIDATION_ERR	16	The requested change to the document would make it invalid.

```
DOMDocumentType $domimpl->createDocumentType(
    [string qualifiedName[, string publicId[, string systemId]]])
```

Creates a document type declaration with the specified *qualifiedName* (i.e., *prefix:name*), the public identifier for a well-known or application-standard document type *publicId*, and the system identifier for the DTD (that is, the URL where an external DTD may be found).

```
bool $domimpl->hasFeature(string feature, string version)
```

Returns TRUE if PHP's DOM implementation supports the specified *feature* of the specified *version*. Features include Core, XML, HTML, Views, Stylesheets and more. For a full list, see the DOM specification.[4]

DOMNode

Due to inheritance, all nodes in the DOM (documents, elements, attributes, etc.) support the methods and properties in this class.

Methods

```
DOMNode $node->appendChild(DOMNode newnode)
```

Adds *newnode* as the last child of this node. Returns the added node.

```
DOMNode $node->cloneNode([bool deep])
```

Creates and returns a copy of this node (and if *deep* is true, all descendant nodes).

```
bool $node->hasAttributes()
```

Returns TRUE if this node is an element that has attributes.

```
bool $node->hasChildNodes()
```

Returns TRUE if this node has children.

```
DOMNode $node->insertBefore(DOMNode newnode[, DOMNode refnode])
```

Adds *newnode* as a child of this node, placing it before *refnode* in the child order (or adding it as the last child if *refnode* is not given). Returns the added node, which must be used if further changes to the node are required.

---

[4] http://www.w3.org/TR/2000/REC-DOM-Level-2-Core-20001113/introduction.html#ID-Conformance

`bool $node->isSameNode(DOMNode node)`

Returns TRUE if *node* and this node are one and the same. Two different nodes can have identical content—this method will still return FALSE.

`bool $node->isSupported(string feature, string version)`

Checks if the specified *feature* in the specified *version* is supported by this node. See the `hasFeature` method of `DOMImplementation`.

`string $node->lookupNamespaceURI(string prefix)`

Returns the namespace URI associated with the given *prefix* for this node.

`string $node->lookupPrefix(string namespaceURI)`

Returns the namespace prefix associated with the given *namespaceURI* for this node.

`$node->normalize()`

Normalizes this node according to standard XML normalization rules in preparation for comparison with potentially equivalent nodes. Whitespace is collapsed, adjacent text nodes are collapsed, etc.

`DOMNode $node->removeChild(DOMNode oldnode)`

Removes the child node *oldnode* from this node. Returns the removed child, or NULL if it could not be removed.

`DOMNode $node->replaceChild(DOMNode newnode, DOMNode oldnode)`

Removes the existing child *oldnode* and replaces it with *newnode*. Returns the removed child.

Properties

attributes
> A `DOMNamedNodeMap` (essentially an associative array) containing the attributes of this node and their values, or NULL if this node is not an element. Read-only.

baseURI
> The absolute URI of this node, or NULL if it is unknown. Read-only.

childNodes

A DOMNodeList of the children of this node. Read-only.

firstChild

The first child of this node, or NULL if there are no children. Read-only.

lastChild

The last child of this node, or NULL if there are no children. Read-only.

localName

The local name of this node in a namespace-aware document, or the full element name if no namespace is assigned. Read-only.

namespaceURI

The namespace URI of this node in a namespace-aware document, or NULL if none is specified. Read-only.

nextSibling

The node immediately following this node, or NULL if this node is the last child of its parent. Read-only.

nodeName

The name of this node (e.g. the element or attribute name). Read-only.

nodeType

The type of the node. See Table A.2 for the list of possible values. Read-only.

nodeValue

The value of this node (e.g. the text content or attribute value).

ownerDocument

The DOMDocument object for the document to which this node belongs. Read-only.

parentNode

The parent node of this node. Read-only.

prefix

The namespace prefix of this node in a namespace-aware document, or NULL if none is specified.

previousSibling

The node immediately preceding this node, or NULL if this node is the first child of its parent. Read-only.

textContent
The text content of this node including all descendants. If written to, all children will be replaced with a text node with the specified content.

Table A.2. DOMNode Type Constants

Constant	Value	Object Class
XML_ELEMENT_NODE	1	DOMElement
XML_ATTRIBUTE_NODE	2	DOMAttr
XML_TEXT_NODE	3	DOMText
XML_CDATA_SECTION_NODE	4	DOMCharacterData
XML_ENTITY_REF_NODE	5	DOMEntityReference
XML_ENTITY_NODE	6	DOMEntity
XML_PI_NODE	7	DOMProcessingInstruction
XML_COMMENT_NODE	8	DOMComment
XML_DOCUMENT_NODE	9	DOMDocument
XML_DOCUMENT_TYPE_NODE	10	DOMDocumentType
XML_DOCUMENT_FRAG_NODE	11	DOMDocumentFragment
XML_NOTATION_NODE	12	DOMNotation
XML_HTML_DOCUMENT_NODE	13	DOMDocument
XML_DTD_NODE	14	DTD nodes are not represented in PHP's DOM representation. These constants are included as defined in the DOM standard for completeness.
XML_ELEMENT_DECL_NODE	15	
XML_ATTRIBUTE_DECL_NODE	16	
XML_ENTITY_DECL_NODE	17	
XML_NAMESPACE_DECL_NODE	18	

DOMNodeList

Essentially an array of DOMNode objects, objects of this class may be iterated through with a PHP foreach loop.

Methods

```
DOMNode $nlist->item(int index)
```

Fetches the DOMNode at position *index* in the list (0 for the first DOMNode).

Properties

length
> The number of DOMNodes in the list. Read-only.

DOMNotation

Represents a notation declared in the document's DTD. Extends DOMNode, inheriting all of that class's properties and methods.

Properties

publicId
> The public ID of a well-known or application-standard notation. Read-only.

systemId
> The system ID of a notation, often a URL that enables the processing application to read data of the type indicated by the notation. Read-only.

DOMProcessingInstruction

Represents a processing instruction (i.e., `<?target data>`) in an XML document. Extends DOMNode, inheriting all of that class's properties and methods.

To create a new DOMProcessingInstruction object directly, use the class's object constructor:

```
$pi = new DOMProcessingInstruction(string target[, string data]);
```

where *target* is the processing instruction's target and *data* is the data contained in the processing instruction.

Don't Use the Constructor!

If you directly create a new DOMProcessingInstruction object, it will be read-only until you add it to the document (e.g. with **appendChild**). To create a writable DOMProcessingInstruction, use the DOMDocument object's **createProcessingInstruction** method instead.

Properties

data
>The data string contained in the processing instruction.

target
>The target of the processing instruction. Read-only.

DOMText

Represents a string of plain text in an XML document. Extends DOMCharacterData, inheriting all of that class's properties and methods.

To create a new DOMText object directly, use the class's object constructor:

```
$text = new DOMText([string value]);
```

where *value*, if specified, is the text string in the node. If no value is specified, an empty text node is created.

Don't Use the Constructor!

It is standard practice to create a new text node using the createTextNode method of the DOMDocument object with which it should be associated.

Methods

```
bool $text->isWhitespaceInElementContent()
```

Returns TRUE if this text node contains only whitespace, the document has been validated, and the DTD requires that the parent element of this text node contains only child elements (no text nodes). In other words, returns TRUE if this text node is nonsignificant whitespace for validation purposes (and likely application purposes).

```
DOMText $text->splitText(int offset)
```

Splits this text node into two text nodes, where this node will contain text content up to specified *offset* and the new node will contain the remaining content (if any). The new node is inserted as a sibling following this node in the document (if it has a parent node), and is returned as a DOMText object.

Properties

wholeText
Returns the text of this and all adjacent text nodes in the document (including expanded entities). Read-only.

DOMXPath

An object of this type enables XPath queries to be applied to an XML document.

To create a new DOMXPath object, use the class's object constructor:

```
$xpath = new DOMXPath(DOMDocument doc]);
```

where *doc* is the document to which queries will be applied.

Methods

```
bool $xpath->registerNamespace(string prefix, string namespaceURI)
```

Registers a namespace *prefix* for a *namespaceURI* with this object, so that XPath expressions that include a namespace prefix will correctly map that prefix to the equivalent namespace in the document.

```
mixed $xpath->evaluate(string expression[, DOMNode contextnode])
```

Evaluates an XPath *expression* returning either a single node object (e.g., a DOMElement) or a DOMNodeList containing all the matching nodes. The expression is evaluated relative to the specified *contextnode*, or relative to the root element if none is specified.

```
mixed $xpath->query(string expression[, DOMNode contextnode])
```

Works just like evaluate, except that the result is always returned as a DOMNodeList, even if only a single node matches the query.

Properties

document
The document that this object will query. Read-only.

Function Listing

In addition to the objects listed above, the DOM API includes the following standalone function:

```
DOMElement dom_import_simplexml(SimpleXMLElement node)
```

Converts a SimpleXML element object into a DOMElement, which may then be imported into a DOMDocument (using its importNode method) and used with the DOM API.

SimpleXML Functions

SimpleXML is new to PHP 5. As its name implies, it provides a simplified way to access the content of XML documents.

Function Listing

The following SimpleXML functions are used to load an XML document or fragment.

```
SimpleXMLElement simplexml_import_dom(DOMNode node[,
    string class_name])
```

This function takes a node object from the DOM API and converts it into a SimpleXML representation of the document or fragment. If an error occurs, FALSE is returned instead.

```
SimpleXMLElement simplexml_load_file(string filename)
```

This function will convert the XML code in *filename* into a SimpleXML representation of the document or fragment. If an error occurs, FALSE is returned instead.

```
SimpleXMLElement simplexml_load_string(string data)
```

This function will convert a string of XML code (*data*) into a SimpleXML representation of the document or fragment. If an error occurs, FALSE is returned instead.

SimpleXMLElement Methods

When an XML document or fragment is loaded with SimpleXML, a `SimpleXMLElement` object is the result. This object supports the following methods:

```
string $simplexml->asXML()
```

Converts this document or fragment into a string of XML code.

```
SimpleXMLElement $simplexml->attributes()
```

Returns a `SimpleXMLElement` object that may be treated as an associative array of attribute names to attribute values for this element.

```
SimpleXMLElement $simplexml->children()
```

Returns a `SimpleXMLElement` object that may be treated as an array of the children of this element.

```
array $simplexml->xpath(string path)
```

Evaluates the XPath expression given in *path* relative to this SimpleXML node. Returns an array of `SimpleXMLElement` objects that match the query.

Appendix B: CMS Administration Tool

In this appendix, we're going to finish the CMS administration tool. We're going to pick up where we left off in Chapter 7, to build administrative forms and components for our remaining content types. When we're finished, the administration tool will be able to handle Web copy and news items, not just articles; it will also allow you to manage administrators, authors, and categories.

Picking Up Where We Left Off

In Chapter 7, which was the last point at which we spent significant time on the CMS administration tool, we built a login and verification page, an administrative index page, and the forms and logic required to list, add, edit, and delete articles.

In this appendix, we're going to repeat this process for Web copy, news items, authors, site administrators, and categories. The first two items, Web copy and news items, will be very similar in functionality and structure to articles; the last three will be a good opportunity to examine some alternative ways of handling XML information.

Every time we add another set of pages to the administration tool, we want to provide access to those pages on the administrative index page. When we're done, our administrative index content will look like Figure B.1.

Let's get started.

Managing Web Copy

Web copy is very similar to articles in terms of its structure, although it does use different XML elements. It's also similar to articles in terms of its function; however, Web copy items are used in the kinds of Web pages that are more typically likened to "About Us," "Contact Us," and other such pages.

Users often want to know who authored an article; with Web copy, this is usually not the case. Web copy typically has to include a headline and navigation label that's appropriate to the site's navigation; not so with articles—usually, they're retrieved via a search request. These slight variations in structure and function prompted me to separate Web copy from articles in the design of our CMS.

Figure B.1. The appearance of our administrative index page.

To refresh your memory, here's the code of a typical Web copy content item:

File: **xml/webcopy20040903112345.xml**

```
<?xml version="1.0" encoding="iso-8859-1"?>
<webcopy id="webcopy20040903112345">
  <headline>Creating an XML-powered CMS</headline>
  <navigationlabel>XML CMS 101</navigationlabel>
  <description>Here are some articles that will further your XML
    knowledge.</description>
  <pubdate>2004-01-20</pubdate>
  <status>live</status>
  <body><![CDATA[
  <h1>Creating an XML-powered CMS</h1>
  <p>Are you tired of waiting around for your "IT Guy" or
    expensive designer to update your web site? Well, those days
    will be long forgotten if you buy our XML-powered CMS! With
    this revolutionary new tool, you can make quick and easy
    updates to your own web site! Forget all the hassles! It
    slices, it dices!</p>
```

```
]]></body>
</webcopy>
```

You'll notice right away that the `webcopy` element has an `id` attribute composed of the string `webcopy` with a time stamp appended in the format *YYYYMMDDHHMMSS*. In this regard, the `id` uniquely identifies each Web copy document—the article's `id` fulfills the same function.

You'll also notice that we use a CDATA section inside the `body` element of Web copy, as we did with articles. Some may view this as a controversial decision, but it will save us a lot of time, as we won't have to validate this text. Of course, it would be to your advantage to make sure that you're using XHTML-compliant markup in these sections.

Unlike the article content type, we do not have `authorid`, `categoryid`, or `keywords` elements in the Web copy content type. And we have a `navigationlabel` element to provide a shorter version of the headline for concise titles in navigation systems.

Web Copy Index Page

Let's build the first page associated with the Web copy content type: an index page that will list all Web copy documents, provide us with the opportunity to create new ones, and allow us to edit and delete existing Web copy documents.

As with our article management page, we must first include our access control and common include files:

File: **webcopytool.php** (excerpt)

```php
<?php
  include 'security.inc.php';
  include_once '../common.inc.php';
?>
```

Next up is some pretty standard HTML boilerplate. Again, this is strikingly similar to the article management page:

File: **webcopytool.php** (excerpt)

```html
<!DOCTYPE html PUBLIC "-//W3C//DTD XHTML 1.0 Transitional//EN"
    "http://www.w3.org/TR/xhtml1/DTD/xhtml1-transitional.dtd">
<html xmlns="http://www.w3.org/1999/xhtml">
<head>
<meta http-equiv="Content-Type"
```

```
      content="text/html; charset=iso-8859-1" />
<title>Web Copy Index</title>
<link rel="stylesheet" type="text/css" href="../xmlcms.css" />
</head>
<body>
<h1>Web Copy Index</h1>
<p><a href="webcopytool_create.php">Create New Web Copy</a></p>
<p><a href="index.php">Cancel</a></p>
```

Next, we use a `while` loop and SimpleXML to process the `xml` directory and pull out all the XML files whose filenames start with `webcopy`. These candidates are inspected with SimpleXML, which we use to pull unique IDs and headlines into a HTML list, with links to edit and delete each Web copy document:

File: **webcopytool.php (excerpt)**

```
<ul>
<?php
$handle = opendir($fileDir);
while (($file = readdir($handle)) !== FALSE) {
  if (is_dir($fileDir . $file)) continue;
  if (!eregi("^webcopy.*\.xml$", $file)) continue;

  $wcFile = simplexml_load_file($fileDir . $file);
  echo '<li>' . htmlentities($wcFile->headline);
  echo ' <a href="webcopytool_edit.php?id=' . $wcFile['id'] .
    '">edit</a>';
  echo ' <a href="doWebcopyDelete.php?id=' . $wcFile['id'] .
    '">delete</a></li>';
}
?>
</ul>
</body>
</html>
```

This page displays as shown in Figure B.2.

Figure B.2. The Web copy index page.

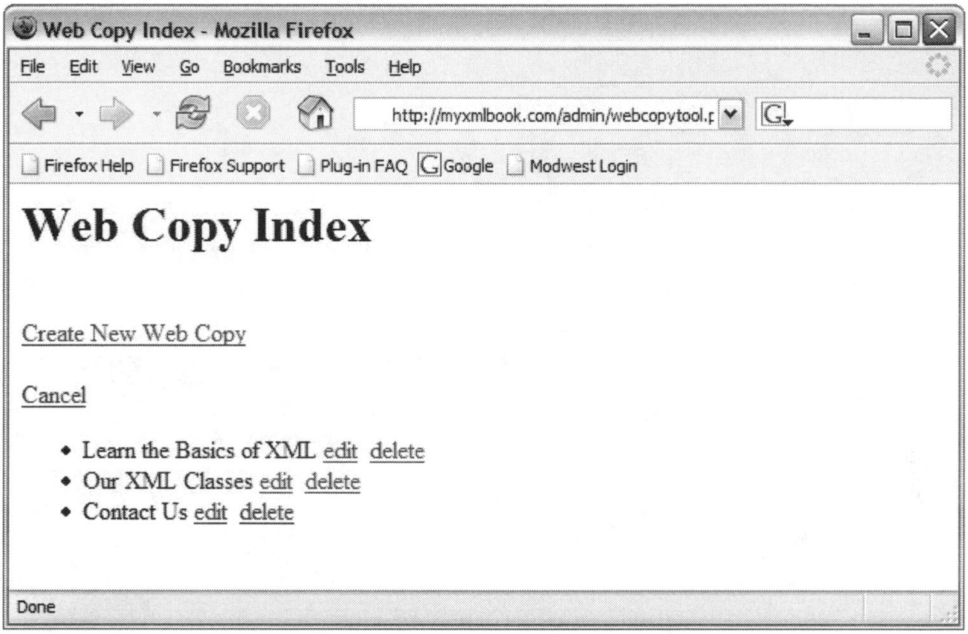

Web Copy Creation Page

The next step is to build the form that allows us to create new Web copy items. This is essentially a very simple form that posts its contents to a PHP file, doWebcopyCeate.php, which does all the heavy lifting.

Here is the markup and code for the form:

File: **webcopytool_create.php**

```php
<?php
include 'security.inc.php';
?>
<!DOCTYPE html PUBLIC "-//W3C//DTD XHTML 1.0 Transitional//EN"
    "http://www.w3.org/TR/xhtml1/DTD/xhtml1-transitional.dtd">
<html xmlns="http://www.w3.org/1999/xhtml">
<head>
<meta http-equiv="Content-Type"
    content="text/html; charset=iso-8859-1" />
<title>Create New Web Copy</title>
<link rel="stylesheet" type="text/css" href="../xmlcms.css" />
```

```
<link rel="stylesheet" type="text/css" href="forms.css" />
</head>
<body>
<h1>Create New Web Copy</h1>
<p><a href="webcopytool.php">Cancel</a></p>
<form action="doWebcopyCreate.php" method="post">
<div class="fields">
  <p>
    <label for="headline">Headline</label>
    <input type="text" id="headline" name="headline" class="text"
      />
  </p>
  <p>
    <label for="headline">Navigation Label</label>
    <input type="text" id="navlabel" name="navlabel" class="text"
      />
  </p>
  <p>
    <label for="status">Status</label>
    <select id="status" name="status">
      <option value="in progress">In Progress</option>
      <option value="live">Live</option>
    </select>
  </p>
  <p>
    <label for="description">Description</label>
    <textarea id="description" name="description"></textarea>
  </p>
  <p>
    <label for="body">Web Copy Body (HTML)</label>
    <textarea id="body" name="body"></textarea>
  </p>
</div>
<div class="actions">
  <input type="submit" value="Add Web Copy" />
  <input type="reset" value="Reset" />
</div>
</form>
</body>
</html>
```

Because this form is very similar to that generated by the `articletool_create.php` file we wrote in Chapter 7, I won't spend much time on it. You can see what it looks like in Figure B.3.

Figure B.3. The Web copy creation form.

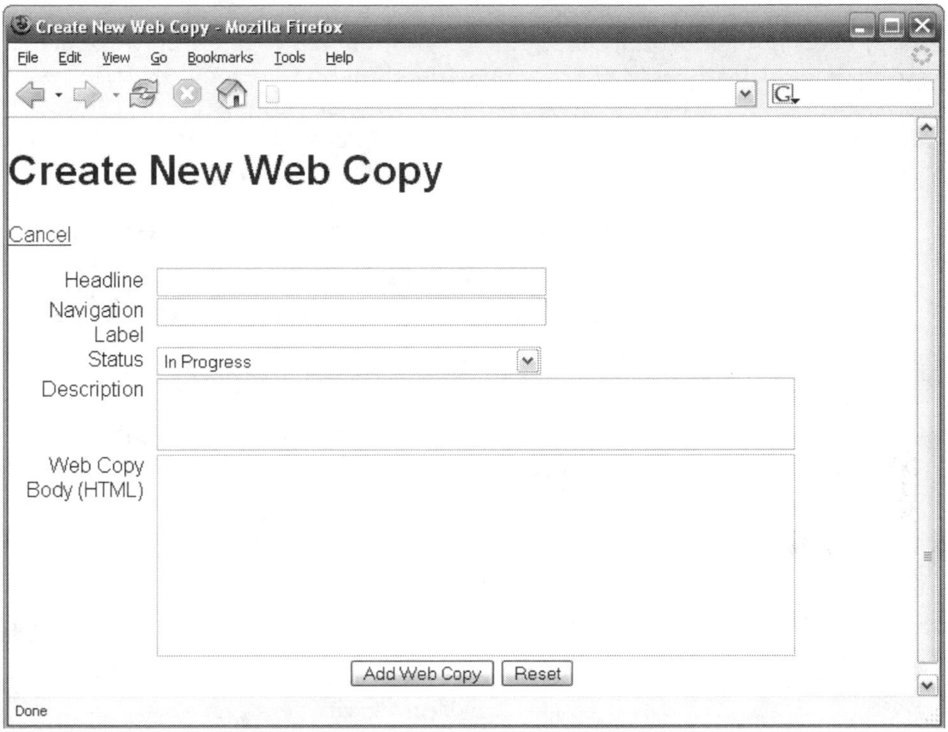

New Web Copy Processing Script

The doWebcopyCreate.php file takes the submitted form values from webcopy-tool_create.php and turns them into a valid XML file. It's modeled very closely on the doArticleCreate.php file, which is used by the system to create articles.

In the first part of the file, we need to create a new DOMDocument, then create the file's root element, webcopy. Note that we're using the DOM here to create a new XML document from scratch:

File: **doWebcopyCreate.php (excerpt)**

```php
<?php
include 'security.inc.php';
include_once '../common.inc.php';

$doc = new DOMDocument();
```

```
$root = $doc->createElement('webcopy');
$root = $doc->appendChild($root);
```

Next, we add a unique id attribute to this root element. The way we generate the unique identifier is to use PHP's date function, and prepend the string web-copy to the result. Just in case, we also have to check to ensure that no other Web copy file has the same unique ID. If we do detect a collision, we add one second to the timestamp in our id attribute and check again:

File: **doWebcopyCreate.php** (excerpt)

```
$timestamp = date('YmdHis');
do {
  $id = 'webcopy' . $timestamp++;
} while (file_exists($fileDir . $id . '.xml'));
$root->setAttribute('id', $id);
```

Next, we create our headline, navigationlabel, description, pubdate, status, and body elements:

File: **doWebcopyCreate.php** (excerpt)

```
$head = $doc->createElement('headline');
$root->appendChild($head);
$htext = $doc->createTextNode($_POST['headline']);
$head->appendChild($htext);

$navlabel = $doc->createElement('navigationlabel');
$root->appendChild($navlabel);
$navtext = $doc->createTextNode($_POST['navlabel']);
$navlabel->appendChild($navtext);

$desc = $doc->createElement('description');
$root->appendChild($desc);
$dtext = $doc->createTextNode($_POST['description']);
$desc->appendChild($dtext);

$pub = $doc->createElement('pubdate');
$root->appendChild($pub);
$pubtext = $doc->createTextNode(date('Y-m-d'));
$pub->appendChild($pubtext);

$stat = $doc->createElement('status');
$root->appendChild($stat);
$stext = $doc->createTextNode($_POST['status']);
$stat->appendChild($stext);
```

```
$body = $doc->createElement('body');
$root->appendChild($body);
$cdata = $doc->createCDATASection($_POST['body']);
$body->appendChild($cdata);
```

Last, but not least, we write to the file and return the administrative user to the Web Copy Index page.

File: **doWebcopyCreate.php** (excerpt)

```
$filename = $fileDir . $id . '.xml';
$doc->save($filename);

header('location: webcopytool.php');
?>
```

Web Copy Editing Page

The next step in the process is to create a page from which we can edit Web copy items. This page is identical to `webcopytool_create.php` with the exception that it must open the specified XML file and load the existing values into the appropriate fields.

For this purpose, we'll use SimpleXML. For example, we can open an XML file with:

File: **webcopytool_edit.php** (excerpt)

```
$file = simplexml_load_file($fileDir . $_GET['id'] . '.xml');
```

We can display a value, such as a headline, in a form field like this:

File: **webcopytool_edit.php** (excerpt)

```
<input type="text" id="headline" name="headline" class="text"
    value="<?php echo htmlentities($file->headline); ?>" />
```

Here's the entire form. Notice that we do a simple check to ensure that the page does receive an ID of some kind through HTTP GET.

File: **webcopytool_edit.php** (excerpt)

```
<?php
include 'security.inc.php';
include_once '../common.inc.php';

if (!isset($_GET['id']) || $_GET['id'] == '' ||
    !file_exists($fileDir . $_GET['id'] . '.xml')) {
```

```php
  header('location: webcopytool.php');
  exit;
}
$file = simplexml_load_file($fileDir . $_GET['id'] . '.xml');
?>
<!DOCTYPE html PUBLIC "-//W3C//DTD XHTML 1.0 Transitional//EN"
    "http://www.w3.org/TR/xhtml1/DTD/xhtml1-transitional.dtd">
<html xmlns="http://www.w3.org/1999/xhtml">
<head>
<meta http-equiv="Content-Type"
    content="text/html; charset=iso-8859-1" />
<title>Edit Web Copy</title>
<link rel="stylesheet" type="text/css" href="../xmlcms.css" />
<link rel="stylesheet" type="text/css" href="forms.css" />
</head>
<body>
<h1>Edit Web Copy</h1>
<p><a href="webcopytool.php">Cancel</a></p>
<form action="doWebcopyUpdate.php" method="post">
<input type="hidden" name="id" value="<?php
    echo htmlentities($_GET['id']); ?>" />
<div class="fields">
  <p>
    <label for="headline">Headline</label>
    <input type="text" id="headline" name="headline" class="text"
        value="<?php echo htmlentities($file->headline); ?>" />
  </p>
  <p>
    <label for="headline">Navigation Label</label>
    <input type="text" id="navlabel" name="navlabel" class="text"
        value="<?php echo htmlentities($file->navigationlabel);
        ?>" />
  </p>
  <p>
    <label for="status">Status</label>
    <select id="status" name="status">
      <option value="in progress"
          <?php if ((string)$file->status == 'in progress')
          echo 'selected="selected"'?>>In Progress</option>
      <option value="live"
          <?php if ((string)$file->status == 'live')
          echo 'selected="selected"'?>>Live</option>
    </select>
  </p>
  <p>
    <label for="description">Description</label>
```

```
      <textarea id="description" name="description">
<?php echo htmlentities($file->description); ?></textarea>
  </p>
  <p>
    <label for="body">Web Copy Body (HTML)</label>
    <textarea id="body" name="body">
<?php echo htmlentities($file->body); ?></textarea>
  </p>
</div>
<div class="actions">
  <input type="submit" value="Update Web Copy" />
  <input type="reset" value="Reset" />
</div>
</form>
</body>
</html>
```

As you can see, this form posts to a file named doWebcopyUpdate.php. This file has much the same functionality as doWebcopyCreate.php, except that it has to update a piece of Web copy, not create one from scratch.

Web Copy Update Processing Script

This script is almost exactly the same as doWebcopyCreate.php, except that:

1. It deletes the file it's currently working on before writing a new file.

2. It doesn't have to work quite as hard to come up with a unique ID, as one has already been assigned to the content item.

Why did I choose to delete the XML file and then create a new file with the same identifier? Because replacing XML nodes in place can be both complicated and expensive, so makes more sense just to recreate the file from scratch.

Here's the code. I've highlighted in bold the two lines that differ from doWebcopyCreate.php:

File: **doWebcopyUpdate.php**

```php
<?php
include 'security.inc.php';
include_once '../common.inc.php';

$doc = new DOMDocument();
$root = $doc->createElement('webcopy');
```

```php
$root = $doc->appendChild($root);

$id = $_POST['id'];
$root->setAttribute('id', $id);

$head = $doc->createElement('headline');
$root->appendChild($head);
$htext = $doc->createTextNode($_POST['headline']);
$head->appendChild($htext);

$navlabel = $doc->createElement('navigationlabel');
$root->appendChild($navlabel);
$navtext = $doc->createTextNode($_POST['navlabel']);
$navlabel->appendChild($navtext);

$desc = $doc->createElement('description');
$root->appendChild($desc);
$dtext = $doc->createTextNode($_POST['description']);
$desc->appendChild($dtext);

$pub = $doc->createElement('pubdate');
$root->appendChild($pub);
$pubtext = $doc->createTextNode(date('Y-m-d'));
$pub->appendChild($pubtext);

$stat = $doc->createElement('status');
$root->appendChild($stat);
$stext = $doc->createTextNode($_POST['status']);
$stat->appendChild($stext);

$body = $doc->createElement('body');
$root->appendChild($body);
$cdata = $doc->createCDATASection($_POST['body']);
$body->appendChild($cdata);

$filename = $fileDir . $id . '.xml';
unlink($filename);
$doc->save($filename);

header('location: webcopytool.php');
?>
```

Web Copy Delete Processing Script

The final thing we have to do is create a script to delete Web copy items.

Here's the code:

File: **doWebcopyDelete.php**

```php
<?php
include 'security.inc.php';
include_once '../common.inc.php';

$filename = $fileDir . $_GET['id'] . '.xml';
unlink($filename);

header('location: webcopytool.php');
?>
```

Managing News Items

News items are designed to contain those short snippets of information that are posted on our site's left-hand side navigation area. Here's a refresher illustrating what a news item might look like:

File: **news20041014061004.xml**

```xml
<?xml version="1.0" encoding="iso-8859-1"?>
<news id="news20041014061004">
  <authorid>1</authorid>
  <categoryid>1</categoryid>
  <headline>XML CMS Almost Ready!</headline>
  <url>http://www.myxmlbook.com/</url>
  <description>The XML CMS is finally almost ready for shipping.
  </description>
  <pubdate>2004-10-14</pubdate>
  <status>live</status>
  <keywords>xml</keywords>
</news>
```

You'll notice that the news content item has many of the same elements as our articles, including `authorid`, `categoryid`, `headline`, `description`, `pubdate`, `status`, and `keywords`. It doesn't have a `body` element, but it contains a unique element, `url`.

For the administration system, we're going to follow the same pattern we used for Web copy and articles, so I'll present the code for each of the forms and scripts with little or no commentary.

News Item Index Page

Here's the main news management page. Notice that it behaves in exactly the same way as the other content item index pages.

File: **newstool.php**

```php
<?php
include 'security.inc.php';
include_once '../common.inc.php';
?>
<!DOCTYPE html PUBLIC "-//W3C//DTD XHTML 1.0 Transitional//EN"
    "http://www.w3.org/TR/xhtml1/DTD/xhtml1-transitional.dtd">
<html xmlns="http://www.w3.org/1999/xhtml">
<head>
<meta http-equiv="Content-Type"
    content="text/html; charset=iso-8859-1" />
<title>News Index</title>
<link rel="stylesheet" type="text/css" href="../xmlcms.css" />
</head>
<body>
<h1>News Index</h1>
<p><a href="newstool_create.php">Create New News Item</a></p>
<p><a href="index.php">Cancel</a></p>
<ul>
<?php
$handle = opendir($fileDir);
while (($file = readdir($handle)) !== FALSE) {
  if (is_dir($fileDir . $file)) continue;
  if (!eregi("^news.*\.xml$", $file)) continue;

  $wcFile = simplexml_load_file($fileDir . $file);
  echo '<li>' . htmlentities($wcFile->headline);
  echo ' <a href="newstool_edit.php?id=' . $wcFile['id'] .
      '">edit</a>';
  echo ' <a href="doNewsDelete.php?id=' . $wcFile['id'] .
      '">delete</a></li>';
}
?>
</ul>
</body>
</html>
```

News Item Creation Page

```php
<?php
include 'security.inc.php';
include_once '../common.inc.php';
?>
<!DOCTYPE html PUBLIC "-//W3C//DTD XHTML 1.0 Transitional//EN"
    "http://www.w3.org/TR/xhtml1/DTD/xhtml1-transitional.dtd">
<html xmlns="http://www.w3.org/1999/xhtml">
<head>
<meta http-equiv="Content-Type"
    content="text/html; charset=iso-8859-1" />
<title>Create New News Item</title>
<link rel="stylesheet" type="text/css" href="../xmlcms.css" />
<link rel="stylesheet" type="text/css" href="forms.css" />
</head>
<body>
<h1>Create New News Item</h1>
<p><a href="newstool.php">Cancel</a></p>
<form action="doNewsCreate.php" method="post">
<div class="fields">
  <p>
    <label for="headline">Headline</label>
    <input type="text" id="headline" name="headline" class="text"
    />
  </p>
  <p>
    <label for="author">Author</label>
    <select id="authorid" name="authorid">
      <?php
        $authors = simplexml_load_file($fileDir . 'authors.xml');
        foreach ($authors->author as $author) {
          echo '<option value="' . htmlentities($author['id']) .
            '">' . htmlentities($author->name) . '</option>';
        }
      ?>
    </select>
  </p>
  <p>
    <label for="category">Category</label>
    <select id="categoryid" name="categoryid">
      <?php
        $cats = simplexml_load_file($fileDir . 'categories.xml');
        foreach ($cats->category as $cat) {
```

```
            echo '<option value="' . htmlentities($cat['id']) .
                '">' . htmlentities($cat['label']) . '</option>';
        }
    ?>
    </select>
</p>
<p>
    <label for="status">Status</label>
    <select id="status" name="status">
        <option value="in progress">In Progress</option>
        <option value="live">Live</option>
    </select>
</p>
<p>
    <label for="keywords">Keywords</label>
    <input type="text" id="keywords" name="keywords" class="text"
        />
</p>
<p>
    <label for="description">Description</label>
    <textarea id="description" name="description"></textarea>
</p>
<p>
    <label for="url">URL</label>
    <input type="text" id="url" name="url" class="text" />
</p>
</div>
<div class="actions">
    <input type="submit" value="Add News Item" />
    <input type="reset" value="Reset" />
</div>
</form>
</body>
</html>
```

New News Item Processing Script

File: **doNewsCreate.php**

```php
<?php
include 'security.inc.php';
include_once '../common.inc.php';

$doc = new DOMDocument();
$root = $doc->createElement('news');
$root = $doc->appendChild($root);
```

```
$timestamp = date('YmdHis');
do {
  $id = 'news' . $timestamp++;
} while (file_exists($fileDir . $id . '.xml'));
$root->setAttribute('id', $id);

$author = $doc->createElement('authorid');
$root->appendChild($author);
$atext = $doc->createTextNode($_POST['authorid']);
$author->appendChild($atext);

$cat = $doc->createElement('categoryid');
$root->appendChild($cat);
$ctext = $doc->createTextNode($_POST['categoryid']);
$cat->appendChild($ctext);

$head = $doc->createElement('headline');
$root->appendChild($head);
$htext = $doc->createTextNode($_POST['headline']);
$head->appendChild($htext);

$url = $doc->createElement('url');
$root->appendChild($url);
$utext = $doc->createTextNode($_POST['url']);
$url->appendChild($utext);

$desc = $doc->createElement('description');
$root->appendChild($desc);
$dtext = $doc->createTextNode($_POST['description']);
$desc->appendChild($dtext);

$pub = $doc->createElement('pubdate');
$root->appendChild($pub);
$pubtext = $doc->createTextNode(date('Y-m-d'));
$pub->appendChild($pubtext);

$stat = $doc->createElement('status');
$root->appendChild($stat);
$stext = $doc->createTextNode($_POST['status']);
$stat->appendChild($stext);

$key = $doc->createElement('keywords');
$root->appendChild($key);
$ktext = $doc->createTextNode($_POST['keywords']);
$key->appendChild($ktext);
```

```
$filename = $fileDir . $id . '.xml';
$doc->save($filename);

header('location: newstool.php');
?>
```

News Item Editing Page

```php
<?php
include 'security.inc.php';
include_once '../common.inc.php';

if (!isset($_GET['id']) || $_GET['id'] == '' ||
    !file_exists($fileDir . $_GET['id'] . '.xml')) {
  header('location: newstool.php');
  exit;
}
$file = simplexml_load_file($fileDir . $_GET['id'] . '.xml');
?>
<!DOCTYPE html PUBLIC "-//W3C//DTD XHTML 1.0 Transitional//EN"
    "http://www.w3.org/TR/xhtml1/DTD/xhtml1-transitional.dtd">
<html xmlns="http://www.w3.org/1999/xhtml">
<head>
<meta http-equiv="Content-Type"
    content="text/html; charset=iso-8859-1" />
<title>Edit News Item</title>
<link rel="stylesheet" type="text/css" href="../xmlcms.css" />
<link rel="stylesheet" type="text/css" href="forms.css" />
</head>
<body>
<h1>Edit News Item</h1>
<p><a href="newstool.php">Cancel</a></p>
<form action="doNewsUpdate.php" method="post">
<input type="hidden" name="id"
    value="<?php echo htmlentities($_GET['id']); ?>" />
<div class="fields">
  <p>
    <label for="headline">Headline</label>
    <input type="text" id="headline" name="headline" class="text"
        value="<?php echo htmlentities($file->headline); ?>" />
  </p>
  <p>
    <label for="author">Author</label>
```

```php
    <select id="authorid" name="authorid">
      <?php
        $authors = simplexml_load_file($fileDir . 'authors.xml');
        foreach ($authors->author as $author) {
          if ((string)$author['id'] == (string)$file->authorid) {
            echo '<option value="' . htmlentities($author['id']) .
                '" selected="selected">' .
                htmlentities($author->name) . '</option>';
          } else {
            echo '<option value="' . htmlentities($author['id']) .
                '">' . htmlentities($author->name) . '</option>';
          }
        }
      ?>
    </select>
</p>
<p>
  <label for="category">Category</label>
  <select id="categoryid" name="categoryid">
    <?php
      $cats = simplexml_load_file($fileDir . 'categories.xml');
      foreach ($cats->category as $cat) {
        if ((string)$cat['id'] == (string)$file->categoryid) {
          echo '<option value="' . htmlentities($cat['id']) .
              '" selected="selected">' .
              htmlentities($cat['label']) . '</option>';
        } else {
          echo '<option value="' . htmlentities($cat['id']) .
              '">' . htmlentities($cat['label']) . '</option>';
        }
      }
    ?>
  </select>
</p>
<p>
  <label for="status">Status</label>
  <select id="status" name="status">
    <option value="in progress"
        <?php if ((string)$file->status == 'in progress')
        echo 'selected="selected"'?>>In Progress</option>
    <option value="live"
        <?php if ((string)$file->status == 'live')
        echo 'selected="selected"'?>>Live</option>
  </select>
</p>
<p>
```

```
    <label for="keywords">Keywords</label>
    <input type="text" id="keywords" name="keywords" class="text"
        value="<?php echo htmlentities($file->keywords); ?>" />
  </p>
  <p>
    <label for="description">Description</label>
    <textarea id="description" name="description">
<?php echo htmlentities($file->description); ?></textarea>
  </p>
  <p>
    <label for="url">URL</label>
    <input type="text" id="url" name="url" class="text"
        value="<?php echo htmlentities($file->url); ?>" />
  </p>
</div>
<div class="actions">
  <input type="submit" value="Update News Item" />
  <input type="reset" value="Reset" />
</div>
</form>
</body>
</html>
```

News Item Update Processing Script

File: **doNewsUpdate.php**

```php
<?php
include 'security.inc.php';
include_once '../common.inc.php';

$doc = new DOMDocument();
$root = $doc->createElement('news');
$root = $doc->appendChild($root);

$id = $_POST['id'];
$root->setAttribute('id', $id);

$author = $doc->createElement('authorid');
$root->appendChild($author);
$atext = $doc->createTextNode($_POST['authorid']);
$author->appendChild($atext);

$cat = $doc->createElement('categoryid');
$root->appendChild($cat);
$ctext = $doc->createTextNode($_POST['categoryid']);
```

```
$cat->appendChild($ctext);

$head = $doc->createElement('headline');
$root->appendChild($head);
$htext = $doc->createTextNode($_POST['headline']);
$head->appendChild($htext);

$url = $doc->createElement('url');
$root->appendChild($url);
$utext = $doc->createTextNode($_POST['url']);
$url->appendChild($utext);

$desc = $doc->createElement('description');
$root->appendChild($desc);
$dtext = $doc->createTextNode($_POST['description']);
$desc->appendChild($dtext);

$pub = $doc->createElement('pubdate');
$root->appendChild($pub);
$pubtext = $doc->createTextNode(date('Y-m-d'));
$pub->appendChild($pubtext);

$stat = $doc->createElement('status');
$root->appendChild($stat);
$stext = $doc->createTextNode($_POST['status']);
$stat->appendChild($stext);

$key = $doc->createElement('keywords');
$root->appendChild($key);
$ktext = $doc->createTextNode($_POST['keywords']);
$key->appendChild($ktext);

$filename = $fileDir . $id . '.xml';
unlink($filename);
$doc->save($filename);

header('location: newstool.php');
?>
```

News Item Delete Processing Script

File: **doNewsDelete.phpdoNewsUpdate.php**

```php
<?php
include 'security.inc.php';
include_once '../common.inc.php';
```

```
$filename = $fileDir . $_GET['id'] . '.xml';
unlink($filename);

header('location: newstool.php');
?>
```

Managing Authors, Administrators, and Categories

I'm going to cover authors, administrators, and categories together because in terms of function and structure, they are all very similar. Instead of each author, administrator, or category residing in a separate file (as is the case for articles and news items), what we're talking about here are lists of authors, administrators, and categories. We can take advantage of this fact in the way that we display and update the listed information.

Let's go through each of these lists, one at a time, so you can see how we handle these kinds of structures.

Managing Authors

First, here's a sample author listing. You'll notice that it's essentially a list of authors and related information:

File: **authors.xml**

```xml
<?xml version="1.0" encoding="iso-8859-1"?>
<authors>
  <author id="1">
    <name>Tom Myer</name>
    <byline>myerman</byline>
    <email>tom@myerman.com</email>
  </author>
  <author id="2">
    <name>Joe Blow</name>
    <byline>joe</byline>
    <email>joe@myerman.com</email>
  </author>
  <author id="4">
    <name>Bill</name>
    <byline>bill</byline>
    <email>bill@myerman.com</email>
```

```
    </author>
  </authors>
```

Because we're presented with a list, we have an opportunity to update the entire file with one form, adding, editing, and deleting items through a unified interface. But first, let's provide an interface to simply view the list of existing authors:

File: **authortool.php**

```php
<?php
include 'security.inc.php';
include_once '../common.inc.php';
?>
<!DOCTYPE html PUBLIC "-//W3C//DTD XHTML 1.0 Transitional//EN"
    "http://www.w3.org/TR/xhtml1/DTD/xhtml1-transitional.dtd">
<html xmlns="http://www.w3.org/1999/xhtml">
<head>
<meta http-equiv="Content-Type"
    content="text/html; charset=iso-8859-1" />
<title>Author Index</title>
<link rel="stylesheet" type="text/css" href="../xmlcms.css" />
</head>
<body>
<h1>Author Index</h1>
<p><a href="authortool_edit.php">Edit Author Listing</a></p>
<p><a href="index.php">Cancel</a></p>
<ul>
<?php
$authors = simplexml_load_file($fileDir . 'authors.xml');
foreach ($authors->author as $author) {
  echo '<li>' . htmlentities($author->name) .
      ' (' . htmlentities($author->email) . ')</li>';
}
?>
</ul>
</body>
</html>
```

Figure B.4 illustrates how our Author Index Page will display.

Figure B.4. The Author Index page.

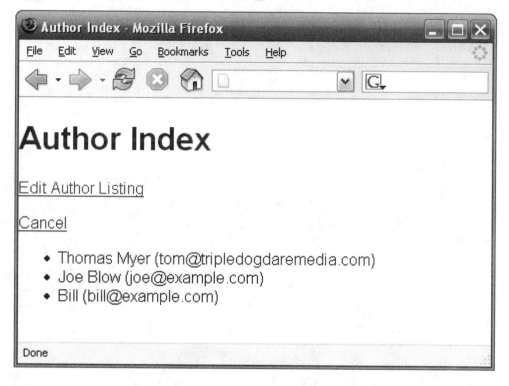

When an administrative user clicks on Edit Author Listing he or she sees the Edit Authors page, the page shown in Figure B.5.

This page essentially consists of a single form that loads the values from the XML file into the appropriate form fields. On each line that's already populated, the administrator is given the opportunity to delete existing authors. Furthermore, the administrator has the chance to add up to three more authors (though this can easily be modified in the code, or scripted to be made more flexible).

Here's the PHP and HTML code that creates this page. It begins similarly to all our other administrative pages: by loading our two include files, and then outputting the HTML boilerplate:

Figure B.5. The Edit Authors page.

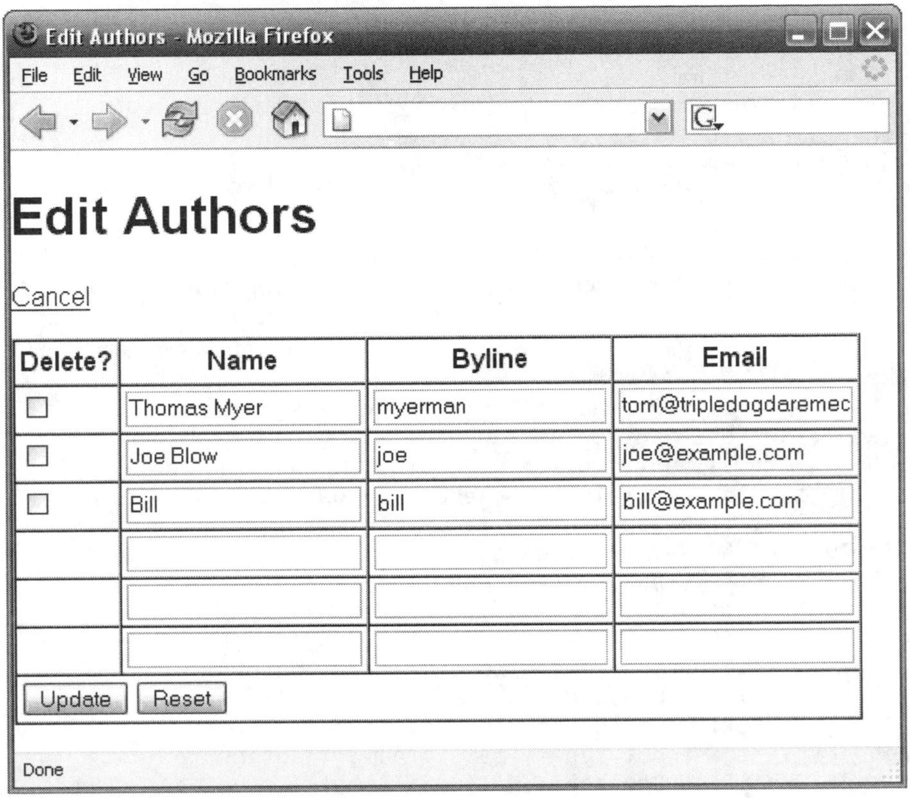

File: **authortool_edit.php** (excerpt)

```php
<?php
include 'security.inc.php';
include_once '../common.inc.php';
?>
<!DOCTYPE html PUBLIC "-//W3C//DTD XHTML 1.0 Transitional//EN"
    "http://www.w3.org/TR/xhtml1/DTD/xhtml1-transitional.dtd">
<html xmlns="http://www.w3.org/1999/xhtml">
<head>
<meta http-equiv="Content-Type"
    content="text/html; charset=iso-8859-1" />
<title>Edit Authors</title>
<link rel="stylesheet" type="text/css" href="../xmlcms.css" />
</head>
<body>
<h1>Edit Authors</h1>
```

```
<p><a href="authortool.php">Cancel</a></p>
<form method="post" action="doAuthorsUpdate.php">
<table border="1" cellspacing="0" cellpadding="3">
  <tr>
    <th>Delete?</th>
    <th>Name</th>
    <th>Byline</th>
    <th>Email</th>
  </tr>
```

We can then use SimpleXML to load up and loop through the authors one at a time, in order to create form elements that contain the proper information:

File: **authortool_edit.php (excerpt)**

```
<?php
$authors = simplexml_load_file($fileDir . 'authors.xml');
foreach ($authors->author as $author) {
  echo "\t<tr valign=\"top\">\n";
  echo "\t\t<td><input type=\"checkbox\" name=\"author[" .
      htmlentities($author['id']) . "][delete]\" " .
      "value=\"true\" /></td>\n";
  echo "\t\t<td><input type=\"text\" name=\"author[" .
      htmlentities($author['id']) . "][name]\" value=\"" .
      htmlentities($author->name) . "\" /></td>\n";
  echo "\t\t<td><input type=\"text\" name=\"author[" .
      htmlentities($author['id']) . "][byline]\" value=\"" .
      htmlentities($author->byline) . "\" /></td>\n";
  echo "\t\t<td><input type=\"text\" name=\"author[" .
      htmlentities($author['id']) . "][email]\" value=\"" .
      htmlentities($author->email) . "\" /></td>\n";
  echo "\t</tr>\n";
}
```

Note that the form fields are specifically named to produce a PHP array in the processing script, from which the various values for each existing author may be accessed (e.g. $_POST['author'][1]['name']).

Additionally, our form includes three blank rows of fields for new authors to be added:

File: **authortool_edit.php (excerpt)**

```
for ($i = 0; $i < 3; $i++) {
  echo "\t<tr valign=\"top\">\n";
  echo "\t\t<td></td>\n";
  echo "\t\t<td><input type=\"text\"
```

```
        name=\"newauthor[name][]\" /></td>\n";
   echo "\t\t<td><input type=\"text\"
        name=\"newauthor[byline][]\" /></td>\n";
   echo "\t\t<td><input type=\"text\"
        name=\"newauthor[email][]\" /></td>\n";
   echo "\t</tr>\n";
 }
 ?>
 <tr><td colspan="4">
   <input type="submit" value="Update" />
   <input type="reset" value="Reset" />
 </td></tr>
</table>
</form>
</body>
</html>
```

This form posts to doAuthorsUpdate.php, in which we will use DOM functions to update the existing authors.xml file. Since more than one administrator may be working with the list of authors at once, we can't simply rebuild a new authors.xml file based on the form submission, because any changes submitted by another administrator since the form was generated would be lost.

So to start, we load our include files and then load up our existing authors.xml file[1] and grab a reference to the authors element. We also create a couple of additional variables, $maxId and $deleteFailures, that we'll need later on in the script.

File: **doAuthorsUpdate.php** (excerpt)

```
<?php
include 'security.inc.php';
include_once '../common.inc.php';

$doc = new DOMDocument::load($fileDir . 'authors.xml');
$root = $doc->documentElement;
$maxId = 0;
$deleteFailures = array();
```

We can then loop through the existing authors in our XML file:

File: **doAuthorsUpdate.php** (excerpt)

```
foreach ($root->getElementsByTagName('author') as $xAuthor) {
```

---

[1]The script assumes such a file exists, so to initialize an empty copy of the CMS, you will need an authors.xml file with no author entries.

First up, we'll get the ID of each author in the XML file. Because we may need to add new authors to the file, we'll take this opportunity to keep track of the highest author ID:

File: **doAuthorsUpdate.php** (excerpt)

```
$id = $xAuthor->getAttribute('id');
if ($maxId < (int)$id) $maxId = (int)$id;
```

For each author in the file, we'll check for a corresponding submitted set of author details. This approach neatly avoids attempts to update authors that have just been deleted by another administrator, and doesn't touch any authors that were just added:

File: **doAuthorsUpdate.php** (excerpt)

```
if (isset($_POST['author']) and
    isset($_POST['author'][$id])) {
  $author = $_POST['author'][$id];
```

If the Delete? checkbox was checked for this author, we want to remove the corresponding entry from the XML data. But before we can do that, we must first check if there is any existing site content that is attributable to the author. What should happen if existing content is found is up to you, really: you could simply delete the offending content; you could assign the content to a special "anonymous" author ID; or you could prompt the user for a course of action. For this example, we'll skip the deletion and collect the author's ID in an array variable, $deleteFailures, which we'll present to the user at the end of this script.

File: **doAuthorsUpdate.php** (excerpt)

```
if (isset($author['delete']) and $author['delete'] == 'true')
{
  $okToDelete = TRUE;
  $handle = opendir($fileDir);
  while (($file = readdir($handle)) !== FALSE) {
    if (is_dir($fileDir . $file)) continue;
    if (!eregi("^(article|news).*\.xml$", $file)) continue;
    $contentItem = simplexml_load_file($fileDir . $file);
    if ((string)$contentitem->authorid == (string)$id) {
      $okToDelete = FALSE;
      break;
    }
  }
  if ($okToDelete) $root->removeChild($xAuthor);
  else $deleteFailures[] = $id;
```

If Delete? wasn't checked, we simply update the entry with the details that were submitted:

File: **doAuthorsUpdate.php** (excerpt)

```php
    } else {
      $name = $xAuthor->getElementsByTagName('name');
      $name = $name->item(0);
      $name->nodeValue = $author['name'];

      $byline = $xAuthor->getElementsByTagName('byline');
      $byline = $byline->item(0);
      $byline->nodeValue = $author['byline'];

      $email = $xAuthor->getElementsByTagName('email');
      $email = $email->item(0);
      $email->nodeValue = $author['email'];
    }
  }
}
```

Next up, we must process any new author entries that have been submitted. For a new author entry to be valid, we'll require that it at least have a name:

File: **doAuthorsUpdate.php** (excerpt)

```php
if (isset($_POST['newauthor'])) {
  foreach ($_POST['newauthor'] as $author) {
    if (isset($author['name'] and trim($author['name']) != '')) {
      $xAuthor = $root->appendChild($doc->createElement('author'));
```

With the element created and appended to the XML data, all that's left is to set its ID attribute (one greater than the current maximum ID value) and add the data elements for the submitted name, byline, and email address:

File: **doAuthorsUpdate.php** (excerpt)

```php
      $xAuthor->setAttribute('id', ++$maxId);
      $xAuthor->appendChild($doc->createElement('name',
          $author['name']));
      $xAuthor->appendChild($doc->createElement('byline',
          $author['byline']));
      $xAuthor->appendChild($doc->createElement('email',
          $author['email']));
    }
  }
}
```

With all the requested changes to our XML data done, we can overwrite authors.xml with our updated version:

File: **doAuthorsUpdate.php** (excerpt)

```
unlink($fileDir . 'authors.xml');
$doc->save($fileDir . 'authors.xml');
```

If any requested author deletions were unsuccessful, we'll redirect the browser to a page that displays a relevant error message, passing it the list of failed author IDs in the query string:

File: **doAuthorsUpdate.php** (excerpt)

```
if (count($deleteFailures) > 0) {
  $qs = '?';
  foreach ($deleteFailures as $id) {
    $qs .= "id[]=$id&";
  }
  header('location: authortool_deletefail.php' . $qs);
```

But if all goes well, then we'll simply redirect the browser back to the main author management page:

File: **doAuthorsUpdate.php** (excerpt)

```
} else {
  header('location: authortool.php');
}
?>
```

That's it for the author update processing script. For the sake of completeness, here's the page that displays failures to delete authors:

File: **authortool_deletefail.php**

```
<?php
include 'security.inc.php';
include_once '../common.inc.php';
?>
<!DOCTYPE html PUBLIC "-//W3C//DTD XHTML 1.0 Transitional//EN"
    "http://www.w3.org/TR/xhtml1/DTD/xhtml1-transitional.dtd">
<html xmlns="http://www.w3.org/1999/xhtml">
<head>
<meta http-equiv="Content-Type"
    content="text/html; charset=iso-8859-1" />
<title>Delete(s) Failed</title>
<link rel="stylesheet" type="text/css" href="../xmlcms.css" />
</head>
```

```
<body>
<h1>Delete(s) Failed</h1>
<p>Failed to delete the following authors, who still have content
   on the site. Remove or reassign their content items first, then
   try again.</p>
<ul>
<?php
$authors = simplexml_load_file($fileDir . 'authors.xml');
foreach ($id as $authorId) {
   echo '<li>' . $authors->xpath("author[@id='$authorId']/name") .
      '</li>';
}
?>
</ul>
<p>Any other requested changes have been made.</p>
<p><a href="authortool.php">Back to Author Listing</a></p>
</body>
</html>
```

Managing Administrators

Here's the administrator listing. As you'll see, its structure is very similar to that of the authors listing:

File: **admin.xml**

```
<?xml version="1.0" encoding="iso-8859-1"?>
<admins>
  <admin id="1">
    <name>Joe</name>
    <username>joe</username>
    <password>$1$O64.HQ..$x912Oh1I1HFylTPJmJR/k/</password>
    <email>joe@myerman.com</email>
  </admin>
  <admin id="2">
    <name>Bill</name>
    <username>bill</username>
    <password>$1$Ep5.7h4.$R6iGqy.Wj2Dz8SAE9WG31O</password>
    <email>bill@myerman.com</email>
  </admin>
  <admin id="3">
    <name>Tom</name>
    <username>tom</username>
    <password>$1$Cl/.j3..$QcjxGtxqYxOVNp3QanGnPO</password>
    <email>tom@myerman.com</email>
```

```
    </admin>
</admins>
```

Encrypted Passwords

As you can see, the password values are encrypted for added security. So that you can use the sample `admin.xml` file included in the code archive for this book, you need to know that the initial password of all three administrators stored in that file is `password`.

We're going to process administrators in much the same way we processed authors.

File: **admintool.php**

```php
<?php
include 'security.inc.php';
include_once '../common.inc.php';
?>
<!DOCTYPE html PUBLIC "-//W3C//DTD XHTML 1.0 Transitional//EN"
    "http://www.w3.org/TR/xhtml1/DTD/xhtml1-transitional.dtd">
<html xmlns="http://www.w3.org/1999/xhtml">
<head>
<meta http-equiv="Content-Type"
    content="text/html; charset=iso-8859-1" />
<title>Admin Index</title>
<link rel="stylesheet" type="text/css" href="../xmlcms.css" />
</head>
<body>
<h1>Admin Index</h1>
<p><a href="admintool_edit.php">Edit Admin Listing</a></p>
<p><a href="index.php">Cancel</a></p>
<ul>
<?php
$admins = simplexml_load_file($fileDir . 'admin.xml');
foreach ($admins->admin as $admin) {
  echo '<li>' . htmlentities($admin->name) .
      ' (' . htmlentities($admin->email) . ')</li>';
}
?>
</ul>
</body>
</html>
```

File: **admintool_edit.php**

```php
<?php
include 'security.inc.php';
include_once '../common.inc.php';
```

```
?>
<!DOCTYPE html PUBLIC "-//W3C//DTD XHTML 1.0 Transitional//EN"
    "http://www.w3.org/TR/xhtml1/DTD/xhtml1-transitional.dtd">
<html xmlns="http://www.w3.org/1999/xhtml">
<head>
<meta http-equiv="Content-Type"
    content="text/html; charset=iso-8859-1" />
<title>Edit Admins</title>
<link rel="stylesheet" type="text/css" href="../xmlcms.css" />
</head>
<body>
<h1>Edit Admins</h1>
<p><a href="admintool.php">Cancel</a></p>
<form method="post" action="doAdminsUpdate.php">
<table border="1" cellspacing="0" cellpadding="3">
  <tr>
    <th>Delete?</th>
    <th>Name</th>
    <th>Username</th>
    <th>New Password</th>
    <th>Email</th>
  </tr>
  <?php
  $admins = simplexml_load_file($fileDir . 'admin.xml');
  foreach ($admins->admin as $admin) {
    echo "\t<tr valign=\"top\">\n";
    echo "\t\t<td><input type=\"checkbox\" name=\"admin[" .
        htmlentities($admin['id']) . "][delete]\" " .
        "value=\"true\" /></td>\n";
    echo "\t\t<td><input type=\"text\" name=\"admin[" .
        htmlentities($admin['id']) . "][name]\" value=\"" .
        htmlentities($admin->name) . "\" /></td>\n";
    echo "\t\t<td><input type=\"text\" name=\"admin[" .
        htmlentities($admin['id']) . "][username]\" value=\"" .
        htmlentities($admin->username) . "\" /></td>\n";
    echo "\t\t<td><input type=\"text\" name=\"admin[" .
        htmlentities($admin['id']) . "][password]\" /></td>\n";
    echo "\t\t<td><input type=\"text\" name=\"admin[" .
        htmlentities($admin['id']) . "][email]\" value=\"" .
        htmlentities($admin->email) . "\" /></td>\n";
    echo "\t</tr>\n";
  }
  for ($i = 0; $i < 3; $i++) {
    echo "\t<tr valign=\"top\">\n";
    echo "\t\t<td></td>\n";
    echo "\t\t<td><input type=\"text\"
```

```
        name=\"newadmin[$i][name]\" /></td>\n";
    echo "\t\t<td><input type=\"text\"
        name=\"newadmin[$i][username]\" /></td>\n";
    echo "\t\t<td><input type=\"text\"
        name=\"newadmin[$i][password]\" /></td>\n";
    echo "\t\t<td><input type=\"text\"
        name=\"newadmin[$i][email]\" /></td>\n";
    echo "\t</tr>\n";
  }
  ?>
  <tr><td colspan="5">
    <input type="submit" value="Update" />
    <input type="reset" value="Reset" />
  </td></tr>
</table>
</form>
</body>
</html>
```

File: **doAdminsUpdate.php**

```php
<?php
include 'security.inc.php';
include_once '../common.inc.php';

$doc = DOMDocument::load($fileDir . 'admin.xml');
$root = $doc->documentElement;
$maxId = 0;

foreach ($root->getElementsByTagName('admin') as $xAdmin) {
  $id = $xAdmin->getAttribute('id');
  if ($maxId < (int)$id) $maxId = (int)$id;
  if (isset($_POST['admin']) and
      isset($_POST['admin'][$id])) {
    $admin = $_POST['admin'][$id];
    if (isset($admin['delete']) and $admin['delete'] == 'true') {
      $root->removeChild($xAdmin);
    } else {
      $name = $xAdmin->getElementsByTagName('name');
      $name = $name->item(0);
      $name->nodeValue = $admin['name'];

      $uname = $xAdmin->getElementsByTagName('username');
      $uname = $uname->item(0);
      $uname->nodeValue = $admin['username'];

      if (isset($admin['password']) and
```

```
        trim($admin['password']) != '') {
      $pass = $xAdmin->getElementsByTagName('password');
      $pass = $pass->item(0);
      $pass->nodeValue = crypt($admin['password']);
    }

    $email = $xAdmin->getElementsByTagName('email');
    $email = $email->item(0);
    $email->nodeValue = $admin['email'];
    }
  }
}

if (isset($_POST['newadmin'])) {
  foreach ($_POST['newadmin'] as $admin) {
    if (isset($admin['name']) and trim($admin['name']) != '' and
        isset($admin['username']) and
        trim($admin['username']) != '' and
        isset($admin['password']) and
        trim($admin['password']) != '') {
      $xAdmin = $root->appendChild($doc->createElement('admin'));
      $xAdmin->setAttribute('id', ++$maxId);
      $xAdmin->appendChild($doc->createElement('name',
          $admin['name']));
      $xAdmin->appendChild($doc->createElement('username',
          $admin['username']));
      $xAdmin->appendChild($doc->createElement('password',
          crypt($admin['password'])));
      $xAdmin->appendChild($doc->createElement('email',
          $admin['email']));
    }
  }
}

unlink($fileDir . 'admin.xml');
$doc->save($fileDir . 'admin.xml');

header('location: admintool.php');
?>
```

Managing Categories

Finally, here's the category listing, which uses attributes instead of elements to do its job:

File: **categories.xml**

```xml
<?xml version="1.0" encoding="iso-8859-1"?>
<categories>
  <category label="xml" status="live" id="1"/>
  <category label="php" status="live" id="2"/>
  <category label="asp" status="live" id="3"/>
  <category label="javascript" status="live" id="4"/>
  <category label="perl" status="live" id="5"/>
</categories>
```

Despite this structural difference, we handle the information in much the same way we handled authors and administrators. Again, because there isn't much difference, I'll present the code without commentary.

File: **categorytool.php**

```php
<?php
include 'security.inc.php';
include_once '../common.inc.php';
?>
<!DOCTYPE html PUBLIC "-//W3C//DTD XHTML 1.0 Transitional//EN"
    "http://www.w3.org/TR/xhtml1/DTD/xhtml1-transitional.dtd">
<html xmlns="http://www.w3.org/1999/xhtml">
<head>
<meta http-equiv="Content-Type"
    content="text/html; charset=iso-8859-1" />
<title>Category Index</title>
<link rel="stylesheet" type="text/css" href="../xmlcms.css" />
</head>
<body>
<h1>Category Index</h1>
<p><a href="categorytool_edit.php">Edit Category Listing</a></p>
<p><a href="index.php">Cancel</a></p>
<ul>
<?php
$cats = simplexml_load_file($fileDir . 'categories.xml');
foreach ($cats->category as $cat) {
  echo '<li>' . htmlentities($cat['label']) .
      ' (' . htmlentities($cat['status']) . ')</li>';
}
?>
</ul>
</body>
</html>
```

```php
<?php
include 'security.inc.php';
include_once '../common.inc.php';
?>
<!DOCTYPE html PUBLIC "-//W3C//DTD XHTML 1.0 Transitional//EN"
    "http://www.w3.org/TR/xhtml1/DTD/xhtml1-transitional.dtd">
<html xmlns="http://www.w3.org/1999/xhtml">
<head>
<meta http-equiv="Content-Type"
    content="text/html; charset=iso-8859-1" />
<title>Edit Categories</title>
<link rel="stylesheet" type="text/css" href="../xmlcms.css" />
</head>
<body>
<h1>Edit Categories</h1>
<p><a href="categorytool.php">Cancel</a></p>
<form method="post" action="doCategoriesUpdate.php">
<table border="1" cellspacing="0" cellpadding="3">
  <tr>
    <th>Delete?</th>
    <th>Label</th>
    <th>Status</th>
  </tr>
  <?php
  $cats = simplexml_load_file($fileDir . 'categories.xml');
  foreach ($cats->category as $cat) {
    echo "\t<tr valign=\"top\">\n";
    echo "\t\t<td><input type=\"checkbox\" name=\"cat[" .
        htmlentities($cat['id']) . "][delete]\" " .
        "value=\"true\" /></td>\n";
    echo "\t\t<td><input type=\"text\" name=\"cat[" .
        htmlentities($cat['id']) . "][label]\" value=\"" .
        htmlentities($cat['label']) . "\" /></td>\n";
    echo "\t\t<td><select name=\"cat[" .
        htmlentities($cat['id']) . "][status]\">\n";
    echo "\t\t\t<option value=\"live\"" .
        ((string)$cat['status'] == 'live' ? ' selected="selected"'
        : '') . ">live</option>\n";
    echo "\t\t\t<option value=\"in progress\"" .
        ((string)$cat['status'] == 'in progress' ?
        ' selected="selected"' : '') . ">in progress</option>\n";
    echo "\t\t</select></td>\n";
    echo "\t</tr>\n";
  }
  for ($i = 0; $i < 3; $i++) {
```

```
    echo "\t<tr valign=\"top\">\n";
    echo "\t\t<td></td>\n";
    echo "\t\t<td><input type=\"text\" name=\"newcat[$i][label]\"
        /></td>\n";
    echo "\t\t<td><select name=\"newcat[$i][status]\">\n";
    echo "\t\t\t<option value=\"live\">live</option>\n";
    echo "\t\t\t<option value=\"in progress\"
        >in progress</option>\n";
    echo "\t\t</select></td>\n";
    echo "\t</tr>\n";
  }
  ?>
  <tr><td colspan="3">
    <input type="submit" value="Update" />
    <input type="reset" value="Reset" />
  </td></tr>
</table>
</form>
</body>
</html>
```

File: **doCategoriesUpdate.php**

```php
<?php
include 'security.inc.php';
include_once '../common.inc.php';

$doc = DOMDocument::load($fileDir . 'categories.xml');
$root = $doc->documentElement;
$maxId = 0;
$deleteFailures = array();

foreach ($root->getElementsByTagName('category') as $xCat) {
  $id = $xCat->getAttribute('id');
  if ($maxId < (int)$id) $maxId = (int)$id;
  if (isset($_POST['cat']) and
      isset($_POST['cat'][$id])) {
    $cat = $_POST['cat'][$id];
    if (isset($cat['delete']) and $cat['delete'] == 'true') {
      $okToDelete = TRUE;
      $handle = opendir($fileDir);
      while (($file = readdir($handle)) !== FALSE) {
        if (is_dir($fileDir . $file)) continue;
        if (!eregi("^(article|news).*\.xml$", $file)) continue;
        $contentItem = simplexml_load_file($fileDir . $file);
        if ((string)$contentItem->categoryid == (string)$id) {
          $okToDelete = FALSE;
```

```
          break;
        }
      }
      if ($okToDelete) $root->removeChild($xCat);
      else $deleteFailures[] = $id;
    } else {
      $xCat->setAttribute('label', $cat['label']);
      $xCat->setAttribute('status', $cat['status']);
    }
  }
}

if (isset($_POST['newcat'])) {
  foreach ($_POST['newcat'] as $cat) {
    if (isset($cat['label']) and trim($cat['label']) != '') {
      $xCat = $root->appendChild($doc->createElement('category'));
      $xCat->setAttribute('id', ++$maxId);
      $xCat->setAttribute('label', $cat['label']);
      $xCat->setAttribute('status', $cat['status']);
    }
  }
}

unlink($fileDir . 'categories.xml');
$doc->save($fileDir . 'categories.xml');

if (count($deleteFailures) > 0) {
  $qs = '?';
  foreach ($deleteFailures as $id) {
    $qs .= "id[]=$id&";
  }
  header('location: categorytool_deletefail.php' . $qs);
} else {
  header('location: categorytool.php');
}
?>
```

File: **categorytool_deletefail.php**

```
<?php
include 'security.inc.php';
include_once '../common.inc.php';
?>
<!DOCTYPE html PUBLIC "-//W3C//DTD XHTML 1.0 Transitional//EN"
    "http://www.w3.org/TR/xhtml1/DTD/xhtml1-transitional.dtd">
<html xmlns="http://www.w3.org/1999/xhtml">
<head>
```

```
<meta http-equiv="Content-Type"
    content="text/html; charset=iso-8859-1" />
<title>Delete(s) Failed</title>
<link rel="stylesheet" type="text/css" href="../xmlcms.css" />
</head>
<body>
<h1>Delete(s) Failed</h1>
<p>Failed to delete the following categories, which still contain
  content. Remove or reassign their content items first, then try
  again.</p>
<ul>
<?php
$cats = simplexml_load_file($fileDir . 'categories.xml');
foreach ($id as $catId) {
  echo '<li>' . $cats->xpath("category[@id='$catId']/@label") .
    '</li>';
}
?>
</ul>
<p>Any other requested changes have been made.</p>
<p><a href="categorytool.php">Back to Category Listing</a></p>
</body>
</html>
```

Updating the Admin Index Page

With all our tools in place, we can now update our administrative index page to link to them:

File: **index.php**

```
<?php
include 'security.inc.php';
?>
<!DOCTYPE html PUBLIC "-//W3C//DTD XHTML 1.0 Transitional//EN"
    "http://www.w3.org/TR/xhtml1/DTD/xhtml1-transitional.dtd">
<html xmlns="http://www.w3.org/1999/xhtml">
<head>
<meta http-equiv="Content-Type"
    content="text/html; charset=iso-8859-1" />
<title>Welcome to the Admin Index Page</title>
<link rel="stylesheet" type="text/css" href="../xmlcms.css" />
</head>
<body>
<h1>Welcome to the Admin Index Page</h1>
<p>
```

```
    <a href="webcopytool.php">Manage Web Copy</a><br />
    <a href="articletool.php">Manage Articles</a><br />
    <a href="newstool.php">Manage News Items</a><br />
    <a href="admintool.php">Manage Administrators</a><br />
    <a href="categorytool.php">Manage Categories</a><br />
    <a href="authortool.php">Manage Authors</a>
</p>
<p><a href="logout.php">Log out</a></p>
</body>
</html>
```

Summary

Folks, we're done with the administrative tool for our CMS. It can now handle a variety of content types, categories, administrators, and authors. You've finished the project!

Index

Symbols

%, parameter entity prefix, 67
&, general entity prefix, 67, 122
<<<, PHP heredoc syntax, 176
@, XPath attribute selector, 82

A

a0 namespace prefix, 147
about attribute, RDF, 209–210
action attribute, <form> element, 94
ActiveXObject class, 145
administration tool, CMS project, 181–197, 297–337
    administration index page, 186, 297, 336
    administrative login tool, 32, 182
    administrators' login verification, 184
administrative metadata, 26
administrator listings, CMS project, 57, 327–331
alert function, JavaScript, 147
alphabetical sorting, 111–112
appendChild method, 150, 173
applications and Web Services, 221, 223
apply-templates element, XSL, 45
    <xsl:for-each> and, 125
    <xsl:sort> as child of, 111
    book chapter example, 85
arrays
    exported database field names, 254
    search engine results, 128
    SimpleXML attributes within elements, 178
    SimpleXML child element storage, 176

sorting in reverse order, 217
storing retrieved elements in, 170, 322
storing selected categories for headline feed, 217
treating NodeLists as, 141
xml_parse_into_struct function, 264
XML-RPC responses, 230, 242
xu_rpc_http_concise function, 240
arrow notation, PHP, 175–176
article content type, CMS project, 28, 187–197
    counting live articles, 234, 239
    creating articles, 188
    deleting articles, 197
    design changes, 77
    editing articles, 194
ASCII (*see* plain text)
asXML method, PHP, 180
async property, 139
AtomEnabled project, 211
attribute declarations, 65, 73
attribute values
    accessing in SimpleXML, 178
    matching, using XPath, 82, 88, 109
    quoting requirement, 7, 37
    unique attributes, 66
    updating with SimpleXML, 180
    validator error messages, 75
attributes, 8–9
    choice between element storage and, 72
    DOM representation of, 272
    implied and required, 66
    referencing in navtop.inc.php, 98
    use by CMS category listing, 331
    XPath predicate notation for, 82

Extensible Hypertext Markup Language (*see* XHTML)

Extensible Stylesheet Language Transformations (*see* XSLT)

external DTDs, 68
   internal memo example, 76
   linking to, 76

external entities, 68

F

faults, XML-RPC, 230
file paths and XPath, 107
Firefox
   corrected jsTest.html display, 151
   display of raw XML, 20
   display problem with jsTest.html, 145
   serialization bug, 147
   treatment of whitespace, 152
   validating parsers and, 20
firstChild property, 150
flat-file databases, 248
fopen function, PHP, 167
for-each element, XSL, 125
foreach loops, PHP, 176, 213
format attribute, <xsl:number>, 117
formatting, 12
   book chapter example, 84
   collapsible tree formatting, 53
   XSLT whitespace problem, 47
forms, HTML (*see* example PHP files)
frameset DOCTYPE, XHTML, 38

G

general entities, 67
generated text, CSS, 43
getAttribute method, 153
getDomDocument method, Sarissa class, 147
getElementById method, 154

getElementsByTagName method, 142, 170
greater-than symbol, 122

H

handler functions, PHP, 166
hasChildNodes method, 150
headings
   book chapter title elements and, 87
   CMS project homepage title, 100
heredoc syntax, PHP, 176
hierarchical nature of XML, 11
href attribute, including XPath expressions, 135
HTML
   limitations, 2–4
   transforming XML into, 50
   use in CMS content, 30
HTTP headers for XML-RPC requests, 228
HTTP POST requests, XML-RPC use, 224, 229, 237

I

IBM XML4J parser, 22
ID attributes, 66
   categorization and, 158
   creating new articles, 189, 192
   including in links, 135
   Stock Keeping Units, 113
   webcopy element, 299, 304
ID elements, tracking author information, 78
ID variables, CMS project content area, 102
IDREF attributes, 66
IE (*see* Internet Explorer)
if element, XSL, 122
   <xsl:choose> and, 123
if test, 172
implicit templates, XSLT, 46

Y

Books for Web Developers
from SitePoint

Visit http://www.sitepoint.com/books/
for sample chapters or to order!

3rd Edition
Covers PHP5, MySQL4
and Mac OS X

sitepoint

Build Your Own

Database Driven Website

Using PHP & MySQL

By Kevin Yank

A Practical Step-by-Step Guide

PHP 5 Ready

The PHP Anthology

Object Oriented PHP Solutions

Volume I

By Harry Fuecks

Practical Solutions to Common Problems

PHP 5 Ready

The PHP Anthology

Object Oriented PHP Solutions

Volume II

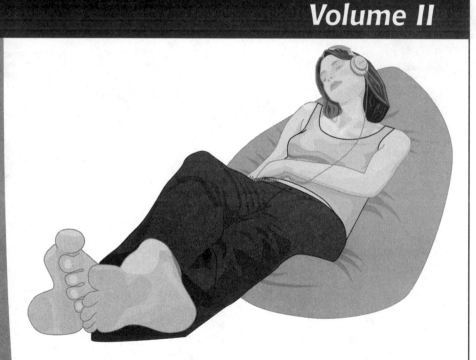

By Harry Fuecks

Practical Solutions to Common Problems

RUN YOUR OWN
WEB SERVER
USING
LINUX & APACHE

BY **STUART LANGRIDGE**
& **TONY STEIDLER-DENNISON**

GET STARTED WITH LINUX AND APACHE — THE EASY WAY!

BUILD YOUR OWN
ASP.NET
WEBSITE
USING
C# & VB.NET

BY ZAK RUVALCABA

THE ULTIMATE ASP.NET BEGINNER'S GUIDE

2ND EDITION

sitepoint®

HTML UTOPIA:
DESIGNING WITHOUT TABLES USING CSS

BY RACHEL ANDREW
& DAN SHAFER

THE ULTIMATE BEGINNER'S GUIDE TO CSS

THE CSS ANTHOLOGY

101 ESSENTIAL TIPS, TRICKS & HACKS

BY RACHEL ANDREW

THE MOST COMPLETE QUESTION AND ANSWER BOOK ON CSS

DHTML UTOPIA:
MODERN
WEB DESIGN
USING
JAVASCRIPT & DOM
BY **STUART LANGRIDGE**

PRACTICAL UNOBTRUSIVE JAVASCRIPT TECHNIQUES

THE JAVASCRIPT ANTHOLOGY

101 ESSENTIAL TIPS, TRICKS & HACKS

BY **JAMES EDWARDS**
& CAMERON ADAMS

THE MOST COMPLETE QUESTION AND ANSWER BOOK ON JAVASCRIPT

BUILD YOUR OWN
STANDARDS
COMPLIANT
WEBSITE
USING
DREAMWEAVER 8

BY RACHEL ANDREW

A PRACTICAL STEP-BY-STEP GUIDE TO MASTERING DREAMWEAVER 8

Flash
MX 2004

sitepoint

The Flash Anthology

Cool Effects &
Practical ActionScript

By Steven Grosvenor

Practical Solutions to Common Problems

Kits for Web Professionals
from SitePoint

Available exclusively from
http://www.sitepoint.com/

Dreaming of running your own successful Web Design or Development business?

This kit contains everything you need to know!

The Web Design Business Kit

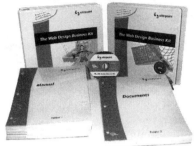

Whether you are thinking of establishing your own Web Design or Development business or are already running one, this kit will teach you everything you need to know to be successful…

Two ring-bound folders and a CD-ROM jam packed with expert advice and proven ready-to-use business documents that will help you establish yourself, gain clients, and grow a profitable freelance business!

Folder 1:
Covers advice on every aspect of running your business:

- *How to sell yourself*
- *How to land bigger jobs*
- *What to charge*
- *How to keep clients for life*
- *How to manage budgets*
- *How to hire & fire employees*
- *And much more*

Folder 2:
Contains 64 essential, ready-to-use business documents:

- *Business Plan*
- *Sample Proposal & Contract*
- *Client Needs Analysis Form*
- *Marketing Surveys*
- *Employment Documents*
- *Financial Documents*
- *And much more*

CD-ROM:
Contains electronic copies of all the business documents in Folder 2, so you can apply them instantly to your business!

- *Ready to apply*
- *Easily customizable*
- *MS Word & Excel format*

The Web Design Business Kit is available exclusively through sitepoint.com. To order, get more information, or to download the free sample chapters, visit:

www.sitepoint.com/books/freelance1/

What our customers have to say about the Web Design Business Kit:

"The Web Design Business Kit (Documents & Manual) is the best marketing tool that I have found! It has changed my business strategies, and my income."

Barb Brown
www.barbbrown.com

"We've already closed 2 deals by following the suggested steps in the kit! I feel like I shouldn't pass the word about this kit to others or risk a lot of good competition!"

Jeneen McDonald
www.artpoststudios.com

"Of everything I have purchased on the Internet, related to business and not, this is (without question) the most value for the money spent. Thank you."

Thom Parkin
www.twice21.com

Fast-track Search Engine Marketing strategies!

The Search Engine Marketing Kit

The Search Engine Marketing Kit contains everything that you need to maximize your Website's traffic, using Search Engine Optimization and Pay-Per-Click advertising techniques.

Comprising a ring-bound folder and a CD-ROM, and packed full of expert advice by author Dan Thies, you'll discover keyword strategies you won't find anywhere else, find out the best ways to optimize pages and build links, learn how to create, optimize and manage advanced pay-per-click campaigns, and much more.

The Folder:

Contains 301 letter-sized pages covering every aspect of Search Engine Optimization (SEO) and Pay-Per-Click (PPC) advertising.

- *Learn advanced keyword research & selection strategies.*
- *Discover how crawlers work and exactly what they do.*
- *Get the lowdown on how search engines set priorities.*
- *Discover the best submission and paid-inclusion tactics.*
- *Avoid getting banned or labeled as a search engine spammer.*
- *Go step-by-step through the pay-per-click advertising process.*
- *Learn "Dayparting", positioning, and targeting strategies.*
- *Detailed advice on preparing to sell your services.*
- *Discover how dynamic websites affect SEO*

The CD-ROM:

Contains tools and documents designed to make the process of Search Engine Marketing much easier.

- *Sample SEM Proposal*
- *Client Assessment Form*
- *Keyword Analysis Worksheet*
- *Directory Planning Worksheet*
- *Sample SEO Presentation*
- *Process Flowchart*
- *Sample SEM Agreement*
- *Site Review Checklist*

To order, get more information, or to download a free sample chapter, visit:

www.sitepoint.com/books/sem1/

What the experts say...

"Those who purchase Dan's kit and put it to good use will be much better prepared to run their SEM businesses, while also serving their clients in a highly professional manner."

Jill Whalen
http://www.highrankings.com
Mar 3rd 2005

"Dan Thies is a search marketing expert who is not afraid to roll up his sleeves and get to the nuts and bolts of search"

Andy Beal, VP Search Marketing.
http://www.KeywordRanking.com
Feb 27th 2005

"Dan Thies breaks down the tactics used by successful search marketing companies in easy to consume bites, allowing you to improve the quality of your services."

Ed Kohler
http://www.HaystackInANeedle.com/
Mar 1st 2005